SACRED SELVES, SACRED SETTINGS

The borders of identity, religion and secularity are contested and analysed in new ways in the social sciences today. Drawing on Hans Mol's sociological study of religion, this volume offers an excellent and broad look into the definition and relationship between these critical issues in the process of identity formation in a plural and diverse society.

Anders Bäckström, Uppsala University, Sweden

Significantly influencing the sociological study of religion, Hans Mol developed ideas of identity which remain thought-provoking for analyses of how religion operates within contemporary societies. *Sacred Selves, Sacred Settings* brings current social-religious topics into sharp focus: international scholars analyse, challenge, and apply Mol's theoretical assertions. This book introduces the unique story of Hans Mol, who survived Nazi imprisonment and proceeded to brush shoulders with formidable intellectuals of the twentieth century, such as Robert Merton, Talcott Parsons, and Reinhold Niebuhr. Offering a fresh perspective on popular subjects such as secularization, pluralism, and the place of religion in the public sphere, this book sets case studies within an intellectual biography which describes Mol's key influences and reveals the continuing import of Hans Mol's work applied to recent data and within a contemporary context.

Sacred Selves, Sacred Settings

Reflecting Hans Mol

Edited by

DOUGLAS J. DAVIES
Durham University, UK

ADAM J. POWELL
Lenoir-Rhyne University, USA

ASHGATE

© Douglas J. Davies and Adam J. Powell 2015

All rights reserved. No part of this publication may be reproduced, stored in a retrieval system or transmitted in any form or by any means, electronic, mechanical, photocopying, recording or otherwise without the prior permission of the publisher.

Douglas J. Davies and Adam J. Powell have asserted their right under the Copyright, Designs and Patents Act, 1988, to be identified as the editors of this work.

Published by
Ashgate Publishing Limited
Wey Court East
Union Road
Farnham
Surrey, GU9 7PT
England

Ashgate Publishing Company
110 Cherry Street
Suite 3-1
Burlington, VT 05401-3818
USA

www.ashgate.com

British Library Cataloguing in Publication Data
A catalogue record for this book is available from the British Library

The Library of Congress has cataloged the printed edition as follows:
Sacred selves, sacred settings : reflecting Hans Mol / edited by Douglas J. Davies and Adam J. Powell.
    pages cm
  Includes bibliographical references and index.
    ISBN 978-1-4724-2526-3 (hardcover) -- ISBN 978-1-4724-2527-0 (ebook) -- ISBN 978-1-4724-2528-7 (epub) 1. Mol, Hans, 1922- 2. Christian sociology. 3. Religion and sociology. I. Davies, Douglas James, editor.
  BX4827.M58S23 2015
  306.6'3--dc23

2014033446

ISBN 9781472425263 (hbk)
ISBN 9781472425270 (ebk – PDF)
ISBN 9781472425287 (ebk – ePUB)

Printed in the United Kingdom by Henry Ling Limited,
at the Dorset Press, Dorchester, DT1 1HD

Contents

List of Tables   *vii*
List of Contributors   *ix*

Introduction   3
Douglas J. Davies

PART I   HANS MOL (RE)CONSIDERED

1   Hans Mol   11
    Adam J. Powell

2   Mol's Sociology: Social Theory, Dialectics and Hegel's Shadow   33
    Louis Greenspan

3   Mol, Science, Religion and Narrative Identity   43
    Ian Weeks and Petra Brown

PART II   REVISITING THEMES:
               PLURALISM, SECULARISM AND CONTESTED BORDERS

4   The Secularization of the Sanctity of Life and Death   67
    Karel Dobbelaere

5   The Public Role of Religion   87
    Roberto Cipriani

6	Religion Fixed and Fickle: The Contemporary Challenge of Religious Diversity *Douglas Pratt*	101
7	From Secularist to Pluralist: Post-World War II Australia *Desmond Cahill*	123
8	Contextual Theology and Religious Discourse in Indonesia *James Haire*	145

Postscript: Reflections of a Sociologist-Priest   165
Gary D. Bouma

Selected Bibliography of Hans Mol   *175*
Index   *177*

List of Tables

4.1	Evolution of the mean scores of justification of euthanasia according to church involvement (1981–2009)	76
7.1	Major religious and secularist groups in Australia: 1911–2011 (in raw numbers)	126
7.2	Major religious and secularist groups in Australia: 1911–2011 (in percentages of total Australian population)	127
7.3	Major religious and secularist groups in 2011 Australia: seven largest source countries	133
7.4	Major religious and secularist groups in Australia X state/territory (in percentages of total state/territory population)	137

List of Contributors

Gary D. Bouma AM is the UNESCO Chair in Intercultural and Interreligious Relations – Asia Pacific, Emeritus Professor of Sociology at Monash University, Australian node of the Religion and Diversity Project, University of Ottawa and President of the Australian Association for the Study of Religions. Author or co-author of over 25 books and 300 articles, he has been invested as a Member of the Order of Australia (AM) for services to Sociology, to Interreligious Relations and to the Anglican Church of Australia.

Petra Brown completed her PhD in philosophy at Deakin University, late in 2012. Her thesis, titled 'Bonhoeffer as Kierkegaard's "Single Individual" in a "State of Exception"', questions the idea that violence can be justified as a 'last resort' through investigating the concept of 'exception' in the writing and action of the German theologian Dietrich Bonhoeffer in conjunction with the writings of Søren Kierkegaard and Carl Schmitt. Brown contributed to the Springer publication, *Secularisations and Their Debates* (2014) and has published 'Bonhoeffer, Schmitt, and the State of Exception', in *Pacifica* (October 2013, vol. 26, no. 3, pp. 246–64).

Desmond Cahill, Professor of Intercultural Studies at RMIT University in Melbourne, has been researching cross-cultural issues and multicultural and multi-faith societies for the past 35 years. His recent focus has been on religion, globalization and interfaith interaction. In 2004, he published with colleagues for the Australian immigration department, *Religion, Cultural Diversity and Safeguarding Australia* in the aftermath of 9/11 and in 2011 for the Australian Human Rights Commission, *Freedom of Religion and Belief in 21st Century Australia*. Since 2000, he has chaired Religions for Peace Australia and in 2008 was elected co-president and deputy moderator of Religions for Peace Asia. In 2010, he was awarded the Order of the Medal of Australia for 'his services to intercultural education and to the interfaith movement'.

Roberto Cipriani is Professor of Sociology at the University of Rome 3. He is past President of the Italian Sociological Association and of the ISA Research Committee for the Sociology of Religion. He has been Editor-in-Chief of *International Sociology*. In 2006 he was 'Chancellor Dunning Trust Lecturer' at Queen's University of Victoria (Canada). His *Handbook of Sociology of Religion* has been translated into English, Spanish, Portuguese, French, and Chinese. At the moment he is President of the Council of National Sociological Associations of the European Sociological Association. Cipriani served alongside Mol in the International Sociological Association in the 1970s.

Douglas J. Davies is Professor in the Study of Religion at Durham University and Director of its Centre for Death and Life Studies. From 1974 to 1997 he taught at Nottingham University after training in Anthropology at Durham and Oxford, and in Theology, again, at Durham University. His research interests in ritual, symbolism and belief include numerous publications on Anthropology and Theology, Mormonism, Anglicanism, Emotions, and Death Studies. He has chaired both the British Association for the Study of Religion and The British Sociological Association's Religion Group. Davies holds an Oxford D.Litt., an Honorary Dr.Theol. of Sweden's Uppsala University, is a Fellow of the UK Academy of Social Sciences and a Fellow of the Learned Society of Wales.

Karel Dobbelaere, Emeritus Professor of the Catholic University of Leuven and the University of Antwerp (Belgium), is an elected Fellow of the Royal Flemish Academy of Belgium for Sciences and Fine Arts and the Academia Europaea. He was President and Secretary General of the International Society for Sociology of Religion, a Visiting Fellow of All Souls College (Oxford), the Nanzan Institute for Religion and Culture (Nagoya, Japan), Sofia University (Tokyo), and the Institut de Recherche sur les Sociétés Contemporaines (CNRS, France). His main fields of interest are secularization, religious and church involvement, pillarization, new religious and sectarian movements.

Louis Greenspan is Professor Emeritus at McMaster University in Hamilton Ontario, Canada. In 1967, he joined the newly formed Department of Religious Studies and from 1970 he worked with Hans Mol who was hired to establish a program on Religion and the Social Sciences. Other activities at McMaster included a role in the founding of McMaster's Arts and Science Program, and service as the director of the Bertrand Russell Editorial Project from 1986 to 1996. Publications include works on Bertrand Russell, articles and an edited volume on the Jewish philosopher Emil Fackenheim, and works on contemporary religion. Since retirement Greenspan has been a frequent traveller to China where he has presented works in Jewish philosophy and contemporary religion to various conferences, especially at the Institute of Religious Studies in Nanjing. Currently he is working on the subject of post-secularism.

James Haire is Professor of Theology, Charles Sturt University (CSU), Canberra, Australia; Executive Director, Australian Centre for Christianity and Culture (ACC&C), CSU; Director, Public and Contextual Theology Research Centre (PACT), CSU; and Extraordinary Professor of Theology, University of Halmahera, Indonesia. An Oxford-trained theologian, he also holds a PhD from the University of Birmingham as well as honorary doctorates from Belfast, Ulster, Griffith University, and the Australian Catholic University. Haire became a Presidential Friend of Indonesia in 2010, and was appointed a Companion of the Order of Australia (AC), Australia's highest civilian award, in 2013.

Adam J. Powell is Coordinator for the graduate programme in Religious Studies at Lenoir-Rhyne University's Centre for Graduate Studies (Asheville, NC, USA). In addition to investigating the life and works of Hans Mol, Powell's research applies sociological and anthropological theory to historical religious issues such as doctrinal development and ritual practice. He holds a PhD from Durham University and has published in such diverse fields as Patristics, Mormon Studies, and the Sociology of Religion.

Douglas Pratt is Professor of Religious Studies at the University of Waikato, New Zealand, and Adjunct Professor of Theology and Interreligious Studies at the University of Bern, Switzerland. He is also an Adjunct Associate Professor (Research) in the School of Political and Social Inquiry, Monash University, Australia. His research interests include interreligious dialogue, Christian–Muslim relations, and issues of religious plurality and extremism. Trained in philosophy and theology, Douglas was in the first student intake for sociology when it was introduced into the University of Auckland. Recent publications include the co-edited *Understanding Interreligious Relations* (Oxford 2013).

Ian Weeks has taught at Melbourne, Yale, McMaster and Deakin Universities and has been a Fellow at the University of Melbourne and the Melbourne College of Divinity. His research is on the relationships between religious and philosophical thought (particularly political philosophy), mainly in the twentieth century in the existentialist and European traditions. He retired in 2003 but has continued with some teaching, writing and supervision of doctoral students and has been Dean at several faith-based tertiary colleges and Chair of their Academic Board.

Dr Hans Mol
Source: Used by kind permission of Margery Harpur.

Introduction

Douglas J. Davies

Today, the issues of identity, religion, spirituality, and secularity are of interest to wider academic circles than ever before. This makes it all the more timely to engage with Hans Mol, a scholar whose creative work offers its own dynamic perspective on human life, values, and commitments. In this volume, each chapter title speaks for itself, with some authors adopting autobiographical and biographical narratives while others strike more theoretical approaches. The scope of these reactions to Mol is extensive and will have the benefit of taking some readers into unfamiliar aspects of social theory, philosophical frames, and geographical contexts. I will not map these out in advance, leaving the information provided in the List of Contributors, alongside their respective chapters, to furnish their own guide to personal, professional, and theoretical encounters with Hans Mol. Suffice it to say that appreciation and critical analysis complement each other, with reflections on Mol's contribution over many decades passing into appropriate critiques and contemporary theoretical developments. What emerges is an unusual interplay of personal and theoretical materials that gives a real sense of how an individual scholar's life and thought interweave. In this particular case the jig-sawed contributions really do show something of the complexity of identity, religion, and secularity that make a life.

A Personal Appreciation

But why this book just now? In answering that question I take leave to introduce this volume autobiographically even though, unlike those able to narrate their personal encounter with Hans Mol, I have only 'met' him through his published work.

The mid 1970s saw me as a young lecturer appointed to develop the study of religion in what had, hitherto, been a firmly traditional Department of

Theology at Nottingham University. My theoretical interests included the way the disciplines of the history of religions and comparative religion often seemed to treat the 'great' world religions as qualitatively different from the 'traditional', 'tribal', or primitive 'religions' that were the customary purview of anthropology. The former were frequently described as 'salvation religions', with the implication that, whatever the latter were, they were not about 'salvation'. Just then I was fresh from strong traditions of anthropology and sociology of religion at Oxford and of theology at Durham universities, and was beginning to try to make sense of some sort of interface between those often diverse streams of thought and academic practice, a task that remains to this day.

One of the voices then heard amidst numerous academic streams dealing with religion, and which struck me with an obvious intellectual intensity, was Hans Mol's. My response was to utilize his *Identity and the Sacred* in my early doctoral work and its ensuing publication as *Meaning and Salvation in Religious Studies* (Davies 1984). This appeared as a monograph in the supplement series – *Studies in the History of Religions* – that complemented the journal *Numen*. In it I sought to develop an analysis of the idea of salvation that integrated ideas from the sociology of knowledge alongside an anthropology of evil. It would be a non-theological definition of 'salvation'. At that time I was preoccupied with 'the paradigm of meaning' and with some aspects of systems-theory, seeking to show, in particular, how plausibility theory could describe salvation in terms of 'cognitive and affective well-being', irrespective of the kind of society under consideration. This approach placed all 'religions' on an even-footing and removed the categorical distinction between 'salvation' religions and other, 'lesser', traditions. In this I found the Australian anthropologist W.E.H. Stanner's work highly influential, though his academic presence in the UK and the study of religion was scarcely visible.[1] It was here that Mol's concern with identity came into the picture, allowing the human process of meaning-making, then so common in phenomenologically influenced sociology (Berger 1969), to spotlight this personal focus of human self-reflection. I was especially interested in the way Mol's work considered 'the significance of general affective dimensions' (Davies 1984: 58–61) – or what we would, today, more directly describe as 'emotions' in this context – and in his intriguing view of 'sacralisation' of identity (Davies 2011). This seemed to me to add a necessary individual dimension to Durkheim's long-standing sociological notion of the 'sacred' as applied to a social group as transformed through ritual, especially given

---

[1] W.E.H. Stanner (1905–81). One might compare Stanner's deeply humane appreciation of indigenous Australian life with that of his age-mate Lévi-Strauss (1908–2009) on some South American peoples.

Durkheim's rules of and for his sociological method that prioritized the group and its sociology rather than individuals and their psychology (Moscovici 1993).

This individualization of the sacred demanded interplay between the individual and some source of identity-conferral, and also opened a valuable mode of analysis of individuals within groups. This made direct sense to me, having already studied aspects both of Mormon and Sikh cultural life, each of which revealed powerful sets of identity-generating phenomena, and served as case studies within the account of 'meaning and salvation' in that early monograph. But the key issue emerging through that monograph, stimulated by Mol's identity-sacralization hypothesis, began to take shape in the question of how the drive for meaning might become a need for salvation in different groups? This prime concern was also fuelled by Max Weber's idea of a group's orientation to the world and need for salvation as well as by the aligned concern of my former supervisor Bryan Wilson's approach to sects and how they coped with 'evil'. Mol's work, taken by me at a rather general level of significance, one that I did not submit to any severe critical analysis, served its own purpose as a general backcloth on identity, meaning, and religion, one that enhanced the status of the individual while other perspectives dictated more on social process.

As one then teaching in a fairly traditional Department of Theology the sacralization hypothesis obviously begged application to such delicate themes as the transformation of Jesus of Nazareth into a deified incarnate Son of God. Might this transformation be an example of the sacralization of identity? As the early Jewish sect of Christians gained their increasing sense of distinctive identity from Jesus, was he not, in turn, sacralized by them? Were the Christian creeds not, perhaps, one clear example of the sacralization of identity? The very grammar of discourse inherent within Jewish mediators of the divine, coupled with the dynamics of an emergent sect, seemed to offer a fruitful arena in which identity-receivers and identity-giver could gain from each other in a form of escalating exchange of attributes[2] in a complex mutual process of sacralizing identities. These were issues that I discussed, for example, with the biblical-linguistic scholar Maurice Casey who saw some relevance in it for his work on Jesus in earliest Christianity, and to a certain extent also with James Dunn, another influential New Testament scholar.

So it was that Mol's insight into the process of sacralizing identity came to influence my own thinking and came to be both implicit in some of my

---

[2] This phrase is, itself, an echo of the early Christian theological idea of *communicatio idiomatum* which described the potential exchange of attributes between Christ's human and divine natures.

general publications (2001: 33–61) and more explicit in some other specific studies (2002: 4; 2000: 200). In teaching, too, Mol's work, especially this sacralization aspect, came to occupy a constant place with many generations of undergraduates being introduced to this concept. I had also suggested to numerous postgraduates that they read Mol. For this influential stream of thought I am most grateful to Hans Mol in terms of my own thinking, teaching, and research, over practically a lifetime of scholarship. The very nature of such academic work is always deeply complex as ideas interplay and the very nature of intellectualism generates its own domain of reciprocities. These sometime involve personal relationships, as with some of the contributors to this collection, but are more frequently embedded within published sources. My own experience has, for example, included writing an unexpected and accidental intellectual biography of a scholar – Frank Byron Jevons – who died before I was born and, finding in that a powerfully enveloping influence of a character who, though dead, still spoke in what becomes a kind of personal voice with its own pervasive ideological and theoretical tone (1991).[3]

Though most of my postgraduates may have read some Mol, the case of Adam Powell, fellow-editor of this volume and former doctoral student, became quite distinctive as Mol's approach made its own intellectual appeal and prompted extensive study, so much so that we decided it would be valuable for him to meet and interview Mol, a venture undertaken with funding from Durham University's Centre for Death and Life Studies. For me this involved vicarious pleasure in that I had never met Mol myself and it was exciting to think of one postgraduate now doing so, and that amidst doctoral studies that had an essentially quite different subject matter.

Moreover, Adam Powell also proposed that we prepare this edited collection in honour of Hans Mol. The interview and basic work for this collection were tasks then undertaken by Adam whilst also completing his own exemplary doctoral studies on the sociology of heresy grounded in a comparative study of early Christian theology and the Mormon world of America's nineteenth century. Accordingly, it is with some considerable gratitude that I thank Adam for all his work and congratulate him on his academic acumen and industry.

So it is that, thanking each of our authors, we offer the following collection of material as a contribution to the history of social theory that carries with it a considerable resonance for religious studies and theological thought and which, in that, reflects brightly on Hans Mol.

---

[3] Jevons was Oxford-educated but long-based at Durham, a nineteenth-century classicist turned anthropologist-historian of religion.

References

Berger, P. (1969) *The Social Reality of Religion*. London: Penguin.
Davies, D.J. (1984) *Meaning and Salvation in Religious Studies*. Leiden: Brill.
Davies, D.J. (1991) *Frank Byron Jevons, 1858–1936: An Evolutionary Realist*. Lewiston: Mellen Press.
Davies, D.J. (2000) *The Mormon Culture of Salvation*. Aldershot: Ashgate.
Davies, D.J. (2001) 'Christianity', in J. Holm and J. Bowker (eds), *Sacred Place*. London: Pinter, 33–61.
Davies, D.J. (2002) *Death, Ritual and Belief*. London: Cassell.
Davies, D.J. (2011) *Emotion, Identity and Religion: Hope, Reciprocity, and Otherness*. Oxford: Oxford University Press.
Moscovici, S. (1993) *The Invention of Society*. Cambridge: Polity.

PART I
Hans Mol (Re)Considered

Chapter 1
Hans Mol

Adam J. Powell

Hans Mol was simply following his mother's example when, at the dawn of the twenty-first century, he set out to compose an autobiography of sorts. For, at the age of 85, Jacoba compiled her life's most vivid memories for the benefit of her family. Although Hans Mol eventually lost track of the whereabouts of this self-published autobiography, his own autobiographical efforts reflect not only an affinity for the strong familial ties often displayed within Dutch culture of which he was a part but also for his mother and the intuition that allowed her to foresee the identity-constructing effect such a volume might have for her posterity. In the same vein, Mol chose to write an autobiography in which he would share as many details of his life as he could recall, assuming that the eyes casting their gaze upon such material would belong to his relatives. The product of this endeavour, self-published in small quantity, was *Tinpot Preacher* (Mol 2003).[1]

Years before, in the introduction to his seminal work *Identity and the Sacred*, Mol reluctantly disclosed a few details of his personal biography. There, for the first time in his publications, he revealed his childhood nickname: '*blikken dominee*' (tinpot preacher) (1976: xi). Initially acknowledging the mocking tone of this appellation as it was spoken by his schoolfellows, Mol seems to have embraced the identity as his life progressed. He was 81 when *Tinpot Preacher* was published, and those decades spanning the distance between boyhood and wisdom had lent a prophetic resonance to the nickname. Martin Redeker, in his biography of Friedrich Schleiermacher, notes that the latter always viewed himself as a preacher rather than a theologian (1973: 199–200). Something similar can be said for Mol who, at 92, is still an honorary minister at St. Andrew's Presbyterian Church in Canberra, Australia. However, beyond

---

[1] Unless otherwise noted, the biographical details of Mol's personal life are taken from this account or from one-on-one interviews conducted in the spring of 2012 between the author and Hans Mol. When the information is solely or additionally available in more easily accessed publications, those sources are cited instead.

the Church, his recognized contributions are not theological but sociological though he has continued to engage enthusiastically in Christian ministry. The clever youth who received the nickname for his ready answers in Sunday-school became both a sociologist and an ordained pastor.[2] For academe, and for many of his colleagues, the former overshadowed the latter. For Mol, however, they were two hats on the same rack (Mol 2008: 271). To accept the title of 'tinpot preacher' was to accept the appraisal of others whilst retaining a role and a faith that was personal and significant.

* * *

Johannis (Hans) Jacob Mol was born on 14 February 1922 in Rozenburg, Netherlands. His childhood, though it included a move from Rozenburg in the south to Ophemert in the centre of the Netherlands, was primarily defined by farm labour. His father, also a Johannis Jacob Mol, earned a diploma from an agricultural school and decided that his best hopes for continuing the family vocation lay in the farmland available for rent from Baron MacKay, a Scotsman who owned most of Ophemert and the surrounding farms. This move, occurring when Mol was only three years old, would prove intellectually fateful for the farmer's son.

Mol's parents were the recipients of liberal educations and had inherited a subculture in the Zeeland islands characterized by a veneration of individuality and self-sufficiency. This progressive bent was precisely what led them to Baron MacKay's land as the latter believed that this variety of farmer would prove much more valuable than the local types who were seemingly committed to the increasingly antiquated feudal model (Mol 1976: xi–xii). At the same time, this proclivity for independence also alienated the Mol family from both the local working class and the social elites of Ophemert. Unable to speak the local dialect but possessing the intellectual capacity to recognize and decry any social injustices originating within the upper-class, Mol's parents struggled to maintain their identity as free-thinking farmers. Eventually, their regard for the powers of reason offered them a unique opportunity to speak out for their fellow farmers. Mol once noted that his mother 'expected much more from radical political action than from praying (ibid.)'. This orientation

---

[2] By all accounts, young Mol certainly was not shy. His quick replies in Sunday school were not isolated events. In his Latin class, the teacher referred to him as Johannis Loquax, a nod to his verbosity.

both to religion and to politics not only resulted in the composition by Mol's parents of progressive letters sent to farmers' newsletters across the nation but in crystallizing Mol's views at a young age. Young Hans believed that the power to effect change resided in the ability to trust rationality. Religion, on the other hand, offered little more than the opportunity to play a pipe organ, the enjoyment of which was somewhat tempered by the necessity of enduring the minister's Barthian sermons (ibid.: xiii).

An Age of Reason

Respect for enlightened thinking was also fostered at the Gymnasium Mol attended in the nearby town of Tiel. The Gymnasium was an academically rigorous school, and it was there at the age of 12 that Mol first encountered a thoroughgoing love of intellectualism. As an adult, Mol claims that this respect for the powers of reason became 'much too ingrained', but there is little doubt that the intensity of the workload and the high expectations of the staff served to establish a solid base for Mol's academic career (1976: xii). Beyond instruction in six languages, the Gymnasium offered a classical education which, alongside other authors, introduced Mol to Plato's thought. The Greek philosopher's probing insights and stirring questions planted a seed of intellectual, existential curiosity that sprouted and thrived years later.

In the meantime, the farmer's son successfully ignored the bullying of his wealthy, upper-class peers and managed to focus his energies on passing the final exams. Such effort was rewarded in 1941 when Mol passed the exams and was, in turn, eligible to attend university. Having spent his life on a farm, witnessing the incessant struggle of those engaged in agricultural lifestyles and the increasing financial difficulties brought on by the Depression and the Nazi occupation of the Netherlands in 1940 Mol and his parents decided that he should not only earn a university education but should be tested at the Psycho-Technical Institute in Utrecht in order to optimise the suitability of Mol to his chosen field of study. Over three days, Mol underwent psychological testing with the result that he would be best paired with the demands and necessary aptitudes of sociology!

Mol, however, was neither amenable nor convinced. He desired that which was growing more elusive in the early days of World War II, a stable career with ample financial incentive. As the Depression spread, Mol's parents had been forced to borrow significant amounts of money and were finding themselves uncertain about their financial future. Mol, who had been sent to the Gymnasium in order to avoid life as a farmer, wanted to ease his parents' burdens. He chose economics instead of sociology and enrolled in the University of Amsterdam.

Envisioning a future career at the large sugar refinery run by a few of his relatives, Mol began studies in economic theory and accounting supplemented by a number of courses in sociology. University work was complicated by the Nazi occupation of Holland. Soon after Mol's studies commenced, food was rationed through a system of ration cards. Students received limited rations, and Mol was forced to ride the train back to his parents' home in Ophemert in order to obtain groceries. This was not simply an inconvenience but led to Mol's first subversive, anti-Nazi action of the war. Transporting suitcases filled with food from Ophemert to Amsterdam, Mol's parents provided him with the address of Jews who needed food. The latter, typically harboured by sympathetic locals, chose not to register for ration cards in an effort to remain elusive. More than once, Mol delivered food to these individuals, risking his own freedom in doing so.

A Reason to Doubt

Mol could not evade the Gestapo indefinitely. He refused to sign an oath of loyalty to the Nazi cause and, though he had attempted to hide in Amsterdam, the secret police located him and sent him off to work in Germany. Almost 45 years after the actual events, Mol recounted the story of his arrest and imprisonment by the Gestapo in *How God Hoodwinked Hitler* (1987). After arriving in Kleinwanzleben, the Germans assigned Mol to work in a sugar factory. This decision was based on Mol's assiduous, intentional display of knowledge concerning the sugar industry. Though the work was forced, the experience and the knowledge gained would eventually prove useful after the war when Mol did, in fact, go to work at his uncle's refinery. In 1943, however, Kleinwanzleben was less an educational venue and more the setting of the most unequivocally defining event in Mol's life.

On 22 December, 1943 the Gestapo detained Mol and three of his friends (ibid.: 7). The young Dutchmen were interrogated and confessed. They were guilty of *Rundfunkverbrechen*, attempting to subvert the Nazi agenda by utilizing a forbidden radio to receive BBC broadcasts whilst engaging in the equally forbidden act of sharing the content of the Allied war updates with other non-Germans (Mol 1976: xiii). Such criminal behaviour was considered seditious par excellence and was suppressed by the threat of death. Expecting the worst, a place among the ranks of concentration camp inmates, Mol learned that he was instead to be sent to a Gestapo prison camp called Rothensee, north of Magdeburg (Mol 1987: 21). For the next three weeks, Mol remained at Rothensee fighting against Nazi cruelty, lice, and an increasing scepticism about his own self-sufficiency.

Mol was relocated to Magdeburg prison to await his trial on 14 January 1944 (ibid.: 39). The trial eventually came after six months of labour in the prison (ibid.: 43). In that time, Mol's understanding of the world transformed. The human psyche became the subject of diligent scrutiny within the monotonous prison system. Mol observed the psychological advantage of the political prisoners, a group defined by their proclivity for independent thought and equally independent survival (ibid.: 53). The Germans did not allow such prisoners to reside together in the same prison cells, so these anti-Nazi individuals faced their new existences alone. Mol, guilty of undermining the Nazi agenda, was just such a prisoner. He found resolve in his political convictions, but began to question the preparedness of his faith in human reason. On three different occasions Mol was asked to join the Waffen SS, once at Rothensee and twice at Magdeburg (ibid.: 58–60). If he had accepted, his case would have been dismissed and the charges dropped. Yet, his political mettle proved up to the task; Mol refused the offer every time.

The irony, however, was that Mol's orientation to life was changing in response to an equivalent change in the world. After six months of intense loneliness and unsolicited lessons concerning the potential for human suffering at Magdeburg, Mol was officially sentenced to one and a quarter years of hard labour at Halle *Zuchthaus* (ibid.: 74). During the ensuing weeks and months, despair and rancour saturated Mol and his fellow inmates, filling the void as hope, dignity, and self-efficacy departed from their minds. He witnessed an outbreak of Typhus, suicide, sexual perversions, nearly died due to infection in his blood, and was forced to uncover unexploded (and highly volatile) bombs. All the while, the intellectual edifice gradually constructed during his childhood and fortified at the Gymnasium attempted to stem the relentless affront presented by the unprecedented experiences of prison.

Looking back on this phase of his life, Mol noted that 'the prison system hated intellectuals and students ... I soon learnt to keep my university education a deep secret' (ibid.: 78). In such a setting, the precepts of rationality as the supreme foundation for the erection of an indomitable identity succumbed to the functionality of religious faith. The former gave way to the latter because, as Mol states, '... in the intellectual world of humanism the basic securities of life have never been radically denied' (ibid.: 76). World War II stole those securities from Mol and from those with whom he shared this harsh existence. With the benefit of hindsight, he explains that his prison sentence altered his identity:

The old Hans Mol with his arrogant belief in the divinity of reason was gone. He had become chastened by the scourge of war, rejection, cruelty and pain. He had stared death in the face, but incongruously death had sent him back on at least three occasions. He had been set on a path of trust and faith from where there was no return (ibid.: 137).

Freedom and Faith

Early in his academic career, Mol held rationality to be culpable both for the considerable advances and achievements of the twentieth century as well as the injurious, yet prolonged, differentiation of society:

> The very principles which have made these economic and technical achievements and adaptations possible (rational analysis and efficient calculation) are structurally unsuited for the provision of a stable frame of reference. However successful rationality may be as a means to achieve ends, it is singularly ill-equipped to provide a uniform world view. Rationality as a norm is essentially divisive. It encourages doubt of assumptions, competes with emotional approaches and obviates cohesion. (Mol 1969: 31)

This divisiveness, this deleterious effect of reason, received significant attention from Mol throughout his tenure as a sociologist of religion. In many ways, the lasting outcome of his prison experiences was veneration of equanimity. His waning confidence in the abilities of human intellect was met by a waxing trust in the efficacy of religious faith. Initially, this newfound perspective altered Mol's response to, and relationship with, those with whom he came into contact.

After the war, Mol briefly returned to his studies in economics at the University of Amsterdam. This proved fruitless and uninteresting, and in 1946 he accepted a position at his uncle's sugar refinery in Dinteloord. As assistant to the chief administrator, Mol was in a position of influence within the factory's hierarchy. Having spent the preceding months attending public lectures on the importance of human rights and management/trade union cooperation, Mol wasted little time in convincing his superior to revive an out-of-print newsletter for the factory employees. *De Kleine Courant* had existed in the early twentieth century and was effective in mollifying management/labour relations. Mol envisioned a sort of recapitulation; the newsletter condoning the primacy of individual rights and the importance of the mutual regulation of wages and profits. In effect, this was a natural corollary to Mol's life-changing encounter with fascism and the subsequent discovery of the need for harmony in society. The latter was fostered during this time but eventually assumed a central and lasting position in Mol's sociological thinking.

Early in his time at the sugar refinery, Mol began a personal journal in which he wrote considerable entries concerned with leadership and business administration. In one such record, he noted an encounter with the planner of a local music concert. The organizer informed Mol that the seating arrangements for the audience were very important; various elites needed to be seated in the first rows. According to his journal, Mol explained to the gentleman that status should not be based on materiality but on the inherent 'quality' of the person. A direct consequence of his prison observations, this sentiment ultimately led Mol to quit his job at the factory. His immediate superior did not value the ideals held with such esteem by this young manager, and the former often vetoed various articles intended for publication in *De Kleine Courant*, arguing that these pieces could incite the labourers. Thus, in 1948 Mol used his own funds to publish all of the vetoed articles together with his resignation letter. In *Identity and the Sacred*, he describes this issue of the newsletter as 'a howling success' and notes that its articles eventually found eager reception with board members and various union officials (1976: xiv). At the age of 81, Mol described the decision to publish the issue as the second best decision of his life, trailing the decision to propose to his wife Ruth in 1952.

Theology and Ministry in Australia

Mol absconded to the shores of Australia before hearing of the response to his resignation. He was booked on the first emigrant ship from the Netherlands to Australia, and it was a voyage that would alter his own life course. On that ship, surrounded by fellow Dutchmen, Mol was chosen to develop a communication network for Dutch immigrants in Australia, disseminating information about their new home in their native language. The task also involved an indubitable religious component. Religion had become increasingly important for Mol in the post-war years, and his fellow immigrants were often members of the Dutch Reformed tradition. Upon arriving in Sydney, Mol set out to investigate the various Christian denominations with the intention of reporting his findings to those immigrants on his network list. This he did, and finding that there was already a strong Presbyterian presence in the country, he and the other Dutch ultimately decided to merge with the pre-existing tradition rather than establish a Dutch Reformed congregation. Mol's contacts with the Presbyterians not only led to his first paid ministry work as 'home missionary' to the Dutch but to his place as a student at St Andrew's College, University of Sydney where he would first study theology in a formal setting.

Though his time at St Andrew's College did not result in a Bachelor's degree, it did provide him with the theological training necessary to be ordained into the Presbyterian Church on 27 February 1952. In the three years prior to his ordination, however, Mol had grown both interested and highly conversant in Christian theology. At the end of his first year, it was reported that he was second in his class. By the time he finished the three-year programme, Mol was awarded the Kenneth Edward prize for the top student in theology. He found that his war experiences and coursework (however limited) in sociology at the University of Amsterdam harmonized well with the work of theologians like Karl Barth and Reinhold Niebuhr. Mol was a self-described 'mediocre student' when studying at the Dutch Gymnasium but quickly became familiar with the productivity engendered by passion.

His theological education also found ready application. Some time before official ordination, Mol began preaching to local Dutch congregations. This immersion in the practical world of theology as well as the corresponding encounter with the needs of the laity influenced Mol in an irreversible way. The same concern he had exhibited for the working classes of Holland emerged again in the form of dedication to the Christians 'in the pews'. More specifically, Mol was increasingly preoccupied with ministry to Dutch believers in Australia, and this European aspect of his ministry resulted in his enrolment at the Institute of the World Council of Churches in 1954. Directed by Henry Kraemer in Bossey, Switzerland this visit to the institute allowed Mol to serve as European tour guide to his new Australian bride, Ruth McIntyre. In addition to visiting Italy, France, and Germany; the couple travelled to Holland where Mol recruited new clergy for the burgeoning community of Dutch Christians in Australia. The trip was successful in this objective and was punctuated by an invitation to meet with Queen Juliana in order to discuss emigration.

Mol's prominence in the Presbyterian Church of Australia was rising dramatically. In 1954, the same year that he was sent to Holland on a recruiting mission, he learned that he had been chosen as a delegate for the upcoming conference for the World Council of Churches. Yet, Hans and Ruth Mol had to decline this opportunity as they were working toward a deadline and would not be returning to Australia. Though he was without the credential of a bachelor's degree in theology, Mol applied to and was accepted into both Princeton and Union Seminaries. Taken with the influential writings of Reinhold Niebuhr, Mol decided to accept the scholarship to Union Seminary and began his studies there in the autumn of 1954.

A Sympathetic Scholar

In a section of *Meaning and Place* entitled 'Myth and Reason', Mol describes his sociological approach as 'sympathetic scholarship' (1983: 67). This method attempts to explicate both 'the differences between myth and reason or religion and science *and* the compensations each provides for the other (original emphasis)'. This description follows Mol's discussion of the shortcomings in the academic study of religion, a function of the scholar's intense faith in the power of rationality and positivism despite the conspicuously non-rational nature of the object studied. One is tempted to analyse such statements only in terms of a harrowing prison experience leading to disillusionment with pure reason. To do so, however, is to fix one's gaze on a small area of the canvas at the expense of the full intellectual portraiture.

Mol's 'sympathetic scholarship', though resting on a foundation formed during World War II, also points us to his encounters with prominent theologians during his time at Union Seminary. His perception of religion, reminiscent of Rudolph Otto's 'numinous' and 'creature consciousness' (1936: 10–11), crystallized as he attended seminars with Reinhold Niebuhr and sat through the lectures of Paul Tillich.[3] The former exhibited a dialectical manner of thinking; this was particularly agreeable to Mol who was first lured into theology by the work of Karl Barth (2010) and the latter's notion of 'dialectical theology'.[4] Tillich, on the other hand, stimulated Mol's thoughts on the transcendence of God and religion, an observation that eventually informed Mol's own definition of religion as 'the sacralization of identity' (1976: 1).[5]

Union and its popular professors, then, served to foment Mol's intellect and focus his curiosities. Working toward completion of a Bachelor of Divinity degree, he chose to specialize in religion and society. The laity was not forgotten. Mol possessed an affinity with Niebuhr's work partly because of its concern for the sinful nature of pride, egoism, and pomposity. This theological assertion

---

[3] Paul Tillich, *Theology of Culture* (New York: Oxford University Press, 1959: 40). It is noteworthy that Tillich acknowledged his own indebtedness to Otto's concepts. However, Mol's indebtedness to Tillich should not be overstated as the latter, arguing for religion as an 'ultimate concern', actually sets out to dissolve the delineation between sacred and profane. Mol, on the other hand, maintains the distinction but accepts and propagates the idea of an ineffable quality to religious phenomena.

[4] Barth's commentary on Paul's letter to the Romans (*Der Römerbrief*) is viewed as the quintessential example of his dialectical theology which emphasizes the various dualities and paradoxes in Christian concepts of the divine such as grace and justice.

[5] Here, sacralization is a process entailing emotional commitment, ritual, and objectivity. Thus, to sacralize is to remove from the mundane and relocate in the transcendent.

easily translated into a concern for all, blurring any boundaries separating the academic 'ivory tower' from the rest of society. In addition, the choice to study religion and society was a direct consequence of having worked exclusively with immigrants in Australia. Mol remained interested in the potential *anomie* felt by religious migrants and sought to examine the intersection of religion and societal patterns.

Unfortunately, the religion and society seminars proved lacklustre. In his autobiography, he describes these courses as 'dull and factual', dismissive of 'the trenchant scrutiny of [Union's anti-evangelism] philosophy by the giants of the seminary, Reinhold Niebuhr and Paul Tillich'. Even so, the sociological nature of the material served an important function; Mol grew increasingly eager to study sociology. After finishing his Bachelor's thesis on the pertinence of Christianity for immigrant adjustment in the spring of 1955, Mol managed to enrol in a joint master's programme with Union and Columbia University. This programme in Christian Ethics allowed Mol to work with Niebuhr at Union whilst signing up for as many sociology courses as he could at Columbia. Thus, he finally began to heed the advice of the Psycho-Technical Institute and the results of his testing there 14 years earlier.

Encouraged by his newfound enthusiasm for sociology, Mol made light work of the graduate requirement for the Master's, finishing both the coursework and the thesis during the 1955 calendar year. Mol's time at Union coincided with the post-stroke years of Niebuhr's career. The eminent theologian only taught a single graduate seminar by this time and restricted the number of students to 12. Fortunately, Mol was admitted and used the opportunity to challenge Niebuhr's criticisms of Barth. As a topic for his thesis, Mol chose to argue that Barth's theological anthropology fitted well with sociological observations. Though few of Mol's classmates agreed, Niebuhr expressed a sincere interest and ultimately served alongside Robert McAfee Brown in supervising the thesis.

Mol developed a steady cadence in his studies and not only earned admission to Columbia University to work toward a PhD in sociology but finished enough of the required courses that, by the spring of 1956, he was elevated to candidacy for the degree. In part, such quick progress resulted from the congenial atmosphere Mol discovered at Columbia. Whereas he expressed discontentment with the religion and society seminars of Union, the sociology department of Columbia facilitated his particular interests, offering courses on the sociology of religion with a young academic named Charles Glock. Glock, later to exert great influence in the sociology of religion, watched as Mol earned high marks in all of the former's classes and, as a result, asked

Mol to become a research assistant. Always the individualist, Mol declined the offer.[6]

Over the next two years, Mol completed the remaining coursework. The late 1950s was an important period for the field of sociology, and Mol undoubtedly benefited from his context. He studied under William Goode, Hans Zetterberg, and Robert Merton. Merton's work intrigued Mol. Indeed, Merton interested many during his career as he rose to prominence as one of the most significant sociologists in history. For Mol, it was Merton's focus on historical sociology and the latter's critical engagement with the work of Max Weber that was appealing. Mol recognized a conceptual overlap between Weber's assertions concerning the Puritan influence on Western capitalism and the first-hand experience with immigrant adjustment Mol had gained during his ministry in Australia. Just as Weber understood religious values to be the catalyst for social and economic change, so Mol began to question whether and to what extent such values were tied to the differences in how evangelical and mainstream clergy of immigrant groups reacted to their new home in America.

This became the topic of Mol's doctoral dissertation. His research was supervised by Merton and Sigmund Diamond. Merton's work received pride of place in the study. In 1936, Merton first published his thesis on the rise of the scientific age in the seventeenth century, arguing that an indissoluble relationship existed between the Puritanism and Pietism of the members of that scientific community and the new age to which they gave birth (1936).[7] Mol critiqued this notion, applying it and Weber's *Puritan Ethic* to the topic of Americanisation policies among immigrant religious communities. The resulting study was successfully defended on 8 December 1960, and the PhD was granted five days later.

Pastor and Professor

The University of Canterbury in Christchurch, New Zealand sent Mol a telegram late in 1961 offering him a lectureship in sociology. The news, though certainly welcome, was met with some hesitation. Not only had Mol just received American citizenship two months earlier, but he was the pastor of Bethel Presbyterian Church in a rural town of Maryland. Shortly after his

---

[6] In his recollection of this event, Mol claims that he always questioned his decision, believing that his own career may have taken a very different path had he accepted Glock's offer.

[7] This initial essay was followed by a fuller discussion of the topic: Robert K. Merton, *Science, Technology, and Society in Seventeenth Century England* (New York: Howard Fertig, 1938).

doctoral studies commenced in 1955, Mol decided to seek out a ministry position. Within months he was asked to become the fulltime pastor of this relatively large congregation (500 members). It was a position he came to relish, as much for what it taught him about American culture as for the moments it provided to exhibit Christian leadership. He and Ruth flourished at Bethel, cultivating deep emotional connections with various members of the community during the years between 1955 and 1961. Mol's dedication to Christian ministry and concern for the religious migrant had not faltered during his time at Union and Columbia. In the summer of 1961, he was asked to help organize the international conference for the World Council of Churches and, just as he had done seven years prior, he served as chaplain onboard the ship to Europe so as to offset the cost of travel whilst serving others in a pastoral role. Thus, the academic offer from the University of Canterbury was accepted but not without strong emotions from both Mol's family and a number of his congregation. He hoped to avoid the ostensible effrontery of forgoing service to the church in exchange for service to the academy, but his waxing interest in the intersection of sociology and religion proved sufficiently compelling. Mol decided that he could amplify his impact on the religious world with a university career. Canterbury provided his first chance to do so (Mol 1976: xv).

In the months leading up to his move to New Zealand, Mol managed to incorporate much of his doctoral research into a book on religious emigration. *Churches and Immigrants* was partially funded by the World Council of Churches who believed that such a topic needed addressing as more and more European churches were transplanted into foreign environs. As is often the case, this first book determined the direction of Mol's early career; of the 17 academic books and monographs Mol authored during his career, 4 of the first 5 dealt explicitly with religiosity and immigration with the other addressing church attendance among the various Christian denominations represented in New Zealand.[8] Only two of these works, however, were actually completed in New Zealand.

At the end of Mol's first year teaching at Canterbury, he was offered a position in the recently established Institute of Advanced Studies of the Australian National University in Canberra, Australia. The position entailed undeniable

---

[8] See: Hans Mol, *Churches and Immigrants* (The Hague: Research Group for European Migration Problems, 1961); *Church Attendance in Christchurch, New Zealand* (Christchurch: University of Canterbury, 1962); *Changes in Religious Behaviour of Dutch Immigrants* (The Hague: Research Group for European Migration Problems, 1965); *Race and Religion in New Zealand* (Christchurch: National Council of Churches in New Zealand, 1966); and *The Breaking of Traditions* (Berkeley: Glendessary Press, 1968).

benefits and, after convincing ANU to make the job tenure-track, Mol accepted with the proviso that he be permitted to finish a second year teaching in New Zealand. It was August 1963 when he bid farewell to New Zealand, a location he still cites as the world's apex of natural beauty, after a scenic flight around Mount Cook the nation's highest peak.

In Canberra, Mol's career began to blossom. Here, in addition to completing a number of projects started in New Zealand, he also published his doctoral thesis (*The Breaking of Traditions*) and either published or concluded the work for three other volumes.[9] As a research fellow, Mol had few teaching responsibilities and could dedicate ample time to his other scholarly pursuits. The forthright position he had always taken with regards to his own Christian faith not only led to research projects in New Zealand, such as that conducted for the National Council of Churches, but also to ministry and writing prospects in Australia. His affiliation with St Andrew's in Canberra, the National Presbyterian Church, commenced during this time.[10] In addition to his preaching, Mol seized an important chance to address a broader lay audience. In 1963, a British bishop named John A.T. Robinson published *Honest to God*, a critique of traditional interpretations of the Bible and approaches to Christian theology. Treading on the path blazed by Mol's former professor, Paul Tillich, Robinson's book incited sustained controversy which reverberated throughout the English-speaking world for a number of years. Consequently, Mol was commissioned by Thomas Nelson Publishing of Australia to write a book about the perceived crossroads faced by Christianity in the antipodes.

The result was *Christianity in Chains*, Mol's first excursion into the realm of trade books. Though aimed at a lay audience, it is unequivocally social-scientific in its perspective. Whilst discussing the problem of religious irrelevance within a secular society, for example, Mol highlights the human need for 'unity and order' as well as the corresponding necessity for social institutions to offer 'a common agreement as to how existence is to be interpreted' (1969: 30). In Mol's estimation, Christianity loses cultural relevance only when it is incapable of cementing human commitment around a set of norms, thus preventing conversion from the secular order to the minority view represented by the Christian churches (ibid.: 26, 32). In the end, however, he concedes an important point:

---

[9] Hans Mol, *Christianity in Chains; Religion in Australia* (Melbourne: Nelson, 1971); and ed., *Western Religion* (The Hague: Mouton, 1972).

[10] As of 2013, Mol ministerial relationship with St. Andrew's is in its fiftieth year.

> Institutional religion did not and does not unify all of life and existence under one common denominator. It is potentially equipped to do this, but in actual fact the individual more often than not adds his role as a church-goer or a Catholic or an Anglican to his many other roles. His religion is a compartmentalised rather than a deep unifying concern. (ibid.: 35)

Almost begrudgingly, Mol acknowledges the inability of religious institutions to function as 'sacred canopies'. Even so, the perspective intimated in *Christianity in Chains* betrays a number of key components of Mol's sociological thinking, elements that crystallized during the ensuing years and coalesced in *Identity and the Sacred*.

Functionalism and Sacred Identity

By 1969, the year Thomas Nelson published Mol's response to *Honest to God*, Mol already had published a number of books and articles in the sociology of religion. Two of the latter went beyond simply summarizing the findings of empirical research, attempting to interpret data and theoretically situate the observed religious patterns of various groups (1963, 1965a). In 'The Function of Marginality', Mol assumes a Weberian stance in his assertion that 'predominant features of our modern Western world, such as rationality, objective observation, efficient management, logical calculation, require marginal attitudes' (1963: 176). A degree of marginalization, in other words, is a requisite for the development of Western values. This emphasis on religious values is present in 'Integration versus Segregation in the New Zealand Churches' as well. Here, Mol notes the Maori resistance to integrated churches and attributes this position to the discomfort felt by Maoris when encountering Western, Protestant values (1965a: 142). More importantly, Mol's approach to his work became increasingly theoretical during this time. Whilst at Columbia, he had attended guest lectures by Talcott Parsons in addition to his usual tutelage under Merton and Glock. As intellectual influences go, Glock's fondness for analysis was only outweighed in Mol's mind by the Weberian, functionalist tendencies of Merton and Parsons. Therefore, the presuppositions that emerge in Mol's early work should occasion little surprise. He understood humanity as possessing an innate drive for order, and he believed religion served to offer an interpretation of reality that had the potential to ameliorate the cancerous disorder lurking in the dark places of society. Further, he was not afraid to follow Weber and others in dedicating much focus to the individual and his or her decisions and values.

The dialectical nature of his theological training also surfaced as his analytical frame of reference came into its own. In a meeting of the Canberra Sociological Society in 1967, Mol was able to utilize this tendency to understand society as an incessant oscillation between two extremes to his benefit. As president of the society, he had helped organize the meeting. In this instance, it entailed a comparison of the sociological and philosophical approaches to religion and morality. Mol honed his theoretical notions, arguing that meaning systems and moral codes both have the potential to harm or integrate religion. Too much of either can lead to debilitating rigidity or fatal inclusivity.

Such theoretical ruminations received a degree of negative attention at Australian National University, however, and Mol was passed over for promotion. His immediate superior in the department did not approve of the time spent on *Christianity in Chains* and hardly recognized the seemingly speculative content of the book. Though Mol was not made a senior fellow, he did receive a research sabbatical for the 1969/70 academic year. The fecundity of his years in New Zealand and Australia were undeniable, and when he set off to spend his sabbatical in the United States he did not suspect that he would not be resuming the same course at the same location one year later.

The United States and Canada

The unique brand of neo-functionalism, if such a label is appropriate, promulgated by Mol was well suited to North America in the late 1960s. His sabbatical of 1969 began with a fall semester at the University of California, Santa Barbara. Replacing Thomas O'Dea, Mol found himself in what should have been an environment hospitable to his approach. Just a few years earlier, Peter Berger and Thomas Luckmann published their groundbreaking work on the sociology of knowledge followed by Berger's application of the same ideas to religion (Berger and Luckmann 1967; Berger 1969). Louis Schneider, whose work Mol admired and who was also a past student of Merton, published *Religion, Culture, and Society* in 1964 and was currently finishing his functionalist contribution (*Sociological Approach to Religion*) the same year Mol arrived. Consequently, Mol's concept of dialectical forces in society and the pressure they exert on humanity's drive for meaning and order were in line with many of the most influential works of his contemporaries.

California, however, presented a different scenario. Cultural revolution was sweeping the continent, and theories and theorists who appeared to defend the status quo were losing respect in areas such as Santa Barbara. Whilst teaching there, Mol noted that one of the most popular courses in the sociology department consisted of various professors appearing before the class in succession and lambasting the great majority of existing social establishments. In response, Mol published an article in *The American Sociologist* in which this socially subversive behaviour on the part of his colleagues was taken to be the natural consequence of years spent withholding personal opinion in the name of objective scholarship (1971b).

From California, Mol then travelled to Marquette University in Wisconsin. He spent the winter semester there and was so well received that he was made an offer for a full professorship. Indeed, within the same week in 1970 Mol was met with four job offers at the tenured, full professor level: from Marquette, University of Calgary, University of Edmonton, and McMaster University. After only six years at Australian National University, Mol faced another career decision. The offers were generous and, in the light of his recent differences with the departmental head in Canberra, Mol could not resist. He chose to accept the position at McMaster, a university with a burgeoning religious studies department. One of three senior researchers in the department, Mol was given a light teaching load and permitted to pursue the publication of his most recent project.

Prior to his sabbatical, Mol collaborated with Margaret Hetherton and Margaret Henty on an ambitious sociological study of religion. International in scope, the data gathered was to be condensed and presented at the 1970 world conference of the International Sociological Association. The conference took Mol to Europe in the summer before his new work commenced at McMaster, and his findings were enthusiastically embraced by the Sociology of Religion Research Committee there. Though the work (*Western Religion*) was not published until two years later, Mol's decision to embark on a career at McMaster proved judicious. Not only was he encouraged in the sociology of religion, a barely nascent field in Australia, but his emergent interest in broader theories of religion enjoyed support from a formidable network of colleagues in all areas of religious studies.

Even as his theoretical ideas brewed, he remained very internationally active. In addition to consistent participation in the *Conference International de Sociologie Religieuse*, he became president of the Sociology of Religion Research Committee of the International Sociological Association in 1974 and assisted with the planning for the VIIIth World Congress of Sociology the same year. Back at McMaster, his past perspectives and experiences gradually culminated in a fully developed theory of religion. The dialectical understanding of society, clearly evident in his earlier work, morphed into a theory focused on identity as a salient analytical tool for the scholar of religion. Closely following the line of thought undergirding the previously mentioned 'The Function of Marginality', Mol published two more papers in which an almost idiosyncratic form of functionalism materialized: 'Secularization and Cohesion' and 'Marginality and Commitment as Hidden Variables in the Jellinek/Weber/Merton Theses on the Calvinist Ethic' (1970, 1974). As is obvious from the latter's title, Mol was not only grappling with his own personal faith experiences and the massive quantity of data gathered in the *Western Religion* project but with the functionalist strands present in the work of Merton and other social-scientists.

Shaken by his father's death in 1971, Mol maintained an intense focus on his young identity theory, presenting papers on the idea in Montreal, Toronto, Cologne, Paris, and Barcelona. Though the wide acceptance of functionalism exhibited during the 1960s crumbled under the shifting values of the Western world, various sociologists still maintained that religion provided identity or integration.[11] New discoveries in biology and psychology ostensibly substantiated this claim, and Mol was attuned to these disparate voices.[12] From Mol's perspective, these sources formed a harmonious whole, a resoundingly firm foundation for a new identity theory of religion.

Having refined the rough contours of his theory over the course of 14 years, eight books/monographs, and numerous articles or conference addresses, Mol finally published *Identity and the Sacred* in 1976. It is appropriate to consider this book his magnum opus. Though it arrived to mix reviews in the field, the volume caused sustained reflection on the intersection of identity and religion for at least 40 years.[13] Here, Mol outlined the details of a comprehensive

---

[11] See: Robert Bellah, ed., *Religion and Progress in Modern Asia* (New York: The Free Press, 1965); Harold Fallding, *The Sociology of Religion: An Explanation of the Unity and Diversity in Religion* (Toronto: McGraw-Hill, 1974); Orrin E. Klapp, *Collective Search for Identity* (New York: Holt, Rinehart and Winston, 1969). Each of these was of particular importance for the development of Mol's theory.

[12] See: Erik H. Erikson, *Childhood and Society* (New York: Norton, 1963); Erikson, *Identity-Youth and Crisis* (New York: Norton, 1968); Erikson, 'Identity, Psychosocial', *International Encyclopedia of the Social Sciences* (New York: Macmillan, 1968). In addition to Erikson's influence from the field of psychology, Konrad Lorenz corroborated a number of Mol's views from a biological standpoint: Konrad Lorenz, *On Aggression* (London: Methuen, 1970).

[13] See Richard Fenn's review in *Journal for the Scientific Study of Religion*, 17(1) (1978): 67–8; and Paul Rule, 'From the Sacred to the Scientific', *Religious Traditions: A New Journal in the Study of Religion*, 1(2) (1978): 72–3. Fenn's review is primarily negative in tone and suggests a circularity to Mol's thinking. Rule's review includes stern criticisms but also refers to the theory as a 'masterly sketch' as long as it is taken to be relevant only for western religions. Rule also notes that Mol's perspective avoids 'the distortions' of competing theories and is 'provocative and solidly anchored in the experiences and beliefs of ordinary men and women'.

sociological theory in which religion is defined as 'the sacralization of identity' (1976: 1), identity is taken to be 'the stable niche that man occupies in a potentially chaotic environment which he is therefore prepared vigorously to defend' (ibid.: 65), and sacralization is 'the process by means of which on the level of symbol-systems certain patterns acquire the same taken-for-granted, stable, eternal, quality which on the level of instinctive behaviour was acquired by the consolidation and stabilization of new genetic materials' (ibid.: 5). Religion was not imagined to be a static *thing*; it was conceptualized as a social process. He explored this process in the light of an underpinning dialectic between integration and adaptation. This allowed Mol to critique the vast majority of existing theories because his accommodated both the integrative quality of religion favoured by the functionalists and the destructive potential of religion highlighted by others.

Upon arriving at McMaster, Mol had quickly published his previous research on religious patterns in Australia (1971a). By 1977, however, Mol was prepared to revisit much of his past work, eager to update the data and apply his recently systematized theory. Using sabbaticals and research fellowships, Mol proceeded to accomplish that goal. In 1982, he published the first two titles in a trilogy: *The Fixed and the Fickle: Religion and Identity in New Zealand* and *The Firm and the Formless: Religion and Identity in Aboriginal Australia*. The third volume was published as *Faith and Fragility: Religion and Identity in Canada* and appeared alongside a new work on Australian religiosity (1985a, 1985b). Mol was brazen in his attempts to demonstrate the utility of the identity theory. The basics of the theory served as the common theme in all of his subsequent academic publications.

The attention garnered not only led to publications but to speaking invitations. Between 1977 and his retirement in 1987, Mol presented five lectures on dialectical thinking at the University of Madras in India, gave the Paine lecture on religion at the University of Missouri, headed the discussion of his edited book on religion and identity at the VIIIth World Congress of the International Sociological Association (Mol 1978), gave the opening address at the 1978 International Conference on the Sociology of Religion in Tokyo, presented the Herman Enns Memorial Lecture at McMaster Divinity College, and opened the XVth Congress of the International Association for the History of Religions in Sydney. Ninian Smart was the respondent for the last of those addresses, and with his closing remarks Mol's exceptionally fruitful academic career effectively came to a close as well.

Officially, Mol retired in 1987 at the age of 65. His prolific publication regimen certainly slowed, but his earnest loyalty to religion did not. In the

16 years he spent at McMaster, Mol maintained a connection to his personal faith. He often spoke at the gatherings of various Christian denominations and exhibited as much fidelity to his Presbyterianism as he did to his identity theory. Retirement simply liberated Mol. He returned to his adopted home, Australia. There he resumed his attendance at St. Andrew's Presbyterian Church where he frequently preached. Many of those sermons were compiled and published in his final book *Calvin for the Third Millennium*, a sincere attempt to fuse social science with the writings of Calvin (Mol 2008).

Conclusion

During his career, Hans Mol wore two hats but bore a constellation of influences. He carried memories of the Holocaust alongside a familiarity with the struggles of religious migrants. An abiding affinity for the theology of Barth coexisted with a trust in the explanatory potential of functionalism bequeathed to him from his mentors. For some, the Holocaust meant the end of God. For some, cultural upheaval meant the end of functionalism. For Mol, each of these underscored only one of two extremes, and he aimed for balance. Mol saw give-and-take between competing social factors and posited that identity is found precisely where humans are able to stabilize this volatility. He was an ostensibly suspect proponent of religious faith, a man whose intellectual leanings and university training seemed to pave the way for strictly secular achievement. Yet, his religious faith operated like a fulcrum, signalling the midpoint between the conflicting experiences of his biography. Validating the sociological theory to which he had committed so much time and effort, Mol ultimately emerged with a sacralized self-definition. He embraced paradox, adopted his childhood nickname, and called himself a 'tinpot preacher'.

References

Barth, K. (2010) [1919] *Der Römerbrief*. Tübingen: Theologischer Verlag Zürich.
Bellah, R. (ed.) (1965) *Religion and Progress in Modern Asia*. New York: The Free Press.
Berger, P. (1969) *The Social Reality of Religion*. London: Faber.
Berger, P. and Luckmann, T. (1967) *The Social Construction of Reality*. London: Lane.

Erikson, E. (1963) *Childhood and Society*. New York: Norton.
Erikson, E. (1968a) *Identity-Youth and Crisis*. New York: Norton.
Erikson, E. (1968b) 'Identity, Psychosocial', *International Encyclopedia of the Social Sciences*. New York: Macmillan.
Fallding, H. (1974) *The Sociology of Religion, An Explanation of the Unity and Diversity in Religion*. Toronto: McGraw-Hill.
Klapp, O. (1969) *Collective Search for Identity*. New York: Holt, Rinehart and Winston.
Lorenz, K. (1970) *On Aggression*. London: Methuen.
Merton, R.K. (1936) 'Puritanism, Pietism, and Science', *The Sociological Review*, 28(1): 1–30.
Merton, R.K. (1938) *Science, Technology, and Society in Seventeenth Century England*. New York: Howard Fertig.
Mol, H. (1961) *Churches and Immigrants*. The Hague: Research Group for European Migration Problems.
Mol, H. (1962) *Church Attendance in Christchurch, New Zealand*. Christchurch: University of Canterbury.
Mol, H. (1963) 'The Function of Marginality', *International Migration*, 1(3): 175–7.
Mol, H. (1965a) 'Integration versus Segregation in the New Zealand Churches', *British Journal of Sociology*, 16(2): 140–49.
Mol, H. (1965b) *Changes in Religious Behaviour of Dutch Immigrants*. The Hague: Research Group for European Migration Problems.
Mol, H. (1966) *Race and Religion in New Zealand*. Christchurch: National Council of Churches in New Zealand.
Mol, H. (1968) *The Breaking of Traditions*. Berkeley: Glendessary Press.
Mol, H. (1969) *Christianity in Chains*. Melbourne: Thomas Nelson.
Mol, H. (1970) 'Secularization and Cohesion', *Review of Religious Research*, 2(3): 183–91.
Mol, H. (1971a) *Religion in Australia*. Melbourne: Nelson.
Mol, H. (1971b) 'The Dysfunctions of Sociological Knowledge', *The American Sociologist*, 6(3): 221–3.
Mol, H., Hetherton, M. and Henty, M. (eds) (1972) *Western Religion*. The Hague: Mouton.
Mol, H. (1974) 'Marginality and Commitment as Hidden Variables in the Jellinek/Weber/Merton Theses on the Calvinist Ethic', *Current Sociology*, 22: 279–97.
Mol, H. (1976) *Identity and the Sacred*. Oxford: Basil Blackwell.
Mol, H. (ed.) (1978) *Identity and Religion*. Beverly Hills: Sage Publications.

Mol, H. (1982a) *The Fixed and the Fickle*. Waterloo: Wilfrid Laurier University Press.

Mol, H. (1982b) *The Firm and the Formless*. Waterloo: Wilfrid Laurier University Press.

Mol, H. (1983) *Meaning and Place: An Introduction to the Social Scientific Study of Religion*. New York: The Pilgrim Press.

Mol, H. (1985a) *Faith and Fragility*. Burlington: Trinity Press.

Mol, H. (1985b) *The Faith of Australians*. Sydney: Allen & Unwin.

Mol, H. (1987) *How God Hoodwinked Hitler*. Tring: Lion Publishing.

Mol, H. (2003) *Tinpot Preacher*. Queanbeyan: Talpa Publishing.

Mol, H. (2008) *Calvin for the Third Millennium*. Canberra: Australian National University Press.

Otto, R. (1936) *The Idea of the Holy*. London: Oxford University Press.

Redeker, M. (1973) *Schleiermacher: Life and Thought*. Philadelphia: Fortress Press.

Robinson, J. (1963) *Honest to God*. London: SCM Press.

Schneider, L. (ed.) (1964) *Religion, Culture, and Society: A Reader in the Sociology of Religion*. New York: Wiley.

Schneider, L. (1970) *Sociological Approach to Religion*. New York: Wiley.

Tillich, P. (1959) *Theology of Culture*. New York: Oxford University Press.

Chapter 2
Mol's Sociology: Social Theory, Dialectics and Hegel's Shadow

Louis Greenspan

Mol's theory, published in 1976 as *Identity and the Sacred*, has been subject to much interrogation – some of it supportive and some critical. Karl Popper has taught us that theories that provoke criticism might be preferable to those that inspire obituaries. If this is true then Mol's theories are still alive. I intend to demonstrate the contemporary relevance of *Identity and the Sacred* through a via dolorosa of highlighting the ideas of the doubters and naysayers. I will not praise or bury Mol's various theses but show that critical engagement with his theories can throw some light on the issues plaguing contemporary discussions of religion and secularization.

Mol and His Detractors

During his time at McMaster University, Mol faced criticism from two different constituencies within the department of Religious Studies. The first were textual scholars who were engaged in the study of Christian, Jewish, Buddhist, or Hindu texts. These individuals objected to what they believed was the bias in Mol's theory towards the construction of one template of religion in all the faith traditions. Textual scholars in religion as well as empiricists in sociology promote social-scientific methodology as the 'narrow topics of study and objects in isolation, whose methods emphasize dissecting rather than synthesizing approaches' (Principe 2011: 21). Mol's theory was alien to this methodology. *Identity and the Sacred* is encyclopaedic in its embrace and inclusive in its range of topics. It addresses topics in religion, including myth, ritual, church denomination and of course, secularization. It also addresses an exhaustive set of concepts in the social and even biological sciences. Such concepts include identity, differentiation, and integration as well as the work of figures such as Émile Durkheim, Talcott Parsons and Robert Bellah. Mol could have restated the statement of Terence, the ancient playwright, who declared in *The Self-Tormentor* 'I consider nothing that is human alien to me' as 'I consider nothing in religion alien to my theory' (Act 1, scene 1, line 25).

For textual scholars and many empiricists such ambitions represent a kind of philosophical and scientific hubris. Textual scholars in particular are concerned to uncover difference and nuance. During Mol's service the most highly regarded and best funded project in his department was a five-year study of the relationship between Rabbinic Judaism and Early Christianity that sought to compare and consider the differences in the concepts of sin, salvation, and repentance in both of these religions and in different texts of the same religion. Their criticisms echoed Hegel's reprimand to Schelling's work on history which he dismissed as 'a dark night where all cows are black' (2005: 94).

The second group of critics, philosophers from East and West, were comfortable with grand theory but not with the Darwinian and social-scientific vocabulary in which Mol had framed his ideas. They did not believe that concepts such as differentiation, integration, or even sacralization could engage the metaphysical or theological depths of either Eastern or Western Religion. They also harboured another misgiving. Mol, as we shall see, is more dismissive of the concept of the secular – both as an explanatory concept in sociology and as an historical or social reality – than most. Nietzsche might have claimed that the secular present is simply Christianity in disguise, but when he announced that God is dead he was admitting that something had changed. The philosophers might have critical accounts of the secular and secularization but none of them denied its importance.

Of course, the issues raised by textual scholars and philosophers still form a regular drumbeat of controversy in the university. The question of piecemeal textual approaches versus general theory will never go away – and is sometime fruitful. But theory has made a comeback. New grand accounts of the relationship between religion and society have appeared in the works of Manuel Castells (1997: 584) and Robert Bellah (2011: 605) among others. Today Mol's work must be measured against these theories. The most significant issue that has emerged in the era of globalization is the reality of pluralism. Philosophers ask whether religions can be formulated in deep first order propositions that demonstrate the unity of all religion but which may appear in different forms. For social scientists the question is whether any political order other than a secular one can mediate among collection of contending religious truths within one society. Mol's theory as it stands has almost no political dimension but is now perhaps compelled to develop one.

Identity and the Sacred in the History of Ideas

Thus far, I have provided a brief sketch of issues in social theory as they emerged in Mol's department and in the wider world of the social sciences and philosophy of religion. These issues remain lively, though they need to be updated and formulated in contemporary terms. At this point, however, I shall treat *Identity and the Sacred* from the perspective of an historian of ideas.[1] It is important to note that sociologists such as Max Weber, and indeed Mol himself, could be treated as philosophers of history. Mol might object to this because he seems bent on presenting his theory as a scientific treatise where sociology and biology intersect. He is concerned to show that the human social structuring that he describes as the struggle for identity, a central concept in his theory, is rooted in the biologies of the animal kingdom. In the animal kingdom, he argues, such struggle is waged with 'ardour and passion' by 'chickens to tree shrews, baboons, gorillas and man' (Mol 1976: 2). This strategy can be traced to Darwin, of course, but it is perhaps ill-advised for Mol's theory, for such an approach ignores the crucial differences between animals and humans. Even so, at one point Mol compares the struggle of social formations to integrate alien phenomena with that of an oyster ingesting sand. It is difficult to comprehend the similarities between the oyster that in this circumstance does not need to change itself, with for example, the Catholic Church addressing the challenge of feminism which poses threats to its identity. This comparison, however, feeds into a deeper problematic theme in Mol's theory, namely the relationship between the rigid fortress like identity he finds in the animal kingdom, and the flexible, open identity he sees as appropriate for humans. This signals tension in his theory. Nevertheless, the tension is of a biological sort and has little bearing on our more historical concerns, attempting to locate Mol's theoretical contribution in various streams of western thought.

---

[1] I co-taught an introductory course on Religion and the History of Social Theories at McMaster University, and I am happy to take this opportunity to thank Mol for the education I received on the history of sociological thought.

Identity Theory: Inflections and Influences

In the opening sentence of *Identity and the Sacred* Mol introduces his theory as follows: 'in this book the term, religion, is used in a very wide sense – as the *sacralization of identity*' (original emphasis) (1976: 1). For the historian (and perhaps the theologian) this formula may seem enigmatic; however, the rest of his writing consists of unpacking this phrase which, whatever else it means, situates religion as an actor in history. In fact, the historicist elements in Mol's theory are reminiscent of those in Hegel. First Mol's theory locates the dynamism of human identity formation in a process that he calls sacralization which is the climactic event in the process of adaptation, accomplished by sequence of differentiation and integration. This is a distant heir to Hegel's account of sublation (*aufheben*), going forward and upward to integrate the new. Mol himself identifies the sacralization process as 'dialectical'. Second, a little-noted feature of Mol's theory is that it is in large part inspired by his own commentary on the unfolding of modern history. In this too he recalls Hegel.

The Light of Durkheim

However Mol's account of religious identity, and of religion *as* identity, is built more on Durkheim's studies of tribal religion than on Hegelian philosophy (Durkheim 1995). Durkheim's analyses demonstrate that religion and the sacred are concentrated on items such as totems or symbols that give a society its moral solidarity. Durkheim's view can be illustrated by an imagined, though realistic, example.

Suppose we consider the activities of a mini society, let us say a military unit, examining how it emerges as what can be called a religious community. Our unit will certainly have daily routine which includes a musical presentation of its anthem, a ritual ceremony of flag raising. In the course of its routine each member hears the narrative of the exploits, its tragedies and its successes. Each member also learns the moral ideals of the unit, such as bravery, loyalty, obedience, and service. These are all concentrated in the exercise of unfurling its banners and in other ceremonials. It would be appropriate to call this a model for the creation of identity, especially as such banners, uniforms, etc., are treated as sacred. Each member would be prepared to give his life to protect these from an enemy in battle. This protected sense of belonging is what Mol calls a religious identity. Likewise the creation of that identity accords with Mol's mechanisms of sacralization: objectification, commitment, ritual and myth. Therefore, the sacralized emblems of this unit are the elements of its identity.

This unit functions like one of Durkheim's tribes; its religion is manifested in sacred symbols. Indeed Mol endorses Durkheim's account of sacralization but within limits, 'While I agree that almost anything can be sacred the emphasis here is on process, on the fluid transition from the profane to the sacred' (1976: 6). He points out that Durkheim separates the sacred and the profane while his account is built on their interaction. Mol accuses Durkheim of too static an account of religious identity offering nothing to account for the dynamics of identity formation.

In response, Mol insists upon a dialectic which is set in motion by the need for 'adaptation', driven by the inevitability of 'differentiation' and the resulting necessity of 'integration'. A fluid example of the dynamic that Mol describes might be illustrated by the history of Vatican 2. In the beginning, before Vatican 2, the Church tended to turn inward – as was the case with the Catholic Church of the thirties. In doing so, it attempted to resist change. Yet the resistance was met by currents of post war liberalism and tolerance which created demands within the Church for ecumenical dialogue. This in turn resulted in Vatican 2 – a renewal of the Church which jettisoned obligatory Latin liturgy, its ancient doctrines about the Jews, and so on. Note that for Mol the presence of religion as that which provides an imprimatur to change is most evident when it announces closure to the process of change as for example when it rejects the demands of feminism. For Mol, this is a moment of integration and consolidation. Sacralization he declares is 'a sort of brake applied to unchecked infinite adaptations in symbol systems for which there is less evolutionary necessity' (ibid.: 5). But is there a formula for applying the brake?

The Shadow of Hegel

How does Mol's dialectic of differentiation and integration compare with the dialectic of Hegel? The similarities seem evident but no firm answer can be given. One important implication of Hegel's dialectic is that dynamic history is progressive. History moves towards a goal of spiritual self-understanding. For example in Hegel's account the dialectical tension between the religion of Judaism and the religion of ancient Greece is resolved by the synthesis of both that we know as Christianity. Another example, Hegel's celebrated account of the combat between master and slave ends in a kind of draw from which something new, stoicism, emerges. Mol's examples lack the same specificity but still seem to leave open the possibility of something like historical progress. For example, Mol hints at a progressive pattern when he states that though religion establishes 'integration' and order, 'Too much order leads to stagnation and hardening of the arteries.' Yet, a question remains: is the transition from identity to identity necessarily progressive? In the 1930s, Germany moved from a democratic identity to a fascist identity. This transition follows the dynamics of identity formation, but how can it be thought of as progress? Moreover, while Mol insists on adaptation and fluid process, on dialogue and outreach, he also insists on 'fortress identity'. He notes 'the vitality of precisely those religious organizations which delineate themselves most resolutely from their secular environment' (ibid.: 30). Consequently, the similarity between Hegel's notion of progress and Mol's sense of attaining balance in the dialectic is clearer than Mol's explication of the means to that end.

Even so, we should also note that Mol's theory – like Hegel's – alludes to and even tries to explain our own contemporary history. In Mol's account we are suffering from the unravelling of the Protestant Reformation, which attacked and overthrew the Catholic Church, the central locus of identity in European history. Protestantism, he argues, especially in its Calvinist form, succeeded in responding to the elements of differentiation that appeared in early modern Europe, namely the cities, industrialism and their offspring, individualism. Calvinism succeeded in sacralizing (religionizing) the identity of these hitherto marginal formations, as a church offered them a social religious identity and therefore enhanced stability. Secularism appeared as a merely negative force, in the form of the free floating rationalism and individualism which undermined all social identity causing a species of demoralized ennui to set in and thus producing our present identity crisis. This view of the modern world is not original, nor is it meant to be. It follows the work of R.H. Tawney and Max Weber and gives us the roots of Mol's theoretical account of secularization.

Mol's Secularization

Indeed, the historical account above raises the very central question of Mol's oeuvre. He is typically dismissive of secularization, believing the term to be nearly useless for the sociological study of religion. Accordingly, his approach to secularization is the most controversial theme in his theory. He took strong exception to the widespread use of this term both in describing historical reality as well as in sociological theory. In a rejoinder to an article by social scientist Richard Fenn who contended that it was no longer possible for 'cultural integration to develop around any set of religious symbols' (1972: 16),

Mol took the author to task for limiting religion to the traditional supernatural faiths and insisted that religious expression can be found in a 'kaleidoscopic variety of sacralization patterns' (Mol 1976: 2). This perception is, of course, rooted in the work of Durkheim where religion, it seems, is everywhere. Not only are there no atheists in foxholes there are none anywhere unless you count atheism as another religion.

Certainly Mol's downgrading of secularism is the boldest, most contentious and most puzzling part of his theory. Such downgrading has baffled sociologists, philosophers and religious believers since the time of Marx and Weber. Early on, sociologists assumed the validity of the secularization hypothesis. This hypothesis stated that the advance of science and education that is the modernizing of any society would strip off the religious cloak that held it together. Peter Berger, an eminent sociologist of religion who regretted the universal emergence of the secular still yielded to its inevitability as 'the process by which sectors of society and culture are removed from the domination of religious institutions and symbols?' (1967: 107). As for philosophers, some cast anathemas on the secular and others welcomed it as a vehicle for emancipation. But none rejected it as a chimera. The same is true in common sense uses of the term. Most of us have at some time said things such as 'Football is so and so's religion' or as moralists say 'sex is the modern source of religious ecstasy', but few who make these statements mean to imply that they consider this use of 'religion' as equivalent to 'Religion' as applied to the traditional faith communities. In dismissing the secular, Mol seemed to be swimming against a tidal wave.

Yet, since the late 1970s, we have been in the grips of a global explosion of religious fundamentalism. By the 1990s sociologists began using the term 'post secularism', and Peter Berger announced that the secularization hypothesis may have to be rethought. In such circumstances, Mol might be thought of as prophetic. Mysteriously, Mol never discusses this new phenomenon. He never announces his triumph over all sociological and theological observers. We shall see that there might be reasons for this for, after all, the new fundamentalists never dismiss secularism, and indeed they enhanced its profile as their enemy.

The fundamental logical challenge to Mol's treatment of religion and secularism, then, is that while he insists that identity needs boundaries none are needed for religion. Mol, like Hegel, contends that his theory has a contemporary historical dimension. However, the view becomes problematic when Mol sets out to show how this identity crisis might be overcome. His theory implied that the secular momentum of the post-war period could not last, and he certainly seemed to be right. Now, let us look at these decades more closely.

Religious Realities of the Late Twentieth Century

In the 1960s the triumph of the secular was evident in the advanced economies of the West and celebrated in the emerging politics of the developing world. In Canada, for example, Quebec entered the 'quiet revolution' which removed the Catholic Church from its control of education. Moreover, universities severed their connection with religious founders. In Israel, Orthodox Judaism, whose role in preserving Judaism was supposedly taken over by a secular Zionist state, was in historic retreat on the verge of disappearance. In India, the congress party declared the triumph of secularism and in China Confucianism was all but forbidden. Even the Churches proclaimed *le triomphe de la laïcité*. Harvey Cox's volume *The Secular City*, in which he called for a secular tutelage of religion, became the best-selling volume of the story of the English-speaking world. The secularization hypothesis was not only a theory but evident in the lived experience of a process of emancipation.

In the late seventies, however, there was an unanticipated explosion of fundamentalist activism, a development which might have enhanced the credibility of Mol's theory. In Israel, the settler movement whose territorial claims were ratified by Biblical Commandments became the avant-garde of the Right-wing Likud party. In the United States the Christian Right (then called the Moral Majority) became the avant-garde of the Republican Party, and a fundamentalist movement led by a traditionalist ayatollah who established a mediaeval theocracy came into power in Iran. Others were to follow, such as the orthodox Hindu Movement BJP which came into power in India (and may again in the near future). As previously mentioned, sociologists such as Peter Berger gradually began to take account of the change and began to proclaim an era of 'post secularism'.

However, even this worked out differently from what Mol had anticipated. Mysteriously Mol never comments on this account even though he had said that new identities are bubbling beneath the surface of modern alienation. Mol never took account of this development and perhaps there are good reasons. Just as Marx might have watched the unfolding of the Soviet Union and said, after T.S. Eliot, this is not what I meant at all, Mol might have watched the unfolding of militant religious identity and said the same.

Conclusion

In his account of the secular world, Mol noted the proliferation of various foci of identity, lamenting the role of secularism and rationalism in fostering the unravelling of secure religious identities. But the identities that have emerged are far from what he seemed to be hoping for. A new identity was to restore a universal order. Instead, we have almost universal mayhem and conflicts between religion and the secular that we have not seen in centuries.

The new world of identities is to a large degree the product of globalization which has destroyed much of what had been the secular structure of the 1960s. The dynamism of these identities is well described by Castells as dynamism of exclusion rather than integration, what Castells calls an 'exclusion of the excluded'. These new religious constellations recognize secularism but as their mortal enemy. A chilling example of the triumph of religion as identity is in the home-grown jihadists who, rejecting the flimsy identities they achieved in the west, undertake a universal identity of jihad. They are a source of mayhem rather than integration.

Hans Mol has been a happy and energetic warrior in the sociology of religion. In response to critics he has published over a dozen volumes, restating, updating and refurbishing his theory. Yet, questions remain: does his theory make room for religious pluralism? Does his theory help us make a distinction between the religious and the secular? Finally, does his theory help us understand the religious resurgence that surrounds us today?

References

Bellah, R. (2011) *Religion in Human Evolution*. Cambridge, MA: Belknap Press of Harvard University Press.
Berger, P. (1967) *The Sacred Canopy*. New York: Doubleday.
Castells, M. (1997) *The Power of Identity: The Information Age*, vol. 2. Oxford: Blackwell.
Cox, H. (1966) *The Secular City: Secularization and Urbanization in Secular Perspectives*. New York: Macmillan.
Durkheim, E. (1995) [1912] *The Elementary Forms of Religious Life*. New York: The Free Press.
Fenn, R. (1972) 'Toward a New Sociology of Religion', *Journal for the Scientific Study of Religion*, 11(1): 16–32.
Hegel, G.W.F. (2005) *Hegel's Preface to the Phenomenology of Spirit*. Princeton University Press.
Mol, H. (1976) *Identity and the Sacred*. Agincourt: The Book Society of Canada.
Principe, L.M. (2011) *The Scientific Revolution*. Oxford: Oxford University Press.

Tawney, R.H. (1964) *Religion and the Rise of Capitalism*. Harmondsworth: Penguin.

Terence (1926) *Terence: The Lady of Andros, The Self-tormentor, The Eunuch*. London: Heinemann.

Weber, M. (2004) [1904] *The Protestant Ethic and the Spirit of Capitalism*. London: Routledge.

Chapter 3
Mol, Science, Religion and Narrative Identity

Ian Weeks and Petra Brown

Part I: Religion

Hans Mol and I joined the Department of Religious Studies at McMaster at the same time, in the middle of 1970. We remained colleagues until mid 1987 when I returned to work in Australia. I have met and talked with Hans in Australia since that time. Our discussions at McMaster began over the usefulness of our two disciplines, philosophy and sociology, for the study of religion. I don't think that we ever arrived at a mutually satisfying conclusion to that discussion. Hans was of the view that philosophy was very abstract while sociology was much more empirical. My opinion tended towards the opposite because I took society to be an abstract conception and I thought philosophy was about thinking which was very practical.

At this time, in the early 1970s, philosophy was very preoccupied by questions to do with the nature of language and especially questions about the religious uses of language. The impetus for these studies came from the later work of Wittgenstein, J.L. Austin and others. One of the strands of thinking in this context grew from a remark Wittgenstein made concerning the nature of meaning: he said 'don't ask for the meaning, ask for the use'. Such a remark led some to think that Wittgenstein was suggesting a sociological answer to questions about meaning. In fact what he meant lay at a different level of thought. J.L. Austin provided an interesting example of what Wittgenstein meant by examining the difference between doing something *through* language and doing something *in* language. The former he put in a class of 'perlocutionary' language, where the statements used point beyond themselves to something else, while the latter are a class of 'speech acts' where something is accomplished by the words themselves, which he called 'illocutionary' language. An example of the latter would be the statement made by a marriage celebrant 'I declare you to be husband and wife'. Here the statement is not referring to something else. Rather, the statement constitutes marriage. The differences between representational language and performative language pointed to the many interesting differences in the *functions* that language exhibited. This functional understanding is very clear in Wittgenstein's remark that religion is that which rules in the whole of one's life.

It was not only in Anglo-American philosophy that the concept of function found its place. Ernst Cassirer began to explore the importance of the concept of function as a powerful tool of understanding as early as his *Substanzbegriff und Funktionsbegriff* (1910) and the use of the concept in his work *Zur Einstein'schen Relativitätstheorie* (1921). Subsequently this work was applied in the field of epistemology and then in the enormous work begun in 1921 (volume 1), extended in volume 2 in 1925 and completed in volume 3 in 1929 – *Philosophie der symbolischen Formen*. This immense work is not unlike the work Hans came to do on the nature of identity and its religio-cultural foundations.

Despite the obvious links to contemporary philosophy at the time, Mol was reluctant to make use of these philosophical discussions, and I was puzzled by this. It seemed obvious that these philosophical claims about function would support Mol's claims about the functions of religion. Why did he not use them? I think that his reluctance lay in a concern that such 'abstract' constructions of 'function' would open the door to views of the function of religion that did not fit with Mol's own religious beliefs. Mol, I think, wanted to use the concept of function in a way that would not lead to Marxist or Freudian 'reductionist' accounts of what religion does. Thus, Mol wanted to discuss the 'function' of religion, but in a limited way that did not negate his own religious beliefs as 'essential' to his own identity and thinking in some way. Yet, it was not only Mol's religious beliefs that entailed that he remain wedded to a concept of religious essentialism, it was equally his philosophical understanding of the nature of science that enabled him to conceptualize religion, knowledge and identity as 'essential' and therefore enduring in some way. In this part of the chapter, I test Mol's 'essentialist' views in light of contemporary scientific and religious reflections, and I draw out some of the ethical implications of Mol's views in terms of religious identity.

Mol viewed identity as essential and enduring. This became apparent to me in a discussion that Hans and I had over some years. I began talking to Hans about the work of a psychiatrist I had heard and read at Yale. Robert Jay Lifton specialized in the study of people who had been exposed to very dangerous conditions such as thought reform prisons and US veterans of the Vietnam War.

Lifton became famous for his concept of the 'Protean Self'.[1] His studies suggested that people with strong identities did not survive well in the extreme conditions he was interested in. People who were willing to do whatever was possible to survive were more able to endure extreme circumstances. Lifton thought that these extreme circumstances actually reflected the conditions in which all people lived and so he thought his understanding of the 'Protean Self' was relevant for everyone. Mol became quite upset with this view. He had been in several concentration camps during World War II because he was involved in the YMCA. He survived, he argued, because he had converted to Christianity. In a later interview he wrote, 'God won out over Hitler because the Christian understanding of life is not only true in the long run – but it says God is not on the side of the powerful but on the side of the powerless' (1985). Several years after this Hans produced the promised book on *How God Hoodwinked Hitler* (1987). The assertion that '... God is not on the side of the powerful but on the side of the powerless' was typical of Hans' moral sensibility. At the same time, I think that the concentration camp conversion shaped everything that Hans came to say about religion and the integrity that he experienced. His conversion experience gave Hans a 'strong' sense of identity, radically unlike Lifton's concept of the 'Protean Self'.

Unlike Hans I was struck by the *accidental* character of what he experienced. I am sure that some readers will immediately understand that the accidental character of experience and life is a central concern of the philosophy of Martin Heidegger. His word for this is *Geworfenheit*, which he found in his studies of medieval mysticism, especially in Meister Eckhart. What, I wondered, would have been his experience if he had landed up in one of the camps where Jews were the overwhelming majority of prisoners? This question and the implications of the accidental character of much of our existence arise for me from my understanding of philosophy. It lies at the core of the well-known confrontation between Heidegger and Ernst Cassirer at their meeting in Davos.[2] The differences between Cassirer and Heidegger are fascinating and complicated, but an important theme is their common sense of the great importance of Kant. However they also part company through their understanding of Kant. Cassirer was known as a neo-Kantian and his understanding of Kant, like that of most Anglo-American philosophers, assumes that the important starting point for understanding Kant is Kant's *Critique of Pure Reason*. Cassirer's understanding of the symbolic

---

[1] Lifton used the phrase 'Protean Man' in the late 1960s, well before the publication of his book *The Protean Self* (1993).

[2] Peter Eli Gordon has written a significant book on this debate: *Continental Divide: Heidegger – Cassirer – Davos* (Cambridge, MA: Harvard University Press, 2010).

character of language and knowledge is rooted in Kant's claim that things are unknowable in themselves. Cassirer accepts this claim and takes it be fundamental to all knowledge.[3] What is the significance of this? The First Critique makes a fundamental distinction between how things are 'in themselves' and how they are 'for us' human beings. This is his distinction between 'noumena' and 'phenomena'. Kant's analysis of human experience follows from the phenomena–noumena distinction; experience, for Kant, is necessarily and always a product of intuition and understanding. The consequence of Kant's account is that all experience is in principle understandable; no experience for us is essentially mysterious or transcendent. Cassirer makes an interesting addition to the language Kant uses when he uses the word 'symbol' to designate the objects of our experience. Thus, Cassirer believes in progressive knowledge that eventually comes closer and closer to understanding 'mysterious experiences' in a rational way.

Heidegger is impressed by Kant's First Critique but he disputes the claim that all experience is essentially understandable. The issue here, if it is successful, undermines important parts of the First Critique. While Heidegger's Kant is often much more to do with the *Critique of Practical Reason*, the shorter writings that accompany that book, such as *The Groundwork for the Metaphysic of Morals*, and Kant's Third Critique, *The Critique of Judgement* and its accompanying shorter writings, his writings on the *Critique of Pure Reason* are also at the centre of the debate at Davos. In the Preface to the *Groundwork*, Kant states that the discipline of ethics is governed by freedom and Heidegger is drawn to this as the starting point for philosophy. In fact the radical consequences Heidegger draws from his understanding of freedom has led many philosophers to claim that Heidegger was really a nihilist. Certainly the concept of *Geworfenheit*, to which I referred above, is closely related to a strong understanding of the accidental quality of life, which is the most freedom we can have. The recognition of the accidental condition of humans is at the same time the ground of the possibility of the only kind of freedom we can know. That view is very different from those who think that freedom is either an absolute characteristic or human beings or the consequence of good order and is closer, in some respects, to the view of the ancient Epicureans. Here it should be clear that Heidegger's concept of freedom and the indeterminate nature of human beings is closer to Lifton's account of the 'Protean Self', than Mol's wish for an essential and enduring identity.

The position that Heidegger develops is, in fact, an important part of the development of post-modern philosophy, and it is especially important in the idea of *deconstruction*. Heidegger discovered the elements of this first in the

---

[3] This can be seen in Cassirer's book about Einstein.

tradition of negative mysticism, but then also in the writings of Martin Luther; especially in Luther's use of the idea of *destruction*. One can see the emergence of these ideas in Heidegger's lectures of 1920–21, published as *The Phenomenology of Religious Life* (2004). It is worth emphasizing the fact that Heidegger's early work through to *Zein und Zeit* is deeply influenced by his studies of Christianity in particular.[4]

The use made of Heidegger's philosophy includes Christians such as Bultmann, but also many other thinkers such as Derrida.[5] Heidegger's and Derrida's thought might be difficult but it has many practical applications in literature, psychoanalysis, classics, political philosophy and religious studies, to name only a few fields of application. Intertextuality, for example, is a very practical and detailed study of the ways in which texts are to be understood in the contexts of their writing. Such work is very practical in all contemporary literary studies. Given the role of texts in most religions it should be clear that this philosophical work is not abstract but practical. Indeed in comparison with this research Mol's work appears to be less that 'practical'. By that I mean that there is no experimental evidence involved in his thought.

This leads to my second critique of Mol: his understanding of science. This is demonstrated by the lack of the practical in Mol's work. Underlying Mol's work is a view about the nature of science, especially social science, and a claim that it is an appropriate method for the study of religion. It is important, however, to realize that the claim to be a science in a particular instance must have credibility as a science. Here I think that Mol's approach lets him down. This can be illustrated by a discussion I had with Mol on aspects of science.

---

[4] Heidegger's early work showed a keen interest in religion, and especially in mysticism. From 1923 to 1928 he taught at the University of Marburg. One of his colleagues at Marburg was the New Testament scholar Rudolf Bultmann (1884–1951) whose own work came to be deeply influenced by Heidegger. In his studies of the New Testament, Bultmann came to the view that much of the New Testament was shaped by the writers' understandings of human beings and the world that were part of their culture's science. Bultmann came to call this aspect of New Testament writing *myth*. In order for us to understand the intended teaching of the New Testament we need to *demythologize* such myths. By doing this we will be able to approach the key proclamation of the New Testament, that is, the *kerygma*. It is important to understand that Bultmann also believed that any understanding of the *kerygma* arrived at in any time will itself be a *re-mythologization*. Speaking for his time, Bultmann asserted that such a re-construction would have to be shaped by the philosophy of Martin Heidegger. It is curious that many of the writings about deconstruction omit any reference to Bultmann. His use of Heidegger puts him close to much of deconstruction and his understanding of demythologizing is an early form of deconstruction.

[5] For Heidegger's influence on Bultmann see note 4 above.

Mol was very excited and interested when the idea of the bi-cameral brain was popular. That kind of binary understanding also arose in a seminar we did together for post-graduate students in philosophy and religion at McMaster. The topic was 'Religion and Rationality'. Hans began by drawing up a two-column chart, the first column headed 'Rational' and the second 'Irrational', and then he began filling in the two columns. Mol became quite upset when I asked him whether he was using 'Rational' or Irrational' to define the contents of the columns. Again he had chosen to use a simple binary matrix to develop his view. At that time personal computing was just beginning and there, too, binary mathematics was in use. Others extended the computer model to talk about the brain, suggesting that when a neuron was fired across a synapse it activated the receptor in a binary way. Today that view is questioned. It is thought that the binary action is only the same as an on/off switch, which, after being turned on, behaves in a far more complicated way. This change is reflected in the emerging technology of quantum processing in computers.

This illustration demonstrates a wider problem in Mol's 'scientific' approach. In general terms one has to conclude that there is no sense in which Mol's writing responds to or resembles the development of science in the last 110 years. During that time quantum physics, the special and general theories of relativity and particle physics have fundamentally changed our understanding of reality and our understanding of the nature of science itself. At the present time those changes are being applied to neuroscience and will have profound implications for understanding human consciousness and therefore for any understanding of religious experience. Briefly, these radical changes have replaced the ordered view of the atom and of physics which was a consequence of the Newtonian Revolution in the seventeenth century. In the nineteenth century, Sir James Jeans used the analogy of ripples that spread out in an even pattern when a stone is dropped into a pool of water to describe the patterns of fundamental building blocks of reality. Such thinking has now been replaced by concepts such as quarks or Higgs Boson, and new models of behaviour of sub-atomic particles that require new forms of mathematics and statistics. Central to these developments are ideas that the 'same' event might happen differently in a vast field of possible universes at 'the same time'. Two interpretations followed this understanding. On the one hand, and earlier, there developed a view that brought a previously unthinkable *indeterminism* into the model of the universe which challenged views about causality and time. On the other hand, and later, there developed a view challenging the standard forms of indeterminacy and seeking to replace that concept with a conceptual plurality of possible descriptions of any event.

Heidegger's philosophy reflects this view, which he learnt from Eckhart and Boehme on the one hand and Nietzsche on the other.

The more recent view that there are a number of possible descriptions of any event has overturned many of the 'classical assumptions' regarding causality and time. The implications in terms of knowledge building are significant. In the European Enlightenment and through the nineteenth century it was widely thought that science could be understood as progressive and that in time everything would be understood and science would be complete. More recently, a much more modest view has developed which sees science as incompleteable. Such an account of science is to be found in the work on Scientific Revolutions by T.S. Kuhn. Here the relevance of Heidegger becomes clearer, for Heidegger's account in *Zein und Zeit* is similar to the emerging science. Such a change in the understanding of science is, I think, a problem for the ways in which Mol tries to account for religion in a scientific way.

This leads to my third critique of Mol: his understanding of religion. Mol not only tries to account for religion based on an outdated scientific model, he seems unaware of the history of the concept of religion itself. The first English use of the word 'religion' is not until 1613 when Samuel Purchas published his book *His Pilgrimage, or, Relations of the World and the Religions Observed in All Ages and Places Discovered* ('Religion', Oxford English Dictionary Online 2014). There has been a good deal of recent scholarship that has investigated the emergence of the concept of religion. I have recently read an intriguing book by Leora Batnitzky *How Judaism Became a Religion* (2011).[6] She makes an extended argument that Judaism became a religion only in the late eighteenth and early nineteenth centuries. She is of the view that the concept of religion is an invention of the Protestant Reformation, which described a particular kind of inward architecture and experience, which was absent from Judaism. It was only with Moses Mendelssohn, Batnitzky claims, that Judaism became a religion.[7]

---

[6] More recently I have read Peter Schäfer and Daniel Boyardin on the relationships between Rabbinic Judaism and Christianity in the first few centuries of the Common Era. Their writings build upon the work of another colleague at McMaster, E.P. Sanders, and his team of researchers. The understanding that Jesus lived, taught and died as a Jew, and that his followers, including Paul, were practising and observant Jews, has been changing our understanding of these traditions. Importantly, we can see how many ideas were shared and debated over a considerable time.

[7] Views such as Batnitzky's are at odds with a powerful modern argument proposed by the Canadian scholar Wilfred Cantwell Smith is his famous book *The Meaning and End of Religion* (1962). Cantwell Smith appears to agree with Batnitzky when he attacks the concept of religion as an essentially modern and Protestant idea, but his view is that all religions are matters of a human existential attitude – faith. Placing faith at the centre

Gershom Scholem in 'Reflections on Jewish Theology' takes an even stronger position than Batnitzsky concerning common ways in which Judaism is described. He wrote:

> If I undertake here to reflect on the position and possibilities of Jewish theology today, it should be clear that, as things stand, a systematic disquisition could only be given by someone possessing a fixed standpoint, an Archimedean point as it were, from which these questions could be put into systematic order. I am not among these fortunate ones. (1976: 261)

I take the reference to an Archimedean point as crucial for scholarship and for assessing Mol's point of view. However, I take the matter of an Archimedean point further than Scholem does in this essay, although he does take the implication of his view very far. Thus, is seems to me, that any attempt to say what a religion *is* must in principle regard as relevant the views of *all* people who regard themselves as adherents of that religion and all people who are critics or scholars of that religion.[8] Of course I find some views richer and more profound than others, and I find some lives and texts more exemplary than do others, but many people have other views, other exemplars and other texts. They have a complete right to disagree with me or anyone else. Of course I regard some views as mistaken, but mistaken views also tell us something about the tradition at issue. I do, incidentally, accept the apparently paradoxical fact that this means I accept Mol's views – but only in this general and pluralistic way, which is not what Mol's position entails. I remember with a good deal of pleasure the time when, after discussing these issues, Hans said to me 'You really are very democratic, much more democratic than I thought'.[9] I must confess that I see such a position as vital for our survival and for the survival of religion.

Of course I do not think that what I have said applies only to 'religions'. It seems to me that the sciences are very similar, and that should be reassuring

---

means that Cantwell Smith's argument goes radically against the view of Judaism proposed by Batnitzky. Faith is essentially an inward qualification but not everyone regards faith as important or religious. I think that the Buddhism of the Diamond Sutra poses insuperable problems for such a view. How can one follow such a powerful account of detachment and have faith when faith is deconstructed in that Buddhism?

[8] This point is an elaboration of what Karl Barth said about Feuerbach in his introduction to Feuerbach's selected writings.

[9] For some time I wanted to say to Hans that for me an important doctrine of Protestant Christianity is 'the priesthood of all believers'. This theological view is directly related to my view of democracy and also to the view that no one 'owns' any religion more than all of the followers, including 'experts'.

for it means that science will not come to an end because its work will have been done. Sciences and religions and all other areas of human production and reflection live only as long as they 'live the life of a thousand qualifications', to borrow a phrase from the mid-twentieth-century debates about 'religious language'. All living areas of discovery and reflection find new patterns of meaning and new paradigms of research and exploration and, inter-related with these, new technologies also profoundly change what we know and understand; all of these create changes in traditions, in the ways we understand older traditions and create new traditions. As a Christian philosopher I am endlessly fascinated by the vast panorama of theologies from the past and I expect with delight the millions of new theologies that will come to be as long as there is Christianity. To my delight I do not expect that other old and new traditions will be very different in this regard.

Even more fascinating possibilities open up in other ways. Consider the following experience I had. Some years ago I was invited to spend a few days with a group of Japanese religious leaders who were visiting Australia.[10] I was asked to say some things about the state of religion in Asia, Southeast Asia and Australasia to open the conference. After I said what I had to say there was discussion. The first comment came from the oldest member of the Japanese delegation. He said some nice things but went on to say that my comments reflected a typical problem Westerners showed when speaking about Asia and Asian things. 'Take myself', he said. 'I am known to be the head of official or Temple Shinto. In fact, however, I have three religions'. Now this really caught my attention and I asked him, 'When you say you have three religions is this like having three different roles at the same time, or is it more like having three wives?' A wonderful, almost beatific smile came across his face as he replied, kindly and gently, 'See how difficult you Westerners make it!'[11] Many of us who are shaped in some understandings of our complexes of traditions in the 'West', but including 'the Middle East', have been led to think that religions or traditions *must* be like property or houses; we think that walls and boundaries *must* be

---

[10] Gary Bouma, another contributor to this volume, was also at this weekend.
[11] I have thought about this exchange for quite a long time and have, still, little more than glimpses of what this wise and gentle man meant. It seems clear to me, however, that what he said has a considerable bearing on the topic I have raised. For example, David Hume once remarked that polytheism was more peaceful than monotheism. While polytheism is not free from war and violence, Hume was partly right. An extra god or two, or an extra religion, is unlikely to lead to the kind of killing that monotheism has been associated with. However the history of many countries where polytheism is widespread shows a great deal of violence. This happens when the leadership of the gods becomes an issue.

part of what 'religion' means; we have fought terrible wars because of such ideas. Of course there are important aspects to be found in such understandings but no one can give any credible answer to the questions 'On what basis can this *must* be guaranteed forever?' To me these possibilities do not spell death or secularization. They spell freedom and life ... and also, of course, all the misuses of that as well as the uses.

This leads me to my final concern with Mol's understanding of and approach to religion: the possible ethical implications of his religious essentialism. Gideon Freudenthal's appropriately titled study of the thought of Moses Mendelssohn, *No Religion without Idolatry* (2012), confirms an essential role of iconoclasm for certain varieties of Protestantism because religious women and men cannot help but make various aspects of their experience absolute. Doing that is inevitable for the religious person and the religious community but at the same time, for the sake of religion, that absolutizing must be deconstructed or the religion will soon die. It is the refusal of this dual character of religion that identifies fundamentalism and explains why fundamentalism is a powerful secularizing force in every religion. It must immediately be said that there is no rule about what might be absolutized at any time, nor is there any certainty that a turn against this will happen. This absolutizing, while important, is accidental in when and how it happens, and any solution to it is also accidental despite the wish to be reassured that it is not.

My pluralist view of religion is not without its own problems. In a 'gourmet' and tourist society there is a risk that religions too become fashionable alternatives and they come to be treated in the same way in which one might choose brands of coffee beans. Søren Kierkegaard in the first volume of *Either/Or* illustrates and discusses the first of the three 'Stages on Life's Way', what he calls the 'aesthetic' form of existence. This form of existence Kierkegaard illustrates in a wonderful series of vignettes. The aesthetic form of existence he thinks inevitably leads to despair. The main characteristic of this form of existence is the refusal to choose, a determination to keep all options open in order to be able to experience every possibility. Now it might seem that my deconstruction of any 'essence' of Christianity, and so also of any other living religion, leads to the same aesthetic as that which Kierkegaard identifies. There is, I suppose, some possibility of this for those of us who are scholars in a particular religion. Perhaps this is also a problem for the well-read believer. But the fact that there are in principle almost endless varieties of religious thought and experience does not mean that one could not consider a particular form of one's tradition to have stronger claims upon one's life; nor does the immense diversity of tradition rule out the fact that scholars often draw upon different aspects of their tradition when they write and comment upon their own views.

Early in the history of western philosophy some philosophers asked how one could identify a river when the water in it was constantly changing. There are many different areas of experience and thought where we appreciate the work of someone who, like those ancient philosophers, looks at a field of events or practices and helps us to see a pattern there. But is there only one pattern? And do such patterns last forever? Is the question of identity a help at this point? I doubt it. It smacks too much of customs, borders and long census forms.

Part II: Narrative Identity

In the preceding section, Ian Weeks made an observation based around Mol's concentration camp experience, an experience that was 'essential' to Mol's own religious identity and understanding. Based on conversations about this experience, Weeks was struck by 'the accidental character' of that experience. Mol came to understand his experience in a concentration camp in terms of a religious *narrative* in which God defeated Hitler, siding with the 'powerless' against the 'powerful', a narrative that provided purpose to an event marked by suffering and a profound sense of disorder for Mol:

> Hitler's rampaging, conquering might steamrolling over anguished souls and countries had disregarded God's still, small voice which worked away quietly. The impressive fury and foam of the Reich succumbed to the suffering Servant who gathered in his arms all the victims of Hitler's fuming. Only some of them have lived to tell the story and, as one of the survivors, I feel it incumbent on me to do so. (1987: 10)

This poignant passage illustrates the power of narrative to give an event meaning, to shape one's 'identity' and purpose in response to an event that is deeply disorienting and confronting. It demonstrates the power of 'narrative identity' in making links between disorienting events, and a growing self-awareness of one's own place in that event. In this section of the chapter, I undertake a critical investigation of this concept of 'narrative identity', drawing on the work of Peter Brooks. My intent is not to directly criticize Mol's experience or subsequent interpretation of that experience, but to draw attention to some features of 'narrative identity' that, I suggest, might lie concealed in Mol's attempt to make sense of disorienting events through establishing his own strong sense of identity in this 'narrative' form.

What is *narrative*? It is often thought that narrative is essential to *meaning*. It gives meaning and cohesion to disparate events that otherwise appear as random and therefore unpredictable occurrences that leave us with a sense of vertigo. It enables us to make sense of a person's life, of their happenings, actions and choices. For most people, to live without narrative seems unimaginable, given that 'narrative construction of reality is a basic human operation, learned in infancy, and culturally omnipresent' (Brooks 2011: 139). Without narrative, there is no order and no sense, and perhaps, there is no human *experience* (insofar as all experience becomes understood as experience only on reflection).

Similarly, identity is characterized by order and sense; it is understood to be 'enduring' in some way, even though we may undergo significant changes of identity throughout life. The cohesive part of 'individual identity' is made possible by two components: identification by others and self-identity. Between these two perimeters, the individual is assigned or self-assigns his or her place in the world.

The *narrative identity* of an individual is maintained by a relationship between other-designated or public identity, and self-designated or private identity. Because 'self-designated identity' can only happen in the words we think with and remember, even this sense of identity is not completely 'private'. So, it is the power of the 'public' narrative, the narrative assigned to one by others that comes to be the most persuasive narrative, for the power of narrative lies in its communal sharing and self-validation as the 'right' narrative. When one's narrative includes identification by others as successful and as belonging in society, one's own self-identity tends to be affirmed by this. However, when an individual is identified by others as unsuccessful or not belonging in society, the narrative assigned by others may well shape one's own narrative about oneself. One's narrative told by others tends to outweigh the strength of one's own self-shaped narrative.

Peter Brooks in his *Enigmas of Identity* (2011) investigates both aspects of identity, identification by others and self-identity, in terms of public and private identities. He does this through an exploration of the interplay between the public and private dimensions from the social issues that began in the nineteenth century through to today. Brooks argues that the public concept of identity appeared with the growth of cities, the institutionalization and bureaucratization of the nation state, and as a response to the perceived need to identify the habitual criminal (ibid.: 4). During this time, forms of identification became increasingly sophisticated and normalized, from the use of the police mug shot to identification cards for prostitutes and the invention of fingerprinting. This need to 'identify' the criminal extended to novels. Brooks cites the classic detective story as originating in the increasing urbanization of society, attending to the fears of a mass underclass and its alleged habitual criminal element. According to Brooks, the detective story is an especially pertinent development of this time as it established a 'narrative' account of identity based on the detective's method of pursuing clues. This narrative account is neither deductive, nor fully inductive but moves from seemingly insignificant details and concrete particularities, to an image of a complex reality that is an abstraction from the immediate experiences. As a result, the narrative account of an event brings with it a sense of order as well as inevitability and definiteness (Sherlock Holmes provides a salutary example). In the narrative account of the event, the end of the narrated event is now understood as necessary, as the only possible outcome already contained in the beginning of the narrated event. As Brooks states:

> It is in the peculiar nature of narrative as a sense-making system that clues are revealing, that prior events are prior, and causes are causal only retrospectively, in a reading back from end. (ibid.: 137)

Brooks' account of the invention and popularization of the detective novel points to a nineteenth-century social desire for order, purpose and direction in a time of change and rapid industrialization, where individuals are swept up in a 'machine' beyond their control. Through reading the detective novel, the law-abiding bourgeoisie are reassured that the unpredictable, the anomaly, the criminal, is returned to the social order of the law-abiding citizen. While the same law-abiding bourgeoisie may feel profoundly disoriented through the processes of industrialization, the criminal brought to justice reassures them that the good prevails. The detective story contributes to a larger public narrative in which anxious individuals quell their fears in order to adhere to the greater narrative: that despite many appearances to the contrary, their rapidly changing world moves towards a *telos* that is good for all.

Yet, this narrated account of criminal events is not limited to nineteenth-century detective novels. According to Brooks, this 'narrative account' of the criminal has found its way into the context of modern jurisprudence. Brooks argues that American law courts increasingly turn to a narrative account of identity that now includes a 'doctrine of inevitable discovery', where even illegal methods of obtaining evidence are admissible on the grounds that a trail of clues inevitably led to a specific end – the guilt of the accused.

As Brooks states:

> Standing at the vantage point of the end of the story, the proof that the suspect was in fact guilty of illegal activity, the post-hoc logic of inevitable discovery can be used to justify practically anything – because it is the very logic of narrative, which makes sense by way of its end. (ibid.: 126–7)

Thus, the justice system begins to resemble the confidence of a Sherlock Holmes detective novel that is able to 'identify' (and thereby brings a sense of control over) the alleged habitual criminal in society. Its focus is no longer on 'justice' for particular actions or crimes. The justice system now begins to 'judge' an individual on character, on the total sum of all past actions with a view to predicting likely future events. The outcome of this is that the individual is no longer judged on particular and concrete acts from which he or she, whether through intention or education, is able to 'repent' and turn over a new leaf. Rather, he or she is 'inevitably' or 'necessarily' a criminal. This has two outcomes. The first is that the identity as a 'criminal' is already laid down in events preceding the particular act and the 'habit' of criminal activity is likely to continue after the criminal's day in court. Effectively, the person once identified as a 'criminal' lives his or her entire life under the gaze of the justice system, and by extension, the judgement of society. Secondly, in the logic of narrative, any means necessary can be used to bring the criminal element to light since the end of the narrated event (the guilty criminal) justifies the means.

It is clear therefore that the 'narrative identity', exemplified by the detective novel, is not only of literary interest but has philosophical implications relating to the questions of self-identity, freedom and autonomy in the face of one's identity established by a public narrative. Just as the detective story developed in a time of rapid industrialization and social uncertainty, so the 'doctrine of inevitable discovery' contributes to a larger public narrative in which an anxious society quells its fears in order to adhere to the greater narrative: that despite many appearances to the contrary, the rapidly changing world can be controlled. This world can be controlled, and as befitting the narrative, the means will be justified and shown necessary by the end. In Brooks, this is examined in the context of the nineteenth-century detective novel and modern jurisprudence.

Brooks' investigation of the concept of 'narrative identity' demonstrates the darker side of the power of narrative. I've used Brooks to draw attention to the dangers inherent in 'public-assigned' forms of narrative identities: the danger of designating the other, in one's own narrative, as 'inevitably criminal' and therefore beyond rehabilitation, education or redemption. The power of public narrative lies in its communal and self-validating nature as the 'right narrative', a power that is believed by both the 'judge' and the 'criminal' shaped by and caught up in this narrative.

I now want to draw out some philosophical implications of this, turning to a nineteenth-century philosopher who grappled with the question of 'narrative' precisely during the heady days of the industrialization of society.

The 'Narrative' of Kierkegaard

Søren Kierkegaard appeared on the scene at the tail end of Denmark's 'Golden Age', in a time that was increasingly restless, subjected to the modern process of industrialization. Yet, Kierkegaard did not proscribe a panacea of 'detective novels' to reassure the public of a political order that would ensure good prevailed, while evil received its due punishment. Suspicious of Sherlock Holmes style narratives, Kierkegaard began his own protest narrative, from the edge of European civilization – Copenhagen. How did he do this? The salutary way into Kierkegaard's world is through one of the pseudonyms – Judge Vilhelm, from the second half of *Either/Or* (1988), and the representative of nineteenth-century law and order par excellence. Judge Vilhelm represents the 'ethical sphere' in Kierkegaard's spheres or stages of existence. His identity is shaped and defined through participation in social institutions. Through choosing and embracing a vocation, Judge Vilhelm participates in institutional life and engages in a number of social practices.

Alasdair MacIntyre defines practice as:

> [A]ny coherent and complex form of socially established cooperative human activity through which goods internal to that form of activity are realized in the course of trying to achieve those standards of excellence that are appropriate to, and partially definitive of, that form of activity, with the result that human powers to achieve excellence, and human conceptions of the ends and goods involved, are systematically extended. (1984: 187)

MacIntyre ties 'practice' directly to the Aristotelian account of virtue as excellence in human activity, but not activity understood as a solitary undertaking. It is specifically 'co-operative human activity', including 'arts, sciences, games, politics in the Aristotelian sense, the making and sustaining of family life' (ibid.: 188). Positively, the ethical person is marked by openness, transparency and self-disclosure in a wider world through which the individual lives in 'cooperative human activity'. The social practices that shape the ethical identity are not immutable. But the change to these institutions comes from within, from those who test and work at the boundaries of the institutions. The reflective ethical person recognizes the shifting horizon of social order, but this does not prevent her from making the commitment to the same social order, including the social conventions of 'good and evil': the moral distinctions. The ethicist commits herself to something outside herself, and accepts the sacrifice this may require. Ethical identity finds its fruition in adult participation in society, where each individual contributes to the well-being of the whole.

Judge Vilhelm appears as an exemplary character of MacIntyre's definition of practice. His practice as a Judge is made possible in 'co-operative human activity', and as a Judge, Vilhelm commits himself to that social order, maintaining the social conventions of 'good and evil'. Vilhelm has embraced vocations, as Judge and husband, and has disclosed himself within forms of community, both in the public sphere and the more intimate relationship with his wife. Judge Vilhelm seems to be a unified individual, with congruence between his public and private personas or identities.

Thus, MacIntyre's definition of practice and his understanding of virtue appear in many ways as similar to Kierkegaard's understanding of 'ethical identity', shown in the life of Judge Vilhelm. Yet, to accept this at face value is to seriously misunderstand Kierkegaard's intention in *Either/Or*. The narrative of the Judge cannot be fully understood by his own understanding, just as it cannot be simply accepted based on his social standing as a Judge.

Read beneath the lines, and good Judge Vilhelm not only comes across as sanctimoniously preaching to his wayward nephew 'A', the intended recipient of this correspondence, but also as someone self-deceived about his own identity. This is most clearly seen in the references that the Judge makes to God and his wife throughout the letters. At first glance, it appears that the Judge identifies himself as a religious man. God, sin, repentance and faith weave their way through his rambling prose. For the Judge, there is a blessed harmony between what is required of him as a Judge and what is required of him as a religious man. Yet, Judge Vilhelm keeps 'providence' strictly in place:

> Thus one also believes that there is a providence, and that the soul rests confidently in this conviction, and yet one would never think of venturing to interpenetrate every contingency with this thought to be to conscious of this faith every minute.
> (Kierkegaard 1988: 257)

That is to say, 'providence', God or Christian faith have no essential impact on the identity of Judge Vilhelm, and his Christian identity is not radically different from his social identity.[12] Indeed, the social or public identity of the Judge is made possible, secured, by his understanding of the place of providence. Providence guarantees or secures the law and order of society, and the stability of society is evidence that the existing social order is the expression of providence. In the Judge's account of providence, 'criminal' elements of society 'sin' because they fail to recognize the authority of this divinely sanctioned order.

Like his view of providence, Vilhelm's wife exists to confirm his place in society. This can be seen in a passage where Vilhelm ostensibly praises the institution of marriage to his bachelor nephew:

> [T]here is one thing for which I thank God with my whole soul, and that is that she is the only one I have ever loved, the first, and there is one thing for which I pray to God with my whole heart, that he will give me the strength never to want to love any other. This is a family devotion, in which she also shares, because every feeling, every mood, gains a higher meaning for me by having her share in it. (ibid.: 9)

For the Judge, marriage is a church where he is both priest and congregation (ibid.). Yet, his wife remains unnamed in *Either/Or*, suggesting that her thoughts are concealed and inseparable from his. Her identity is based first and foremost on his identity, her happiness secondary to his happiness. Just as with God, she is part of 'providence' – evidence of, and a guarantee that the Judge is in the 'right place' in the social order. Just as the criminal in society needs to recognize the 'divine order' in place, so the Judge's wife needs to recognize that the 'order' of their intimate relationship is also the result of providence.

Merold Westphal describes Judge Vilhelm as 'an Aristotelian for whom right reason is to be defined in terms of the man of practical wisdom, and a Hegelian, for whom ethics is always a matter of *Sittlichkeit*', of familial and social institutions (1996: 24). Because the Judge understands identity and ethical life in terms of familial and social institutions, he repeatedly urges his nephew to marry, to find employment and to commit himself to social roles and personal relationships. Yet, Kierkegaard is not willing to give Judge Vilhelm the final word on his nephew. For the Judge, his identity as Christian, Danish citizen, Judge and husband amount to the same thing. For Kierkegaard, Vilhelm embodies sanitized, bourgeoisie Danish Christianity. As such, Judge

---

[12] Rudd argues that Vilhelm's outlook is 'essentially secular, and his religion is an adjunct to his ethics. His position is that of one who accepts a certain religion because it is bound up with the culture, history, and traditions of the society with which he identifies. This is ... [in]compatible with Christianity as it understands itself' (1993: 142).

Vilhelm represents the New Testament example of the hypocrite, the Pharisee who proclaims his thanks in the temple that he is not like robbers, evildoers and adulterers (Luke 18: 11). He has chosen the way of duty and is therefore justified before God.

In his socially secure place, the Judge uses others (God, his wife, his nephew) to shore up and confirm his own self-identity, an identity (Judge/husband/caring uncle) that is self-validating in both public and private spheres. It certainly appears from the letters themselves that neither the public nor his wife has ever given him cause to question his own self-confidence about his place of belonging. One imagines Vilhelm to be an avid consumer of detective novels that reassure him the divine economy is still at work, rewarding the good and punishing the evil.

Because he imagines himself already justified, Judge Vilhelm, paragon of the community, is further from God than the sinner, in this case, the recipient of the correspondence: the Judge's wayward nephew – the anonymous 'A', who embodies the 'aesthetic' form of existence, mentioned by Ian Weeks earlier. Judge Vilhelm is further from God than his nephew because the Judge is essentially self-deceived about his own identity.

Narrative as a Form of Self-Deception

Kierkegaard's mature view of the self is given in *The Sickness unto Death* and is characterized by its relations to itself, to other persons and to God. Here, Kierkegaard refers to the self as being established by two distinct poles, 'of the infinite and the finite, the temporal and the eternal, of freedom and necessity' (1980: 13). The relation is not static, but a dynamic tension between two ends. According to Beabout and Frazier, the poles of finitude and infinitude, freedom and necessity, correspond to the poles of sociality and individuality in the self (2000: 82–4). The self's finitude represents the self's historical situatedness. These are the conditions and constraints imposed on the self by its particular historical circumstances and its social nexus, or the various relations with fellow human beings. This aspect is the self's sociality and maps onto the concept of 'narrative identity' that I've discussed so far. However, since the self is not completely determined by its historical context and its relations with others, it also has the capacity for self-reflection and self-determination that is characteristic of the self in its individuality. This suggests that part of identity comes about through one's *own* 'narrative', the story the self tells about one's *own* life. However, lest this suggests 'narrative identity' is possible and reliable in terms of an Aristotelian 'middle way', the so-called distinct poles are in Kierkegaard's view not at all clear for the individual involved, since the capacity for clarity (the clarity necessary to constitute an accurate or realistic account of 'narrative identity') is severely hampered by an even stronger capacity for 'self-deception'.

It is in his reflections on self-deception that Kierkegaard most lucidly comes to represent the modern turn towards suspicion. Brooks investigated this in terms of public suspicion of a criminal element that brings with it an attendant proclivity for judgement of undesirable others. In Kierkegaard, this form of suspicion is turned inward, towards the single individual who must turn the gaze of judgement constantly on their own motives, lest they become 'self-deceived'. As Kierkegaard seemed to understand, whether 'narrative identity' is understood in terms of one's *own* self-narrated story, or whether it is understood as determined by the 'social', the cohesion and clarity desired by individuals and society is simply unattainable when we ourselves are the narrators.

Kierkegaard presents an alternative account of narrative identity. It is a narrative that is shaped by suspicion of one's own motives, and the motives of one's own society. Unlike the detective novel, which validates society's 'suspicion' of the other and encourages the demonization of the 'wrong', creating the category of the damned, Kierkegaard encourages us to turn our suspicious gaze first and foremost on ourselves. When we turn our suspicious gaze on ourselves, the narrative of the detective story fails. When we turn the gaze on ourselves, individually and collectively, the narrative sense of inevitability falls apart. The happy conclusion, that evil has been contained, is replaced by the grim reality that evil lurks within and is not so easily eradicated. For this reason, Kierkegaard is often charged with encouraging individualism; however, it seems that his single individual is not characterized by such isolation. Throughout his corpus, Kierkegaard explores the individual in a context of social settings. His pseudonyms are constantly in conversation with other characters, and in some ways the pseudonymous writings are in conversation with Kierkegaard himself. Thus, in many ways, Kierkegaard's entire oeuvre presents a narrative that remains open-ended. Indeed, even if we accept that Kierkegaard's concept of the 'single individual' is characterized by isolation, it can be read in a positive way. We can understand Kierkegaard as providing a voice, *a narrative*, for the individual who has been designated the Other by a dominant and powerful public narrative, where the combined voices of the many serve to drown out the quiet protests of the one. However, we should be clear that Kierkegaard's 'solitary individual' is always seen by God.

Conclusion

Hans Mol, by his own account, was also seen by God in a sense. I began this section with a comment on Hans Mol's identity as a Christian, a narrative that provided purpose to an event marked by suffering and a profound sense of disorder. Because of his survival, Mol felt it was incumbent on him to tell his story, on behalf of those who died. Yet, in telling the story of his own survival, Mol made of the Nazi regime a demonic enemy that could only be overcome by the intervention of the divine. And in placing the event in the context of a Christian narrative, Mol linked the Nazi regime to the Christian concept of 'sin' and lent it a tone of inevitability:

> My easy student view of the world – if only Nazism can be eradicated everything will be fine – began to be replaced slowly by a sense of inevitability of evil not just in others, but also in myself. Wasn't this mixture of good and bad both in the SS guards and in my fellow prisoners called 'sin' in the drivel I had so decisively rejected in my youth? (1987: 8)

In some ways, then, Mol's narrative account shares important characteristics identified by Peter Brooks in terms of the detective novel and the doctrine of 'inevitable discovery'. One who is identified as a 'sinner' in Mol's account will live his or her entire life under that judgement, such a person is released from this only by the grace of a God who restores order to the life of the individual and the world.

Mol describes *How God Hoodwinked Hitler* as 'the story of Christian growth during the darkest period of my life', an account that was itself 'completely re-written and interpreted' from the 'old, yellowing manuscript ... an arrogant piece of work ... embarrassing bits were left out and too many boring details left in' (ibid.: 9–10). Herein lies both the power and weakness of narrative identities. In telling his story of central events that occurred in his youth, historical events are interpreted and reframed in terms of Mol's identity later in life. Mol's account suggests much growth and understanding of himself has taken place in this time, and at no point does he describe himself as 'heroic' in any way for having survived. Yet the greater Christian narrative in which the event is framed as a battle between 'good and evil' has all the hallmarks of Brook's investigation of narrative identity in the nineteenth century. Furthermore, Mol's Christian narrative is always in danger of becoming, as Kierkegaard understood it, justification of one's own self and social order as being divinely instituted in some way.

What, then, is the problem of narrative identity? Narrative identity, shaped and affirmed in social institutions and validating social norms, is always in danger of becoming a 'detective story' in which we identify and bring to justice 'criminal elements' that endanger the narrative we tell about ourselves: a narrative that is more likely to be a wishful fabrication rather than an honest evaluation of who we are individually, and as a Western society. But life is unlike stories: we do not experience its beginnings or its conclusion in anything like the ways in which stories make such matters clear and definite. With this in mind, we now leave Mol's narrative behind in order to discuss the contemporary status of many of the same sociological issues that once received Mol's identity-focused analysis.

References

Batnitzky, L. (2011) *How Judaism Became a Religion*. Princeton: Princeton University Press.

Beabout, G. and Frazier, B. (2000) 'A Challenge to the "Solitary Self" Interpretation of Kierkegaard', *History of Philosophy Quarterly*, 17(1): 75–98.

Brooks, B. (2011) *Enigmas of Identity*. Princeton: Princeton University Press.

Cassirer, E. (1955) *Philosophie der symbolischen Formen*. Volumes 1 and 2. New Haven: Yale University Press.

Doniger, W. (2009) *The Hindus: An Alternative History*. Oxford: Oxford University Press.

Freudenthal, G. (2012) *No Religion without Idolatry*. Notre Dame: University of Notre Dame Press.

Heidegger, M. (2004). *The Phenomenology of Religious Life*. Bloomington: Indiana University Press.

Kierkegaard, S. (1980) *The Sickness unto Death*. Princeton: Princeton University Press.

Kierkegaard, S. (1988) *Either/Or: Part I*. Princeton: Princeton University Press.

Lifton, R.J. (1993) *The Protean Self: Human Resilience in an Age of Fragmentation*. New York: Basic Books.

MacIntyre, A. (1984) *After Virtue*. Notre Dame: University of Notre Dame Press.

Mol, H. (1985) *The Hamilton Spectator*, April 27: n.p.

Mol, H. (1987) *How God Hoodwinked Hitler*. Tring: Lion Publishing.

Monk, R. (2014) *Robert Oppenheimer: Life inside the Center*. New York: Anchor Books.

'Religion, n'. OED Online. March 2014. Oxford University Press. Available at: http://www.oed.com.ezphost.dur.ac.uk/view/Entry/161944?redirectedFrom=Religion& (accessed 7 April 2014).

Rudd, A. (1993) *Kierkegaard and the Limits of the Ethical*. Oxford: Clarendon Press.

Simmons, J.A. and Minster, S. (2012) *Reexamining Deconstruction and Determinate Religion*. Pittsburgh: Duquesne University Press.

Smith, W.C. (1962) *The Meaning and End of Religion*. New York: Macmillan.

Westphal, M. (1996) *Becoming a Self*. West Lafayette: Purdue University Press.

PART II
Revisiting Themes: Pluralism, Secularism and Contested Borders

Chapter 4

The Secularization of the Sanctity of Life and Death[1]

Karel Dobbelaere

In 1975, at the thirteenth Conference of the ISSR in Lloret de Mar (Spain), I was commissioned – by the Council of the ISSR on the proposal of Hans Mol, who was then President of the Research Committee 22: Sociology of Religion of the International Sociological Association (ISA) of which I was the secretary – to write a trend report on secularization theories to be published in *Current Sociology* (Dobbelaere 1981). Since then I have extended my study on secularization, strongly influenced by theoretical insights of Niklas Luhmann linked to the notion of functional differentiation. This allowed me to elaborate a theoretical and methodological approach of the process of secularization. A new synthesis of my thinking was published in 2002 (Dobbelaere 2002, see also 2007 and 2009) that was tested empirically with the help of my colleague Jacques Billiet on data from the successive waves to the European Value Study (EVS) and especially from the Religious and Moral Pluralism (RAMP) study (Billiet et al. 2003). In this chapter, I continue that work – first

---

[1] The invitation to write a chapter for this *Festschrift* in honour of Hans Mol gives me the opportunity to express to him my gratitude for having stimulated me to work on secularization. My PhD dissertation was a typical study of 'normative integration' in the Catholic Church, measured on the basis of beliefs, practices and ethical norms (Dobbelaere 1966). The multivariate analysis was done on the basis of gender, age, social class, social mobility and family background, a type of study that was characteristic of studies in political sociology and about involvement in social organizations. However, the impact of social structures on integration in the church emerged in the data. Lower social classes living in lower-class neighbourhoods were less integrated in the Church than those living in socially mixed neighbourhoods; the level of church religiosity of women professionally involved was similar to that of men – it was the housewives who were more religious than men; and upwardly mobile persons were more involved in the Church than their parents – the inverse was true for those downwardly mobile. This stimulated me to rethink my sociological work. Due, in part, to Hans Mol's influence, I realized the importance of analysing changing social structures and their impact on the religious involvement of people.

influenced by Hans Mol – by presenting the theoretical frame of the process of secularization and illustrating it with empirical studies done in Europe, particularly in Belgium. In the second section, I use central concepts of the theory of secularization to analyse the changing conceptions of fundamental notions of the juridical system to point out its secularization.

The Process of Secularization

The study of secularization implies an analysis at three levels – societal secularization at the macro-level, organizational secularization at the meso level and individual secularization and compartmentalization at the individual level – and the study of their interrelatedness.

The Macro Level: Societal Secularization

Modern societies are primarily *differentiated along functional lines* that overlay the prior forms of segmentary and social class differentiation, and have developed different subsystems (e.g. economy, polity, science, family and education). These subsystems are similar in the sense that society has equal need of them all, but dissimilar since each performs its own particular function (production and distribution of goods and services; taking binding decisions; production of valid knowledge; procreation and mutual support; and teaching). Their functional autonomy depends of course on their communications with other functional systems and the environment. To guarantee these functions and to communicate with their environment, organizations (enterprises; political parties; research centres and academies; families; schools and universities) have been established (the meso level). Each of these organizations functions on the basis of its own medium (money; power; truth; love; information and know-how) and according to the values of its subsystem and its specific norms.

Regarding religion, these secular subsystems affirm their autonomy and reject religiously prescribed rules, i.e., their *autonomization* – e.g., the emancipation of education from ecclesiastical authority; the separation of Church and state; the rejection of church prescriptions about birth control, abortion and euthanasia; the decline of religious content in literature and arts; and the development of science as an autonomous secular perspective. Consequently, the religious influence is increasingly confined to the religious subsystem itself. Thus, the sociological explanation of societal secularization starts with the process of functional differentiation and the autonomization of the so-called secular subsystems. As a consequence, religion becomes a subsystem alongside the so-called secular subsystems, losing in this process its overarching claims over those other subsystems. On the global level, one could of course point to countries that are not secularized because 'church and state' are not functionally differentiated – Iran for example.

The examples given of the autonomization of the subsystems may suggest that this consequence only occurs as a result of *manifest* secularization. However, we must also be aware that there are forms of *latent* secularization. Take for example the introduction of the clock (Laeyendecker and Veerman 2003: 18–37). From the twelfth century onwards, it became evident that the development of science, industry and trade required other systems to measure and regulate time than the one that offered the bells of the churches and monasteries, which punctuated the sequences of prayer. The invention of the clock and the instalment of clocks on the highest towers of towns – which gave it maximum visibility – offered the possibility to emancipate time from its religious connotations and as a consequence to secularize it, at the turn of the fourteenth century. Time lost its canonical significance and its sacred character. This phenomenon amplified in the following centuries with, among others, the arrival of railroads and, later, planes which imposed international coordination of time. One should also note the development of the media, which are today the great coordinators of time for many families. In this way, time was progressively dissociated from its transcendental dimension. It is henceforth considered under the control of humans who regulate it in function of technological or economical requirements (e.g., summer and winter time). This is a very good example of latent secularization since this consequence was 'unintended and unrecognized' (Merton 1959: 63).

The Meso Level: Organizational Secularization

In the second part of the nineteenth century in Belgium, under the impact of changing parliamentary majorities, the radical liberals were able to implement a secularist policy with the help of an emerging Socialist party. By law, a liberal government reduced the impact of the Catholic Church in charitable work, in culture, in poor relief, and in allocating study grants, which reduced the impact of the Church in important sectors of society. Ultimately, each municipality was compelled by law (1879) to establish at least one school where religious instruction was not part of the compulsory curriculum and, from then on, the schoolteachers in these schools had to be certified by a state school, a move which excluded teachers who had studied in Catholic Teachers'

Training Colleges. The Church for its part reacted strongly in sermons, by making enquiries in the confessionals and refusing the sacraments. The conflict over the schools stimulated Catholic leaders to erect private Catholic schools duplicating the state school system, which started the 'pillar' system intended to protect Catholics from the secular world. The concept of 'pillar' and the process of 'pillarization' are translations of the Dutch terms *zuil* and *zuilvorming* to describe the special structure of vertical pluralism typical of Dutch society. Such structures were also present in Austria and Switzerland (Righart 1986). Pillarization illuminates the processes of secularization: on the one hand, it emerged as a radical reaction to the process of functional differentiation in the country and on the other hand, it collapsed nearly a century later as a result of the individual secularization of its members.

At the start, organizational 'dikes' were established to prevent the secularization of the church's flock. The clergy and part of the religious elite started creating an environment segregated from the more and more secularized world. In fact, they reverted to an older process of differentiation: segmentary differentiation, that is, the duplication of services in those sectors that were differentiated from the Church, to check the impact of secularization and to preserve church control over the Catholic part of the population. If the state and the differentiated subsystems were no longer to be organized around a religious ideology, especially the schools and the professional world (hospitals, media, trade unions, sick funds and culture), then the new civil liberties provided the opportunity to establish religious inspired organizations to protect believers from the secular, that is, an a-religious or anti-religious ideology. Once established, these organizations were gradually organized into a more and more centralized pillar of which a party was the political expression. Hence, in Stein Rokkan's terms (1977: 565), we can speak about an institutionalized pillar interlocking a political and a corporate channel. By the 1950s, a comprehensive Catholic pillar was consolidated in Belgium.

A century after the emergence of the pillar, it became clear that the 'dikes' did not prevent the secularization of the flock. From the second part of the 1960s a process of individual secularization set in. This change in the Catholic population provoked an acute crisis in the Catholic pillar, and its leadership organized study sessions and conferences in which the following questions were debated: what is a Catholic school, a Catholic hospital, a Catholic youth movement, a Catholic trade union ...? They asked themselves whether they should go on providing pillarized services. It was in this period that a new legitimation of the pillar was developed: 'Socio-Cultural Christianity'. Research (Billiet and Dobbelaere 1976: 59–99; Laermans 1992: 204–14) documented that the core philosophy no longer consisted of the strict religious rules of the Catholic Church, but rather referred to so-called typical values of the gospels such as stewardship; social justice; a humane approach toward clients and patients or the *Gemeinschaftlichkeit* of Christian institutions; welfare and well-being; the realization of social justice; and solidarity between social classes with special attention to marginal people. These are values that have a universal appeal, but which are not specifically Christian. However, backed up by a religious source, the gospels, and occasionally solemnized with religious rituals, the values acquire the type of sacred aura Mol repeatedly (as we have seen in previous chapters) associated with the process of religious identity. This new collective consciousness or identity is still symbolized by a 'C', referring to Christian, that is evangelical, instead of to Catholic, the latter being considered to have a more restricted appeal and to be more confining. This 'Socio-Cultural Christianity' functions now as the sacred canopy for the segmented Catholic world of olden days (Dobbelaere and Voyé 1990: 6–8). This process of *organizational* secularization on the meso level is a good example of the adaptation of these organizations to individual secularization in the Catholic world.

However, the secularization of the pillar was not simply the result of a *manifest* adaptation of the collective consciousness; it was also *latently* set in. The influx of students, due to the democratization of education in the 1950s, required financial aid from the state for the Catholic school system, but that implied legal regulations: the state imposed required levels of professional certification of the teachers, which most priests and religious personnel, who traditionally had taught in Catholic schools, did not have. Professional lay people were hired whose reference was no longer the Church but the profession. Religion, that in the past had infused the teaching of subjects like history and literature, became a class among other classes; the selections and the interpretation of the materials of these secular subjects was no longer oriented by religious motives. Professionalization of the teachers promoted the secularization of the Catholic school system latently, not consciously and intentionally. And the same happened in Catholic hospitals. Religious personnel that, in the past, supervised the wards and the operating theatres in Catholic hospitals, imposing the moral norms of the Church, disappeared gradually for lack of vocations and were replaced by professional lay people. The medical doctors and nurses became more and more specialized and followed professional norms rather than church norms. In other words, in both institutions, religion became more and more marginalized as a class among other classes, and the chaplaincy a service among other hospital services. The secularization of the Catholic schools and hospitals was not intended by the teachers, neither by the medical doctors, it occurred latently as a result of changes in society: democratization, professionalization and a growing lack of competent religious personnel (Dobbelaere, Billiet and Creyf 1978; Dobbelaere 1979).

Individual Secularization and Compartmentalization

From 1967 to 1973, church practice on weekends diminished from 43 per cent by more than 10 percentage points in Belgium, in the Flemish part even from 52 per cent by nearly 15 percentage points, i.e. by more than 1.5 to even 2.5 percentage points per year, and this continued, although at a lower rate: the older generation of church goers was not replaced any more by the young adults. In 2009, more than 50 per cent younger than 55 years old declared that they were unchurched, half of them since two or more generations (Voyé and Dobbelaere 2012a: 147–8). Also a large number of seminarians and priests were respectively leaving the seminars and the priesthood at the end of the 1960s and the early 1970s. Concerning beliefs, even if a majority confirmed their belief in God, the image of God changed progressively from the traditional Catholic belief into a belief expressing itself in a God conceived as 'some sort of spirit or life force' (ibid.: 153). The negative reaction, amongst others expressed in an open letter to the Belgian bishop by more than 400 Catholic Flemish intellectuals, against the papal encyclical *Humanae Vitae* (1968) which forbade artificial contraception, indicated that a large majority of lay Catholics rejected certain ethical norms of the Church. This became very clear in the successive waves of the European Values Study, which indicated over the years that a positive attitude towards abortion, euthanasia, divorce and homosexuality was rising quickly (Draulans and Billiet 2012: 125). Finally, the results of an evaluation of confidence asked about 18 national and international institutions in the EVS waves of 1990, 1999 and 2009, revealed that the high confidence rate of the Catholic Church declined over these 20 years to low or no confidence at all (Abts et al. 2012: 185), a Church that in the early nineties had the second highest positive score now had the lowest score. These are all indicators of individual secularization in the Belgian population, and the impact on organizational secularization was clearly shown above.

Connected with individual secularization is compartmentalization or 'secularization in mind', i.e. that people think that the churches should not intervene or impose their views in so-called secular subsystems. We registered this negative attitude in a study done in 13 Eastern, Nordic and Western European countries, called RAMP (Religious and Moral Pluralism) in 1997–99.

Compartmentalization varied with church commitment. 'People with a low commitment to their church (were) prone to prevent secular institutions being affected by religious influences' (Billiet et al. 2003: 153). And we found no differences between members of Protestant churches or the Catholic Church. This was also clearly expressed in the EVS-study wave of 2008–09. In France, 78 per cent are in agreement with the statement 'Religious leaders should not influence government decisions' (Dompnier 2009: 259), in other so-called Catholic Western European countries, the EVS-data registered an agreement on this statement of 75 per cent in Belgium, 71 per cent in Spain, 66 per cent in Italy and 52 per cent in Portugal (Dobbelaere et al. 2014: in press). According to the EVS-study of 2008–09, even those practising weekly reject church interventions in political matters, 50 per cent were in agreement with compartmentalization in Belgium, France and Italy, and 45 per cent in Spain and Portugal (ibid.). And as already mentioned, many Catholics also rejected the rules on birth control expressed in the papal encyclical *Humanae Vitae* on the grounds that it is the parents who decide about the number of children for their family and the contraceptive methods to be used. Thus, we see the manner by which individual secularization, and the compartmentalization with which it is linked, affects religiosity and behavioural choices. Of course, it is even more important to recognize the social consequences that occur when such individual secularization combines with the aforementioned societal and organizational forms.

Life and Death: The Collapse of the Sanctity of Human Life?

Having presented the theoretical frame of secularization theory, we will now apply it to a concrete social case: the juridical subsystem. Peter Singer argues that in the early 1990s the nearly 2,000-year-old traditional western ethic on the sanctity of human life collapsed. This ethic holds that all human life, 'irrespective of its nature or quality', has 'intrinsic value'. Due to its collapse, he states, we can achieve 'a better approach to life-and-death decision-making' (Singer 1996: 1–4). Is this correct?

The Euthanasia Practice in Belgium

Below, after analysing the secularization of the Belgian juridical subsystem, I will discuss both the reaction of the Catholic professionals towards the law and finally how the population evaluates euthanasia.

The Secularization of the Juridical Subsystem

The decline of religious beliefs and church involvement, the related increase of religious pluralism and the fast growing positive attitude towards bodily self-determination, i.e. abortion, euthanasia, divorce, homosexuality and suicide (see supra 1.3 individual secularization), were favourable factors for a wave of secularization of the juridical subsystem, which started with the law on the partial liberalization of abortion in Belgium in 1990. The Socialist parties, which were coalition partners of the Christian parties, joined the opposition to lead with the Liberal parties an alternative majority to approve the draft law in parliament. A number of leading members of the Socialist and Liberal parties are members of atheistic Masonic Lodges. The Christian parties voted against the law, Belgian bishops issuing relevant doctrinal documents. In an appeal to the population at large, they expounded their doctrinal and pastoral position and warned Catholics that individuals who cooperate 'effectively and directly' in abortions 'exclude themselves from the ecclesiastical community'. In 1999, and again in 2003, the Christian parties lost the elections and thus have not been part of the federal government for eight years. During this period, more measures of secularization in the juridical subsystem were adopted. In 2002, two laws were passed on the liberalization of the use of drugs and on euthanasia and, in 2003, a law on the marriage of homosexual couples (Dobbelaere 2008: 75–7).

Since 2002, a Belgian law permits physician-performed euthanasia under strict due care conditions when a patient asks for it and is in a condition of constant and unbearable physical or psychological suffering resulting from a serious and incurable disorder caused by illness or accident for which medical treatment is ineffective and if there is no possibility of improvement. This law was opposed by political parties with a Christian signature. The Belgian bishops again issued doctrinal messages in which they refer to papal documents and expose their ethical standpoint, arguing that euthanasia is deliberately causing death by transgressing a centuries-old norm 'You shall not kill' and, consequently, violating God's law.

The Catholic Professionals and the Law on Euthanasia

Caritas Catholica Flanders (CCF) – an overarching Catholic organization including Zorgnet Vlaanderen (Union of Institutions for Treatment) – has issued a document in which they distance themselves somewhat from the position of the Church. They underscore that the ethical declaration of the Church contains values and principles that are valuable *in general*. However, clinical practice implies *concrete cases* for which exceptional circumstances may play an important role. Reflecting on the application of the law they distinguish three types of *physically* ill patients. Concerning competent terminally ill patients the Caritas document considers that euthanasia may be acceptable if palliative sedation does not help anymore and the patient has constant and unbearable pains. As far as incompetent terminally ill patients who, in the presence of a witness, have signed an anticipated demand of euthanasia, the Caritas Commission recommends a restrictive usage of such documents. However, they do not accept euthanasia for non-terminally ill patients, neither do they for *psychologically* ill patients. This document was sent for reflection to all hospitals associated with Zorgnet Vlaanderen, suggesting that in each hospital the Ethical Committee produce its own policy document on euthanasia.

In a study of hospitals in Flanders, the Dutch-speaking part of Belgium, it was discovered that 29 Catholic hospitals had submitted such policy documents. According to these documents, 80 per cent permit euthanasia for *competent terminally physically ill patients* along the line of the Caritas document. Indeed, only one does not permit it at all, referring to the position of the Church; the others simply follow the law. As far as euthanasia for *incompetent terminally physically ill patients* is concerned, 23 hospitals sent in a policy document: 5 hospitals do not permit it, the others do permit it; 11 follow the Caritas line, and 7 follow the law. Finally, concerning *non-terminally physically ill patients*, 26 hospitals sent in a policy document; the majority does not permit it. It is clear that policies in the majority of Catholic hospitals are still more permissive than the Caritas document. However, it should be stressed that in these hospitals euthanasia, if applied, is mostly preceded by the palliative filter. Likewise, in some hospitals the doctor also receives advice from an ethics committee and/or an interdisciplinary team (Lemeingre et al. 2008: 294–6).

The Attitude of the Population towards Euthanasia

Thus, we now know the attitude of the politicians who voted the law on euthanasia since they set the criteria permitting physician-performed euthanasia. The Catholic Magisterium, of course, defended the opposite attitude and defined euthanasia as murder whilst Catholic professionals displayed a more permissive attitude depending upon the concrete cases they face.

Here, in order to know the attitude of the general population, we will use the four waves of the European Values Study on the basis of question 243: 'Please tell me whether you think that Euthanasia – terminating the life of the incurably sick – can always be justified (10), never be justified (1), or something in between, using the scale on the card'. In 1981 the global score for Belgium was 3.1, 'rather not justified', since then the global score increased to reach 6.9 in 2009, meaning 'rather justified'. It was in 1990, before the law on euthanasia was voted, that there was a big jump pro, as can be seen in Table 4.1. In 2009, the global score for Europe was just over 4.5, with Denmark having the highest score, nearly 7 (Halman et al. 2012: 114). The global score for France was 6.6 (Berton 2009: 96). Analysing the Belgian scores according to generations, we did not detect a significant trend; however, involvement in the church produced significant differences as can be seen in Table 4.1.

Table 4.1   Evolution of the mean scores of justification of euthanasia according to church involvement (1981–2009)

Church involvement	1981	1990	1999	2009
Core Catholics*	3.3	3.7	4.9	5,6
Modal Catholics*	3.6	4.9	6.0	7,0
Marginal Catholics*	3.4	5.6	6.1	6,8
Unchurched	4.4	6.1	6.9	7,4
Global score (N)	3,6 (1101)	5,1 (1740)	6,1 (1777)	6,9 (1431)

Note: *Core Catholics go to church minimally once a month; Modal Catholics go minimally once a year; Marginal Catholics define themselves as Catholic but do not go to church.
Source: Draulans and Billiet 2012.

Indeed, the justification of euthanasia depends to a certain extent on the level of church involvement; however, over the last 30 years this impact decreased significantly. Unchurched persons are most tolerant, and their score went up from 4.4 in 1981 to 7.4 in 2009. However, during this period tolerance also rose on each level of involvement in the church, even in the category of the core members. In 1981, the attitude of the Catholics did not differ significantly (scores 3.3–3.6) and they considered euthanasia 'nearly never justifiable'. This changed around 1990 as homogeneity in the Catholic world broke down; the score of the modal and marginal church members rose substantially. Marginal Catholics scored higher than the modal Catholics, and the former's score came close to that of the unchurched. The score of the core Catholics did not change much and was significantly lower than the score of the other church members. By 1999, the scores of the core and the modal Catholics rose by more than one point, and the difference between the modal and the marginal members disappeared, approaching the score of the unchurched. However, there was still a marked difference between the core Catholics and the others. The results of the 2009 interviews confirm this difference, but the scores of the modal Catholics, the marginal Catholics and the unchurched are now no longer significantly different, their scores revealing that they have shifted from viewing euthanasia as 'nearly never justifiable' 30 years ago to believing it to be 'rather justifiable' today. The score of the core Catholics takes the middle between unjustifiable and justifiable and is significantly lower than the score of the others.

The Rationalization of the Changing Attitudes

In 2011, Liliane Voyé and I presented a small questionnaire to second year students of the KU Leuven (University of Leuven) and persons taking lectures at the UVTD (Adult University of Davidsfonds) asking them to give explicitly their arguments pro or contra euthanasia after indicating their position on the scale, which was a reproduction of question 243 of the EVS questionnaire. We collected 194 valid responses. The university students were predominantly 19 years old, and those of UVTD were in the great majority older than 60. All in all, the respondents were a little more involved in the Catholic Church than their Belgian peers. It was not a representative sample of the Belgian population, but their answers give us an idea of the arguments used by individuals when discussing euthanasia (Dobbelaere and Voyé 2012: 111–16). In both groups, the great majority stated that euthanasia is almost 'always justifiable', and the arguments used were either in *principle* or referring to *circumstances*.

The arguments referring to *principles* were rather short, but forcefully stated. The small group arguing against euthanasia were mostly elderly persons and core Catholics who wrote: 'Life is a gift of God' or 'One must respect life'. Those arguing pro-euthanasia wrote: 'It is the autonomous decision of the person', 'The patient decides' or 'My life is mine' and 'My life is my business'. The latter arguments were given by young and old, church members and unchurched people. To the contrary, the arguments referring to *circumstances* were rather long and centred on the meaning of physical suffering.

Indeed, the meaning of suffering is, for young as well as for old, essential to understand their position towards euthanasia. A large majority thinks that physical suffering has no sense and is pointless: 'A life full of suffering and without perspectives for improvement has no meaning'; 'It is immoral not to deliver people with an incurable illness from their affliction'; 'It is pointless for a human being to have to suffer; in case of an incurable illness one has to deliver them from their agony'. A few suggested that pain is not pointless since it may help people, the sick as well as those surrounding them, to deepen the sense of their life: 'At first suffering may seem meaningless, however it may help to discover and to deepen the meaning of your life'. This way they give suffering a moral sense. However, we did not register the religious sense of suffering: the saving and redeeming effect of it in the hereafter. Connected to suffering, the quality and the meaning of life were evoked by some: 'It is important that life has kept its value and that it is not reduced to simply being there'; 'Not to live further if life has lost all meaning for you or for your family'; 'The quality of life is more important than the quantity'. If other considerations were made – 'It has no sense to put the financial burden on the society to prolong life when all hope of improvement is gone', or 'One cannot ask kin to carry the burden of a life that has lost all quality' – they were always preceded by the specification that they can only be taken into account if there is no hope anymore of improvement and if the sick person suffers from unbearable pains.

What Do We Learn from This Study?

When the political parties with a Christian signature were no longer in a position to block the secularization of the juridical subsystem, the secular parties were able to change the existing laws on abortion, euthanasia and homo-marriages. The Belgian bishops reacted negatively on doctrinal and ethical grounds, giving their arguments against the changes introduced by the three laws in published documents and in press conferences. However, they did not interfere in the political process as, for example, the Italian Episcopal Conference did. The Italian bishops entered actively and vocally into the political field on several occasions. They supported the organization of referenda and gave voting advice on referenda in order to block the secularization of the juridical subsystem. The Vatican also intervened in Italy and was in favour of the actions of the Italian Episcopal Conference. That becomes very clear in the Vatican reaction to the Belgian bishops concerning the ethical laws that were passed there. In their 'Ad Lamina' visit at the Vatican in 2003, the Belgian bishops were accused by Pope John-Paul II of not having 'reacted vehemently' against those laws and 'having let them pass'. In his answer to the Pope, the Belgian archbishop stated that the bishops had clearly exposed the doctrinal vision of the Catholic Church on these matters, but he added that in Belgium, 'The Church has no political power. She can only express her moral opposition ... The Church, in our country', he said, 'is no longer as powerful as she was in the preceding epoch when she was able to make herself heard' (Voyé and Dobbelaere 2012b: 39). In fact, the Church clearly depends on a population not too profoundly secularized, like the Italian population, so that a large number may be mobilized to manifest its opposition to new ethical laws. Since the Belgian population is largely secularized, the church does not have the power anymore to mobilize an opposition against the secularization of the juridical subsystem. Indeed, as was shown, even only a fringe of the Catholic population has a strong negative attitude towards euthanasia.

Thus far, we have pointed out the changes that have occurred and the social positions actively and passively involved in the secularization of the juridical subsystem. However, the major conclusion of the changes in the law on euthanasia and the attitudes towards euthanasia is the de-sacralization of suffering. The Christian idea that suffering has a saving and redeeming effect got lost, which made both suffering and the life of the sufferer seem senseless. This co-produced the de-sacralization of human life in Belgium. It should be noted that euthanasia was also legalized in both the Netherlands and Luxembourg.

Other Cases of a Changing Attitude towards the Sanctity of Human Life

However, not all countries have taken the same road to de-sacralize the traditional view of life and death. The standard view of the law, and of the traditional doctrine of the sanctity of human life in the Judeo-Christian tradition, was that every human life is of equal value. This position was restated quite categorically in 1986 by a judge of the supreme Court of Victoria, Australia: 'the law does not permit decisions to be made concerning the quality of life nor any assessment of the value of any human being' (Singer 1996: 65). However, Singer (ibid.: 60–80) presents the court arguments of two emblematic cases of a patient in persistent vegetative state that departed from this traditional doctrine.

An American Case   A Missouri woman was, after a car accident, in a persistent vegetative state for eight years. Her parents went to court asking for permission to remove her feeding tube. The Missouri Supreme Court 'refused, saying that since (their daughter) was not competent to refuse life-sustaining treatment herself, and the state has an interest in preserving life, the court could only give permission for the withdrawal of life-sustaining treatment if there were clear and convincing evidence that this was what (their daughter) would have wanted. No such evidence had been presented to the court' (ibid.: 61). The parents appealed to the United Sates Supreme Court arguing 'that their daughter had a constitutional right to be allowed to die' which the Supreme Court accepted, but this court also 'accepted the right of the state of Missouri to demand, before permitting this to occur, clear and convincing evidence that it was what (their daughter) would have wanted' (Singer 1996: 61–2). Shortly after this judgement, 'former friends recalled that she had said things to them indicating that she would wish to die, if she were ever in such a situation' (ibid.: 62). Consequently, the state of Missouri did not oppose the parent's application and the lower court accepted that there was now 'clear and convincing' evidence of their daughter's desire 'not to have her life sustained in this situation, and it allowed the feeding tube to be withdrawn' (ibid.).

A British Case A similar case involved a 17-year-old British football fan who was crushed when thousands of supporters were still trying to get into the grounds for an FA Cup semi-final. He was not dead, but his cortex was destroyed; only his brain stem had survived. Neither his family, nor the doctor in charge and a specialist whose opinion was sought, nor the hospital 'could see any benefit to him ... in keeping him alive' (Singer 1996: 57–9). The hospital 'applied to the Family Division of the High Court for declarations that the hospital might lawfully discontinue all life-sustaining treatment' (ibid.: 60). At Family Division an Official Solicitor was appointed as guardian for the patient. He opposed what the doctor in charge was 'going to do, arguing that, legally, it was murder'. The President of the Family Division 'did not accept this view, and he made the requested declarations to the effect that all treatment might lawfully be stopped' (ibid.). The Official Solicitor appealed, and the Court of Appeal upheld the judge's decision; however, the Official Solicitor appealed again. This brought the case before the highest court in the British judicial system, the House of Lords. In each of the three courts that considered the case, the judges came to the same conclusion: 'that the treatment could be discontinued' (Singer 1996: 64). Contrary to the American case, the British judges did not ask what the patient's wishes might have been. The question which they addressed was: 'What is in the best interests of the patient?' (ibid.). Each one of the nine judges involved in the case pronounced in slightly different words that he did not value life that is human only in a biological sense: 'I cannot conceive what benefit his continued existence could be thought to give him', 'the reality of (his) existence outweighs the abstract requirement to preserve life', or '... the patient is not living a life at all. None of the things that one says about the way people live their lives – well or ill, with courage or fortitude, happily or sadly – have any meaning in relation to him', sustaining his life brings him 'no affirmative benefit' (ibid.: 65–7). Singer concludes that in this case 'British law abandoned the idea that life itself is a benefit to the person living it, irrespective of its quality' (1996: 68).

Reflections

Are we, with the British case, 'beyond the sanctity of human life'? A Judge of the Court of Appeal, for instance, said, 'the case for the universal sanctity of life assumes a life in the abstract and allows nothing for the reality of (his) life', and at the House of Lords it was said that the principle of the sanctity of life 'is not an absolute one' (ibid.: 74). In this context, Singer cites a legal scholar from Queens' College, Cambridge, stating that the decision of the case was making 'bad law, largely by approving a consequentialist ethic radically inconsistent with the principle of the sanctity of life' (ibid.: 75), and he concludes:

> the utter hopelessness of (the boy's) condition led the judges to see that technological advances in medicine have made it impossible to retain the principle of the sanctity of human life. Instead they switched to an ethic that sensibly takes into account whether sustaining life will benefit or harm the human being whose life is to be sustained?

The approach of American and British judges was different. If the family wanted the doctors to stop all artificial life-sustaining devices, the American judges wanted to have 'clear and convincing' evidence of the patient's desire. This is similar to the Belgian law on euthanasia concerning incompetent terminally physically ill patients: they must have made a written 'anticipated declaration', before two witnesses, who countersign it to be used as an advance directive. The British judges conversely, addressed the question 'what is in the best interest of the patient', what the living, family and doctors, have to evaluate for the unconscious patient.

Conclusions

The secularization of the sanctity of life and death is a consequence of legislative action (Belgium) favoured by the individual secularization of the Belgian population. In the USA and in Great Britain, it was on the level of the courts that an *organizational secularization* was produced, i.e. the judges referred to the 'quality of life' and did not judge 'every human life of equal value', which is contrary to the traditional doctrine of the sanctity of human life. Our analysis of the attitudes of young and older people in Belgium suggests also that for them the quality of life is very important, not life as such, and that the Christian notion of the saving and redeeming value of suffering is greatly lost.

Finally, it should be underscored that the professionals (Caritas Flanders in Belgium) did not reject the doctrinal position of the Church but highlighted that clinical practice implies concrete cases, much as the British judges did not reject the principle of the sanctity of life and death but found it insufficient for resolving concrete situations. Do these options imply what Singer (1996: 80) suggests: 'the need for a new approach to life-and-death decisions'? Either way, it is clear that in the western world human life has been de-sacralized by laws and the courts responding to a changing evaluation of life by the population, patients and the families. The traditional absolute sacred character of all human life is more and more questioned; it became subject to an assessment of the quality of life.

According to Hans Mol, 'secularization ... is the outcome of differentiations exceeding the capacity of religious organizations to integrate them in the traditional frame of reference' (1979: 35). It is clear that the new definition of life and death emerging in the law on euthanasia (Belgium) and in the court cases (Britain and the USA) seems to exceed the capacity of the traditional Christian churches to integrate them in their traditional frame of reference. This is certainly the case for the Catholic Church. The reaction of Pope John-Paul II to the secularization of the juridical subsystem in Belgium points that out very clearly, as does a recent publication of the Belgian Archbishop. In his recent book (Leonard 2011: 64–5), the latter deplores the numerous current abuses committed by parliament in submitting to a vote 'the most fundamental anthropological parameters'. Implicitly he refers to the Belgian parliament, but we may extend his evaluations to the democratic decisions taken in the parliaments of other countries (France, Italy, Luxembourg, Spain, The Netherlands, Portugal ...). According to him, 'parliament assigned itself the right to decide by majority vote the sense of sexuality, the difference between masculinity and femininity, the significance of the word marriage, the metaphysical connection of the human being to finiteness and death, the quality of embryos deserving or not to be respected, etc.'. He represents the official way of thinking of the Catholic Hierarchy, but his evaluation is overstated. Parliaments decided nothing on these matters. They simply were and are confronted with different worldviews on these matters in their population, and they try to set limits within which people with different views on these moral issues can behave according to their conscience. The state does not impose definitions, but workable situations for its population enabling it to act according to its own ethical views. What Mgr Leonard, a prototype of the Catholic Hierarchy, wants is the imposition of the Catholic vision on life, death, sex, marriage, etc. As long as the Catholic Hierarchy does not understand and accept functional differentiation, it will come in conflict with the polity and the population, demonstrating its incapacity to integrate the changing evaluations in western populations into its own frame of reference. As this situation indicates, therefore, secularization has emerged in Europe as a cultural force with striking relevance far beyond the walls sociology departments. Having explored its import for issues of the sanctity of life and death, our focus now turns to the place of religion and its discourse in secularized European contexts.

References

Abts, K., Swyngedouw, M. and Jacobs, D. (2012) 'Intéret pour la politique et méfiance envers les insttutions. La spirale de la méfiance enrayée?', in L. Voyé, K. Dobbelaere and K. Abts (eds), *Autres temps, autres mœurs. Travaille, famille, éthique, religon et politique: La vision des Belges*. Brussels: Racine Campus, 173–214.

Berger, P. (1967) *The Sacred Canopy: Elements of a Sociological Theory of Religion*. Garden City: Doubleday and Company.

Berton, R.M. (2009) 'Contrôle sur son corps, face au sexe et à la mort', in P. Bréchon and J.F. Tchernia (eds), *La France à travers ses valeurs*. Paris: Arman Colin, 95–7.

Billiet, J. and Dobbelaere, K. (1976) *Godsdienst in Vlaanderen: Van Kerks Katholicisme naar Sociaal-Kulturele Kristenheid?* Leuven: Davidsfonds.

Billiet, J. et al. (2003) 'Church Commitment and Some Consequences in Western and Central Europe', in R.L. Piedmont and D.O. Moberg (eds), *Research in the Social Study of Religion Research in the Social Study of Religion*, Volume 14. Leiden and Boston: Brill, 129–59.

Dobbelaere, K. (1966) *Sociologische analyse van de katholiciteit*. Antwerp: Standaard Wetenschappelijke Uitgeverij.

Dobbelaere, K. (1979) 'Professionalization and Secularization in the Belgian Catholic Pillar', *Japanese Journal of Religious Studies*, 6(1–2): 39–64.

Dobbelaere, K. (1981) 'Secularization: A Multi-Dimensional Concept', *Current Sociology*, 29(2): 3–153.

Dobbelaere, K. (2002) *Secularization: An Analysis at Three Levels*. Brussels: Peter Lang.

Dobbelaere, K. (2007) 'Testing Secularization Theory in Comparative Perspective', *Nordic Journal of Religion and Society*, 20(2): 137–47.

Dobbelaere, K. (2008) 'Two Different Types of Manifest Secularization: Belgium and France Compared', in E. Barker (ed.), *The Centrality of Religion in Social Life: Essays in Honour of James A. Beckford*. London: Ashgate, 69–82.

Dobbelaere, K. (2009) 'The Meaning and Scope of Secularization', in P.B. Clarke (ed.), *The Oxford Handbook of the Sociology of Religion*. Oxford: Oxford University Press, 600–615.

Dobbelaere, K., Billiet, J. and Creyf, R. (1978) 'Secularization and Pillarization: A Social Problem Approach', *The Annual Review of the Social Sciences of Religion*, 2: 97–123.

Dobbelaere, K. and Lauwers, J. (1969) 'Involvement in Church Religion: A Sociological Critique', in *Types, Dimensions and Measures of Religiosity: Acts Xth International Conference on Sociology of Religion, Rome 1969*. Rome: CISR, 101–29.

Dobbelaere, K., Pérez-Agote, A. and Béraud, C. (2014) 'Comparative Synthesis', in K. Dobbelaeare and A. Pérez-Agote (eds), *The Intimate: New Conflicts between Religion and Polity. Laws about Life, Death and the Family in So-Called Catholic Countries*. Leuven: Universitaire Pers Leuven.

Dobbelaere, K. and Voyé, L. (1990) 'From Pillar to Postmodernity: The Changing Situation of Religion in Belgium', *Sociological Analysis*, 51: 1–13.

Dobbelaere, K. and Voyé, L. (2012) 'De Katholieke wereld en de lichamelijke zelfbeschikking: Euthanasie als case', in I. Glorieux, J. Sionger and W. Smits (eds), *Cultuursociologie buiten de lijnen*. Leuven: Lannoo Campus, 101–18.

Dompnier, N. (2009) 'Religion et politique: Regards croisés sur la laïcité', in P. Bréchon and J.-F. Tchernia (eds), *La France à travers ses valeurs*. Paris: Arman Colin, 256–63.

Draulans, V. and Billiet, J. (2012) 'L'Éthique: Le "lourd vaisseau des mœurs" ne prend pas de Brusques virages ... à moins que?', in L. Voyé, K. Dobbelaere and K. Abts (eds), *Autres temps, autres mœurs. Travaille, famille, éthique, religon et politique: La vision des Belges*. Brussels: Racine Campus, 105–43.

Halman, L., Sieben, I. and van Zundert, M. (2012) *Atlas of European Values: Trends and Traditions at the turn of the Century*. Leiden: Brill.

Laermans, R. (1992) *In de greep van de 'Moderne Tijd': Modernisering en verzuiling, individualisering en het naoorlogs publiek discours van de ACW-vormingsorganisaties: een proeve tot cultuursociologische duiding*. Leuven: Garant.

Laeyendecker, L. and Veerman, M.P. (2003) *In de houdgreep van de Tijd: Onze omgang met de tijd in een consumptieve cultuur*. Budel: Damon.

Lemeingre, J., Dierikx de Casterle, B., Denier, Y., Schotsmans, P. and Gastmans, C. (2008) 'How Do Hospitals Deal with Euthanasia Requests in Flanders (Belgium)? A Content Analysis of Policy Documents', *Patient Education and Counseling*, 71: 293–301.

Leonard, Mgr A.-J. (2011) *Agir en chrétien dans sa vie et dans le monde*. Namur: Fidélité.

Luckmann, T. (1967) *The Invisible Religion: The Problem of Religion in Modern Society*. New York: Macmillan.

Merton, R.K. (1959) *Social Theory and Social Structure*. Glencoe: The Free Press.

Mol, H. (1979) 'The Identity Model of Religion: How It Compares with Nine Other Theories of Religion and How It Might Apply to Japan', *Japanese Journal of Religious Studies*, 6(1–2): 11–38.

Righart, H. (1986) *De katholieke zuil Europa: Een vergelijkend onderzoek naar het ontstaan van verzuiling onder katholieken in Oostenrijk, Zwitserland, België en Nederland*. Meppel: Boom.

Rokkan, S. (1977) 'Towards a Generalized Concept of "Verzuiling": A Preliminary Note', *Political Studies*, 25(4): 563–70.

Singer, P. (1996) *Rethinking Life and Death: The Collapse of Our Traditional Ethics*. New York: St. Martin's Press.

Voyé, L. and Dobbelaere, K. (2012a) 'Une Église marginalisée?', in L. Voyé, K. Dobbelaere and K. Abts (eds), *Autres temps, autres mœurs. Travaille, famille,éthique, religon et politique: La vision des Belges*. Brussels: Racine Campus, 144–72.

Voyé, L. and Dobbelaere, K. (2012b) 'Portrait du catholicisme en Belgique', in A. Pérez- Agote (ed.), *Portraits du catholicisme: Une comparaison européenne*. Rennes: Presses Universitaires de Rennes, 11–61.

Chapter 5

The Public Role of Religion

Roberto Cipriani

Introduction

As Chapter 4 suggests, for some decades now specialists of religious phenomena have been heatedly discussing secularization, the death of God, the end of religion, or – to the contrary – a religious reawakening, a return to God, an expansion of the influence of religion. In a number of cases – despite the issues facing some European countries that were previously highlighted by Dobbelaere – there have been reconsiderations, a softening of tone, 180-degree shifts in direction. By way of example, it would be sufficient to refer to Sabino Samele Acquaviva (1971), previously known for his theory of the eclipse of the sacred, and to Harvey Cox (1968), prophet of the secular city. The one was later to specify that he simply meant the end of the magical use of religion (Acquaviva and Stella 1989: 11) while the other, more simply, admitted having been mistaken about the future of religion. Because of these changes of position, the staunchest theorists of a significant return of religious practice too have had to rethink their positions.

Whatever the case, what is lacking is a serious examination of the empirical reality, accompanied by results based on scientifically serious and rigorous investigation, not on preconception. In some instances where reference has been made to it, the approach has been applied only in part, without contextualization and has been too easily over-generalized compared to the variegation and changeability of the scenarios addressed. Above all, insufficient attention has been paid to the significance of historical roots, traditional culture, the socializing function of diffused religion, the weight and influence of confessional organizations, often extremely capillary and efficient in their action (even if immediate appearances might lead one to postulate the opposite).

From Habermas to Böckenförde

The German philosopher-sociologist Jürgen Habermas, by many considered the heir to the so-called Frankfurt School, expresses a certain concern regarding social solidarity. This may be deduced from his greatest work, the theme of which is communicative action (Habermas 1986b: 603–18), the 'normative background' of which is closely interlocked with the authority of the sacred which Habermas recognizes as being the source of ethics. Moral obligation derives, he maintains, from the sacred by means of symbolic mediation, which leads to language (and to the ethics of discourse, that is, to non-instrumental, non-coercive, communicative action). In actual fact, Habermas holds that only a universal type of morality is capable of holding secularized society, which depends on consensus, together (Habermas 1986b II: 669).

Without necessarily accepting and adhering to all the implications contained in Habermasian thinking on communicative action, it is important, nevertheless, to recall that his 'systematics of forms of comprehension' regards four areas:

> (1) ambits of cultural practice, (2) spheres of action where systems of religious interpretation retain powers to guidance such as impact immediately on daily behaviour, and, as a result, on (3) environments of secular, non-religious action, where the store of cultural knowledge is availed of for communication and (4) used to inform focused activities, without the structures of the world view involved being overtly declared as being among the aims of the activities themselves.

This means that the first two ambits are associated directly with the sacred. With regards to the first he states: 'ritual (and sacrificial action) performed by the members of a group correspond to the myth, sacramental practice (and prayer) correspond to the community's religious-metaphysical image of the world, finally, *contemplative* actualization of auratic works of art corresponds to the cultured religion of the early modern age' (original emphasis) (Habermas 1986b: 801). In more explicitly social terms, Habermas maintains that the sacred is grounded in cultural practice (with rites institutionalizing social solidarity; sacraments/prayer institutionalizing the pathways of salvation and knowledge; the contemplative representation of auratic art institutionalizing the fruition of art); the second ambit is concerned with the world views that guide practice (myths; religious and metaphysical images of the world; the religious ethic of conviction; natural rational law; religious citizenship) (Habermas 1986b: 802). Rite and myth belong to archaic society, sacraments/prayers as well as religious and metaphysical images of the world belong to the great ancient civilizations, contemplative representations of auratic art and religious ethical conviction as well as natural rational law and religious citizenship belong to the early modern age.

Even today, religion represents a kind of cognitive challenge in that it bestows content and strength on social norms and, therefore, on solidarity among citizens. Rather than fade (Habermas, Sölle, and Luhmann 1977), religion occupies a place within the public sphere (Habermas 2006a), where it acts as a mediator between two opposites, between fundamentalisms and secularisms. This is how Habermas responds to a provocation by Böckenförde (2007), who denies the secularized state the possibility of guaranteeing its own normative premises (possessed, instead, by the Christian religion) and invokes its reconstruction as a post-secularized state capable of addressing the present-day marked increase in religiosity and in fundamentalist movements.[1]

In actual fact, the Frankfurt sociologist does not believe that the values of religion alone underscore democracy, seeing that democratic rules and procedures also make a contribution. However, he holds that it is indispensable that religions renounce their claims to truth, accept the authority of science and subject themselves to the law of the land. Dissent of both a religious and secular nature must always be taken into consideration. This does not prevent the achievement of reasonable consensus. Destructive secularization is harmful to society itself (Ratzinger and Habermas 2005). Habermas's favourite perspective is illuminist, rationalist (Habermas 2002b) and secularist, although Habermas does not appear totally opposed to religion, as he requires it to engage with the secular world in a manner favourable to dialogue.

In other words, religion is one of the constituents of the life-world (*Lebenswelt*), even if processes of rationalization and secularization have reduced its weight, confining it almost to issues of meaning alone, seeing that the modern concept of consensus has replaced the authority of the sacred. This seems to indicate a crisis of religious legitimation (Habermas 1975) along with an extension of secular concepts of knowledge and, therefore, the notion of a public sphere more and more independent of religion. At the same time, however, Habermas (2006a) attributes a certain importance to the role of religion itself within a common language-diffusion process, which gives rise to a 'linguistic elaboration of the sacred' (Habermas 1986b: 648–96). In short, religious thinking does not fall outside rationality and may be taken into consideration

---

[1] At the same time, however, Böckenförde observes that religion, increasingly free as it is, does not inform public order and is separate from the state, which no longer either represents or protects any religion, though it does not deny it, above all because religion was born before the state.

when seeking to understand the forms and contents of rationalization processes fully. In actual fact, the role of religion has not dissolved, it has simply changed. In any case, communicative action cannot be attributed to conditionings of a religious nature. However, the increasing secularization of society must come to terms with the persistence of religious concepts and the confessional communities that express them (Habermas 2002a: 99–112). Post-secular society is called upon to address its own conception of secular rationality in broader terms as far as the enlargement of the horizons of knowledge is concerned (and in terms of learning about religious thinking too). In other words, the principle of separation between religion and state stands on a 'post-secular' foundation of mutual respect between religion and reason (Habermas 2006b: 19–50). The secular state, however, cannot claim the right to impose its language upon citizens who are believers and who are already obliged by their asymmetrical condition (with regard to non-denominational citizens and a secular state) to seek mediation between faith and secular reasoning, by balancing theology and ethics (Habermas 2006b: 30). This is how it must 'spread its wings', as Habermas (1986a: 202) put it when recalling utopia and hope as theorized by Ernst Bloch.

Believers and Non-believers

Resistance to efficacious communications between believers and non-believers stems, above all, from the insurgence of two fronts also built upon institutional bases: secularity and fundamentalism.[2] Indeed, sociologist Hans Mol illuminated this dichotomy in *Identity and the Sacred*, noting that complex societies of the West tend to create a dialectic between religion and morality in which the former aids the establishment of the later even whilst inevitably moving toward 'rigidification' of moral codes (fundamentalism) (1976: 107–8). Of course, the specific problem of secularity – it must be said – is essentially of European origin, initially French, later and gradually, Italian, Spanish, to become widespread. The seed planted during the age of Enlightenment later took the form and content of the revolutionary events

---

[2] Broadly speaking, both as veritable historically rooted corpora which emerged and established themselves in time, like the various states and churches, and as mindsets or ideologies, born and consolidated thanks to varying degrees of consensus obtained in different historical periods and in different geographical areas and remaining tendentially stable for some time, as in the cases of nihilism, materialism, Marxism, positivism, rationalism, liberalism, secularism, modernism, scientism, existentialism.

of Paris 1789 (and beyond). Of course, the United States of America, during its early stages, was also acquainted with revolution, which did not, however, lead to consequences of a similar nature as far as religious phenomenology was concerned. On the contrary, in North America the link between politics and religion is rather close: the motto on the US coat of arms declares trust in God, and the ritual instatement of the president of the United States makes numerous and repeated references to the Bible and the Christian religion – especially to the Protestant form of Christianity. Religious practice is widespread, as confirmed by several empirical surveys carried out in the United States. In Canada too, especially Québec, there seems to be little tendency to raise issues relating to secularity or, at least, it is not one of the main *foci* of discussion.

Martha Nussbaum (2008) of the University of Chicago, originally an Anglican philosopher and later a convert to the reformed Jewish religion, defends the Mormons' right to polygamy in compliance with her idea of total freedom of conscience and religion (a little like Poulat did, in his 1987 text on freedom and secularity). Yet Nussbaum does not seem to approve the French kind of secularity because, she holds, it is too constraining for believers, who are not invited to express themselves in public. For the Chicago professor, the value of separation between state and Church is secondary compared to equal freedom for citizens, both believers and non-believers. As to the ongoing issue of the refusal of blood transfusion by Jehovah's Witnesses, she opts for the solution that mature, informed adults be free to choose, while their children ought to be safeguarded at all costs. Finally, Nussbaum also advocates including creationism in the syllabi of comparative religious studies though not in science programmes.

Barely south of the United States, in Mexico, we find secularism again, but here expressed in very different terms. This country too had a revolutionary beginning, Zapatism, which marked the end of religion in the public arena, during the first half of the last century. One of the most evident signs of the secular nature of the Mexican state may be said to be the law forbidding the clergy to wear cassocks in public. In short, this norm is intended to make it quite clear that religion is a strictly private matter that should in no way impact at state, and therefore, at public level. In the other states of Central and South America trends in relations between the state and the Churches have followed the vicissitudes of the single nations, which have undergone various kinds of experiences ranging from dictatorship to military government, from pseudo to effective democracy. Interpretations of the events of the past decades have not always been clear or devoid of basic ambiguity. In some instances, there have been cases of cooperation or of ideological non-belligerence between the state and the Churches, with consequences that are still the object of diverging opinion even concerning interpretations of matters of fact.

In Asia, relations between the state and the Churches are associated, essentially, with the types of political regimes in force, but, in general, it is the political authority which establishes the rules and the limitations, independently of the opinions of the interested religious parties. With the odd exception, political power in that part of the world is self-referential and opposes all religious expression that does not comply with the system. A singular case is that of the People's Republic of China where there are two Catholic Churches, one close to the positions of the national state, the other with the Church of Rome as its head. In Japan, on the contrary, the USA's Jeffersonian model prevails; this envisages a neutral state which privileges none of the Gods available, thus preventing Caesar–God dichotomy while favouring the growth of a civil religious society which is both pluralistic and pacific. This explains the agnostic character of the Japanese scholastic system.

The African situation varies according to the dominant religious culture in the single countries but reveals the partial failure of secular-based state interventionist scholastic policies. When Islam is the religion of the majority, it is usually very close to the state and this fact generally prevents the question of secularism from arising at all because of the particular kind of symbiosis existing between the Islamic religion and politics. But Islam (Bozdemir 1996) has had to adapt to animist religious trends, permitting polygamy and forms of syncretism. Relations between secularism and the Christian religions are more complex. In some states, a formal separation between the state and the Churches exists, but, in actual fact, there is no real issue of secularism in Africa because religiosity is widespread and assumes various forms, especially traditional and independent varieties of the animist and Kimbangist creeds. Concluding, we must add that various attempts have been made in Africa to eliminate religion by decree (Madagascar, Benin, Angola, Mozambique, Ethiopia, The People's Republic of the Congo). Little by little secularism has made some headway and become a feature of the majority of state constitutions, but no real debate surrounds the issue which is seen as a foreign import and, therefore, confined mainly to small circles of elitist intellectuals.

As will be outlined in Chapter 7, the predominant reference-model in the Australian context traditionally has been British Anglicanism, although the conditions there are in no way comparable to those of the United Kingdom; in other words, the question of secularism does not seem to present particular differentiations. When all comes to all, then, secularism seems to be an issue of important debate in Europe alone. Above all, one has the impression that all sides seem to be striving to provide a definition of secularism based on a sole parameter. When religiously oriented intellectuals, or the official Church itself, propose a definition, the secular community objects. When the opposite occurs, the criticism comes from the religiously oriented. One must note that it is impossible to disentangle this dilemma unless a joint solution is found, not necessarily one for all seasons, but at least one permitting consensus to be reached as particular issues arise. To demand respect for every definition of secularism would mean, in actual fact, surrendering to the difficulties arising from it and, therefore, resignation to the impossibility of establishing any valid definition at all.

The pivotal point is the public role of religion and religions, or rather, that the public dimension itself becomes the most fruitful arena where ideas and ways of conducting investigations ought to converge. A well-balanced scientific knowledge is the outcome of *epoché*, that is, suspension of judgement before expressing an evaluation, after deep and careful reflection.

It should not be forgotten that there are a-religious, anti-religious and non-religious forms of secularism, expressed by non-believers, as well as varieties of secularity expressed by those professing different beliefs – that is, by those who believe in ways different from the official canon of the Churches or from the statistically more frequent modes of religious expression. This could lead to a boundless range of possible instances of *etsi deus non daretur*. The entire question is part of the scenario of the choices to make according to criteria of responsibility or rationality. Opposite, divergent and polymorphic views are always at work and do not favour easy advancement. In the long run, however, secularism – starting with its own plurality of stances and opinions, which assume concrete form as definitions and decisions (Norris and Inglehart 2011: 53–79) – remains profoundly, essentially, *secular* as long as it foresees and allows for a multitude of perspectives and alternatives beyond its own.

Fundamentalism and Laïcité

In the face of pluralism it is not neutrality but impartiality that is required, above all in the field of ethics and the law, where the power of the state must be exerted regardless of who the object of its legislative or punitive interventions may be. The impartiality of the law entails allowing liberty to embrace religious freedom (the exercise of which includes freedom of thought, association and assembly) as well. This perspective overrides the old principle of *cuius regio, eius religio* because people are no longer obliged to follow the religion of their sovereign, their state or their government.

But an ulterior obstacle exists: fundamentalism, a second hindrance to efficacious dialogue between believers and non-believers which does not mediate, but demands application of the norm in all cases without distinction, failing to recognize the autonomy of interlocutors and insisting on its own reference-principles. At strictly juridical level, the principle of a form of justice which does not take any kind of favouritism into consideration but applies the norm and does not define itself as either secular or religious may prevail, in compliance with the criterion of equality. What does remain open to discussion, however, is the need or otherwise that the positive legal order conform to the objective natural moral law, to the natural moral order (Dalla Torre 2008: 178).

In any case, it is opportune to point out that secularity cannot expect religiosity to adapt to it nor can religion be expected to annul secularity simply to avoid meeting with opposition in the public sphere. To arrive at a similar conclusion, there is much to be done at both religious and political cultural level to provide the new generations especially, but the older generation too, with criteria of discernment sufficiently grounded in terms of a non-ideological type of knowledge. It is rightly held that a good religious education cannot but lead to a vigorous defence of the secularity of the state, without accepting surreptitious interest-grounded formulaic adjustments or agreements of the *do ut des* type, involving undue subjection of the Church by the state or vice versa. The principle of inclusive secularity cannot be considered as being the thin edge of the wedge used to permit the Church to penetrate the state nor, to the contrary, can the public arena be seen as the sphere where the state wields dominion over the Church.

Meanwhile, one might advocate the re-introduction of theology into state university syllabi, to be studied from a non-confessional but a thorough and rigorously scientific point of view, in order to increment interdisciplinary projects like that ground-breaking instance of dialogue between Jürgen Habermas and Joseph Ratzinger (Ratzinger and Habermas 2005). This might light the way to the lowering of barriers of prejudice and resistance, but also and in particular, it might offer ways of enhancing the quality of scientific approaches to themes like secularity and religiosity, bioethics and biological jurisprudence.

According to Böckenförde (2007), religion should cease to be the caretaker of the soul of the state (and, therefore, no longer of either Christian or Muslim or of any other religious tendency) but should operate in society as civil religion capable of influencing the social order through individuals and the indications it provides them. Therefore, one must expect (again, according to Böckenförde) that religion aim at playing a political role in agreement with its very own perspective, that is, the religious point of view. Dwelling on the secularity of the state, Böckenförde seems to suggest a French kind of *laïcité* and prefer the concept of open neutrality towards all creeds (like Germany), but maybe the idea of impartiality would work better in this case and open up a broad enough pathway for the entry of religion or, rather, religions, into the public arena, without confining them, ghetto-like, to the private or at most to the so-called private-social sphere acting in lieu of the state itself. This scenario would permit the full achievement of Jewish, Christian and Islamic religious *Weltanschauungen*, without any kind of discontinuity between faith and action, between spiritual and worldly life. Once again it is a question of finding a balance between state secularity and the religious exigencies of a considerable number of citizens.[3] In this way, it would be possible to recover, as Böckenförde argues, some of the main values of Illuminism: human rights and freedom (of religion too).

There is certainly a link between the *tópos* of secularity and that of pluralism. The one and the other find themselves addressing once more the resilience of religion, which, regardless of the multi-decade surge of secularization, maintains a basic solidity of its own. The reasons for pluralism may be pragmatic, a matter of opportunity: given the persistence of religions the only solution governments seem to opt for is widespread permissiveness. In any case, this choice seems to shirk responsibility for the difficulties created for those who expect greater autonomy and equality, but who instead, are required to give way to others and, to some extent, tolerate them. Thus, inclusiveness becomes tantamount to the exclusion of many who were already present inside a given system. A more pondered kind of inclusiveness should appeal to values like justice, freedom, legitimacy and socio-political duty and accommodate positions at loggerheads with its own pre-existing ones. The risk is that of forcing freedom on those not prepared to accept it and who are entitled by right to disagree, or of asking even of those who do not intend availing of it, so-called equality of respect, a concept still present, as *filótimo*, in Greek village culture (Cipriani, Cotesta, Kokosalakis and van Boeschoten 2002).

---

[3] It is worth noting that much of Hans Mol's theoretical work is built on the assumption that balance is needed for the maintenance of religious identity. Indeed, for Mol the dialectic between identity and adaptability demands that religious adherents walk a line between secular exigencies and religious stability.

Gian Enrico Rusconi (2000) has long been one of the foremost intellectual reference figures in the *querelle* on secularity, thanks to his 40-year-long standing as a cogent and rigorous contributor to the domain of public debate surrounding religion and politics. He is, therefore, a first-class protagonist and interlocutor, attentive, informed and respectful. In his opinion, the novelty of recent times lies in the Churches' intention to contribute to a public ethos. This is a source of conflict for secularity which tends to bar religion from making contributions towards public ethics, as if God did not exist (the well-known *etsi deus non daretur* mentioned earlier). The Churches, in truth, do not object to the secularity of the state but propose a so-called healthy secularity based on their own reference parameters. This leads to secular reaction, which refuses to brook any sort of *diktat* from institutions other than the state itself. The greatest misunderstanding probably stems from the label 'dictator ship of relativism' (De Mattei 2007) which some exponents of so-called Church religion (an old term so dear to Rusconi) attribute to secular statements. On the contrary, such secular statements tend to refer to consensual regulation of ethical principles and their enforcement. On the one hand, stands the authority of the criteria of faith, on the other, those of the citizens as a whole, including believers of various kinds (or 'differently believing', as Rusconi likes to say).

It is held that public, secular ethics can differ, in a tolerable manner, from the ethos of private life; the religious public ethos, on the other hand while appearing more compact, also encounters divergences within the private sphere. The greatest distinction emerges from the different procedures applied by the two perspectives: the secular stance denotes a tendency to decide case by case, while the religious one seeks to draw up a general *corpus* of principles to be applied on all occasions. So, the secular does not accept that the divine trespass on operative choices based on rights proceeding from rationality and consensus. Therefore, it requires the religious subject to adapt to the rules of the secular state. In other words, the convergence between faith and reason finds no support outside Church religion, but the secular position does not at all legitimize, Rusconi adds, the absence of any kind of moral rule. To the contrary, it foresees norms based on a consensual *ethos*, which is not easily accessed. Rusconi, while contesting Böckenförde's thesis (2007) whereby the Christian religion is capable of guaranteeing the normative premises the secular state lacks, observes that the historical roots of Christianity may be transformed, in time, into secular reasons and harmonize in the end with Habermas's request that religions renounce their claims to exclusive truth. Such an action by religious communities could then engender a real, reciprocal dialogue, advancing science and the acceptance of the supremacy of secularity in the field of the law.

Conclusions

Relations between the state and religion/s impact on several politico-territorial realities leading to results that depend heavily on historical contingencies, electoral trends, and systems of government. Indonesia, for example, is a country with a twofold Islamic (just over 87 per cent) and Christian (a little under 10 per cent) presence, alongside two significant religious minorities (Hindu at around 2 per cent and Buddhist at about 1 per cent). In a similar context, as occurs in many other parts of the world (from Ireland to Cyprus, Israel to India, the Sudan to China), the problem of coexistence between diverse religious traditions and cultures within the same territory exists.

Universal history, besides, is a long litany of war and conflict between creeds as well as clashes between politics and religion. In the case of Indonesia, the solution found seems to have emerged thanks to a particular national ideology called *Pancasila* (Intan 2006), within which religion plays a relevant role and which is based essentially on inter-religious dialogue between Muslims and Christians. Neither the Islamic nor the secular character of the Indonesian state would be able, otherwise, to offer a way out. So *Pancasila* was the only possible alternative available if Indonesia intended maintaining its unity and diversity. Being obliged to deal with two conflicting ideologies, the solution *Pancasila* provided showed that Indonesia did not want to be either a secular state where religion was totally absent, nor a religious state founded on one particular faith. In short, 'both Pancasila and "secularization as differentiation" ... allowed one to avoid choosing between a secular state and a largely religious one' (Intan 2006: 18). In other words, according to the principles of *Pancasila* the state remained religious without being theocratic.

This idea of variety within unity was the brainchild of Sukarno (the first president of Indonesia), who, keeping in mind the divisions within Indonesian Islam itself, expounded it on the 1 June 1945 in a speech regarding the five principles of *Pancasila*, a word of Sanskrit and Pali origin indicating five (*panca*) fundaments (*sila*). Originally the five principles were: nationalism, internationalism or humanitarianism, deliberation or democracy, social justice or social well-being, and finally *ketuhanan* or *Lordship*. As can be seen, it was a mixture of Islamic and secular contents, and, indeed, tended to favour the latter. When, however, the principles were reformulated and eventually reduced to one, reference to the Lord was retained and referred to on the basis of his oneness. The unity of the nation was guaranteed by a common reference to the Lord, to be shared by all citizens. Thus, the religious content remained and the nation was not divided but strengthened in its unity by reference to the same Lord. It was, in fact, the oneness of the Lord that satisfied both Muslims and Christians because both considered the idea as being in perfect keeping with their faith. Advocates of the secular state were also gratified by the compromise reached thanks to the existence of a unifying factor in the best interest of the entire Indonesian nation. Later on, however, the situation grew less tranquil and episodes of tension between the various sectors of the Indonesian nation occurred. The principle of sole *Lordship* has, however, contributed towards maintaining a considerable degree of national unity.

However, the situation became more complicated, when, after Sukarno's so-called *Guided Democracy* period, General Suharto came to power. His management of the country led to some reaction at the religious level, especially among sectors of the Islamic population. The conclusive data suggests that the weight of Indonesian religion or religions is considerable, as does the increased influence of Islam within the state, in particular among the members of Suharto's *New Order* government. However, religious action does seem to contribute towards the promotion of democracy and liberation. One cannot overlook the important role played by intellectuals (Islamic and Christian) in favouring the acceptance of *Pancasila*. In actual fact, 'as a lifestyle, *Pancasila* invites Indonesian citizens to found a nation based on human values characterised by inclusion, not by discrimination' (Intan 2006: 222).

It is not our intention to insist on the achievements of the Indonesian case as an example of a solution which is universally replicable. Yet, Indonesia does demonstrate that when secularity is assumed as a value to be defended by the religions themselves, and when religion and religions are taken seriously by the secular world, one can say that virtuous communication has been achieved and that further objectives may be reached. Perhaps, hypothetically speaking, only human dignity cannot be made the object of compromise being a generally recognized non-negotiable value, free from the obligations of reciprocity; it should be respected at all costs, even if others fail to comply. By way of coherence with what has been held so far, it is evident that this last point is not intended as an exception but begs examination and rebalancing on the basis of the outcome of the debate regarding it. Maybe this can become the hypothesis on which to base a kind of secularity and kind of religion which vie with each other in casting off ideology with a view to entering into dialogue without, however, renouncing their own basic principles. Absolute truth is not to be found on either side, but it may be revealed by the participation of both, who cannot fail to concede to others what they ask for themselves. Respect and understanding stem from committed attempts at reciprocal recognition aimed at consciously deliberating on issues of an ethical nature, leading to new horizons for human action and excluding nothing from the domain of possibility.

References

Acquaviva, S.S. (1971) *L'eclissi del sacro nella civiltà industriale*. Milan: Comunità.
Acquaviva, S.S. and Stella, R. (1989) *Fine di un'ideologia: La secolarizzazione*. Rome: Borla.
Bauberot, J. (1990) *Vers un nouveau pacte laïque?* Paris: Seuil.
Bauberot, J. (2003) *Histoire de la laïcité en France*. Paris: Presses Universitaires de France.
Bauberot, J. (2004) *Laïcité 1905–2005, entre passion et raison*. Paris: Seuil.
Bauberot, J. (2007a) 'Laicism', in G. Ritzer (ed.), *The Blackwell Encyclopedia of Sociology*. Oxford: Blackwell, 2529–33.
Bauberot, J. (2007b) *Les laïcités dans le monde*. Paris: Presses Universitaires de France.
Böckenförde, E.-W. (2007) *Diritto e secolarizzazione: Dallo stato moderno all'Europa unita*. Rome and Bari: Laterza.
Bozdemir, M. (ed.) (1996) *Islam et laïcité: Approche globale set régionales*. Paris: L'Harmattan.
Bruce, S. (2002) *God is Dead: Secularization in the West*. Oxford: Blackwell.
Casanova, J. (2000) *Oltre la secolarizzazione: Le religioni alla riconquista della sfera pubblica*. Bologna: il Mulino.
Cipriani, R., Cotesta, V., Kokosalakis, N. and van Boeschoten, R. (2002) *Episkepsi: il villaggio armonioso. Tradizione, modernità, solidarietà e conflitto in una comunità greca*. Milan: Angeli.
Cox, H. (1968) *La città secolare*. Firenze: Vallecchi.
Dalla Torre, G. (2008) 'Laicità: i confini della tolleranza e l'esercizio della libertà', in I. Sanna (ed.), *Emergenze umanistiche e fondamentalismi religiosi*. Rome: Studium, 167–78.
De Mattei, R. (2007) *La dittatura del relativismo*. Chieti: Solfanelli.
De Rita, G. (2008) 'La modernità della Chiesa', *Corriere della Sera*, 13 agosto 2008: 1–39.
Fornero, G. (2008) *Laicità debole e laicità forte: Il contributo della bioetica al dibattito sulla laicità*. Milan: Bruno Mondadori.
Giddens, A. (1990) *The Consequences of Modernity*. Cambridge: Polity Press.
Giddens, A. (1991) *Modernity and Self Identity*. Cambridge: Polity Press.

Giddens, A. (2006) *Fondamenti di sociologia*. Bologna: il Mulino.
Habermas, J. (1975) *La crisi della razionalità nel capitalismo maturo*. Bari: Laterza.
Habermas, J. (1986a) 'Uno Schelling marxista: Ernst Bloch', in R. Cipriani (ed.), *La teoria critica della religione. Il fenomeno religioso nell'analisi della Scuola di Francoforte*. Rome: Borla, 183–203.
Habermas, J. (1986b) *Teoria dell'agire comunicativo. II. Critica della ragione funzionalistica*. Bologna: il Mulino.
Habermas, J. (2002a) *Il futuro della natura umana. I rischi di una genetica liberale*. Turin: Einaudi.
Habermas, J. (2002b) *Religion and Rationality: Essays on Reason, God and Modernity*, edited and with an introduction by E. Mendieta. Cambridge: Polity Press.
Habermas, J. (2006a) 'Religion in the Public Sphere', *European Journal of Philosophy*, 14(1): 1–25.
Habermas, J. (2006b) *Tra scienza e fede*. Rome and Bari: Laterza.
Habermas, J., Sölle, D. and Luhmann, N. (1977) *Il ruolo sociale della religione: Saggi e conversazioni*. Brescia: Queriniana.
Intan, B.F. (2006) *'Public Religion' and the Pancasila-Based State of Indonesia: An Ethical and Sociological Analysis*. New York: Peter Lang.
Mancini, I. (1983) *Il pensiero negativo della nuova destra*. Milan: Mondadori.
Milot, M. (2002) *Laïcité dans le Nouveau Monde: Le cas du Québec*. Turnhout: Brepols.
Mol, H. (1976) *Identity and the Sacred*. Oxford: Basil Blackwell.
Norris, P. and Inglehart, R. (2011) *Sacred and Secular: Religion and Politics Worldwide*. Cambridge: Cambridge University Press.
Nussbaum, M.C. (2008) *Liberty of Conscience: In Defence of America's Tradition of Religious Equality*. New York: Basic Books.
Poulat, É. (1987) *Liberté, laïcité: La guerre des deux France et le principe de la modernité*. Paris: Cerf/Cujas.
Ratzinger, J. and Habermas, J. (2005) *Ragione e fede in dialogo*. Padova: Marsilio.
Rusconi, G.E. (2000) *Come se Dio non ci fosse: I laici, i cattolici e la democrazia*. Turin: Einaudi.
Taylor, C. (2007) *A Secular Age*. Cambridge, MA: The Belknap Press of Harvard University Press.
Weber, M. (1995) [1922] *Economia e società*. Milan: Edizioni di Comunità.
Willaime, J.-P. (2004) *Europe et religions: Les enjeux du XXIe siècle*. Paris: Fayard.

Chapter 6
Religion Fixed and Fickle: The Contemporary Challenge of Religious Diversity

Douglas Pratt

Although secularity engenders questions related to the place of religion in public life, or the interface between religious and non-religious citizens, it is not the only contemporary phenomenon occupying the minds of sociologists of religion. Decades ago, sociologists such as Peter Berger and Hans Mol recognized pluralism as a related force in western culture, a force that was likely to endure and unlikely to prove innocuous for increasingly diverse nations like Australia and the United States. In his book, *The Fixed and the Fickle: Religion and Identity in New Zealand*, Mol undertook 'a social-scientific sketch' of both Maori and Pakeha (European, or non-Maori) religion in New Zealand and he did so through the lens of the sociological identity model of religion:

> This assumes that in any society wholeness (or identity) is constantly jeopardized by fragmentation, conflict, or, more generally, change. The fixed (identity) is constantly 'un-glued' by the fickle (change). The identity model treats religion as one of the means to hold together ('fix' or stabilize) what otherwise would fly apart (through the fickleness of ever-present change). (Mol 1982: 1)

This model is not so much concerned with religion itself as with the 'place of religion in a fundamental, existential dialectic' that characterizes social existence as such. Mol noted the profound change that occurred to Maori religious life and sensibility in the wake of European colonization and evangelization. At the same time, whilst scholars have subsequently referred to the incoming European religious culture as a 'transplanted Christianity' (cf. Davidson and Lineham 1989) Mol rightly observes that the incoming Europeans brought with them their own dialectic: 'migration to the other side of the world meant vast discontinuities with the past' (Mol 1982: 1) even as, in common with all migrants virtually anywhere, the desire to maintain in their new locale their home religious identities and norms – the transplanting of the fixed – was also a powerful guiding influence. Both colonizers and the colonized experienced vast change as a consequence of mutual encounter and uprooted circumstance:

> For both groups the problem arose as to how this change could be absorbed back into a viable meaning-system. How could stability (whether personal, group, or social) be maintained in the face of far-reaching forces of innovation? How could the fixed deal with the fickle? Religion ... had always fixed boundaries and kept chaos at bay. And yet these boundaries were now pierced by arbitrariness, mutability, whimsy, not to mention the forced contact with an alien culture (Maori) or environment (Pakeha). How did religion respond? (ibid.)

Revisiting these issues for the twenty-first century, I will explore the matter of the response – with respect to both Maori and Pakeha (European) – in terms of the mutual encounter of the nineteenth and early twentieth century, in rough parallel to the programme of Chapters 1 and 2 of *The Fixed and the Fickle*. However, whereas Mol, writing as he did in the very early 1980s, paid some attention to the question of race relations and religion, here I will conclude with the issue that has come to the fore since the early 1980s – namely, religious diversity as such. First, however, I shall recount something of the features and factors that contributed to religious identity – the arena of the fixed – of both Maori and Pakeha and also some of the dynamics of novelty and interaction that speak of change – the realm of the fickle – which arose in the context of the encounter of Maori and Christian religious beliefs and sensibilities.

Maori Religion: The Context of Encounter

As James Irwin (1984) observes, myth and religion were inseparable elements of the one overall reality of classical Maori society. Myths narrate primeval origins that lie in a remote past. Their repeated telling 'renews' the sense of the primordial reality out of which present existence has sprung; myth powerfully links the present to the past. Myth effects and establishes the relationship of the human to the world around, and relationship to the gods or sacred powers. Irwin also notes two fundamental religious issues which are dealt with in a people's worldview, that of *identity* and *context*. Identity is found in the answers to the questions 'Where do we come from?' and 'Where are we going?' The context of being/living is determined by the way personal action is related to the universal order of things; the life-settings for relationships and responsibilities. The sacred and the secular mutually interpenetrate; the life of the Maori of classical society was holistic. Irwin sums it up neatly when he remarks:

> Pre-European Maori religion provided structures that kept the people in harmony with the universe as they apprehended it, gave them protection from supernatural dangers, gave means to circumvent disasters that are normally beyond the control of natural man [sic], provided access to supernatural power, maintained access with the sacred and provided the means to deal with ritual pollution caused by breaching religious sanctions, whether deliberate or accidental. (Irwin 1978: 17)

Whilst myth and religion intertwine, it would be nonetheless appropriate to speak of a myth and legend phase that is essentially pre-religious, yet which cannot be ignored when addressing the subject of Maori religion. Such myths express the reflective thinking of a people who, in common with all humanity, seek to understand whence they have come and how the universe as they experience it is structured (cf. Pratt 1993). In this case, from out of the conjunction of the primeval mythic parents, *Rangi* (or *Ranginui*, the sky-father) and *Papa* (or *Papatuanuku*, the earth-mother) are born offspring (70 in total) who become the departmental deities (the 'gods' or *atua*). In the process of establishing their identity and role in emancipation from the parents, they forcefully separate *Rangi* and *Papa* apart, thus resulting in the binary pair of sky-father and earth-mother deity figures. The emergence of all the Maori 'gods' from these two heralds the advent of classical Maori religion. The full panoply of deity, however, may be classified into four categories: Gods of origin, including the Supreme Being (*Io*) together with *Rangi* and *Papa*; 'departmental gods' such as *Tangaroa* (god or *atua* of the seas) or *Tawhirimatea* (god/*atua* of wind) who derive directly from *Rangi* and *Papa*; plus tribal gods (*atua*); and inferior spirits (*wairua*) who evolve subsequently in the unfolding of a mythically construed human history. With many subtle variations on the aetiological narratives, pre-European Maori had a rich religious inheritance and fund of existential guidance. In knowing who we are, where we belong, and where we fit, human beings have a sense of fixedness which is arguably inherent and healthy for human identity; it is the bulwark against chaos and confusion. This fixed reference is often a key function of religion; this was seemingly the case for New Zealand Maori. Then there came the Europeans with their religion, Christianity. The fixed world of Maori religious sensibility was to be forever changed.

Nineteenth-century Christian Missions: Focus of Encounter

The Christianity that arrived first was that of the modern Protestant missionary era of England, soon followed by a form of Catholic missionary endeavour out of France. Although Protestant Christianity continued to diversify even during the nineteenth century, a common core of evangelical theology and practice had emerged such that, by the time of the coming of the missionaries to Aotearoa/New Zealand, there was a fairly clear framework of ideas and presuppositions. These give an insight into the worldview of the Protestant evangelical missionary who came to this remote land and the kind of Christian culture they promoted. The key ideas included a need for *individual conversion* through a personal awareness and conviction of sin in order to gain the salvation freely given by God in Christ; a belief in *providence*, seen in God's direction and leading of the converted to serve God's mission to the world – no matter what trials the Christian had to face, God's purposes would be fulfilled; a concern to transform individuals through personal conversion *and also* to transform society as a whole through reform. As well, there was evidence of the encouragement of *philanthropy* through support given to various voluntary societies that worked to achieve evangelical aims, and a *British nationalist-cum-imperialistic* focus, seen in the way British evangelicals identified with British colonial expansion throughout the world, not just in New Zealand. Sometimes this resulted in conflict between colonial and imperial political aspirations on the one hand, and Christian evangelical commitments on the other. This could arise in respect to a clearly *humanitarian* concern, expressed for example in the struggle to abolish 'inhuman' practices such as, on the wider international front, slavery and the slave trade, and in more local contexts cannibalism, sacrifice, widow-burning ('sati' in India – albeit not known in New Zealand), the exploitation of children, improving the conditions of women and workers in Britain, and so on.

There was, of course, an often *patronizing* and *paternalistic* approach taken when doing things on behalf of others. The Christian colonial missionaries of such evangelical ilk often lacked the ability to be critical of their own self-righteous prejudices and were often very sympathetic towards the faults of their colleagues or compatriots. They were, after all, only all-too-human. As Davidson asserts, 'Missionary attitudes towards other cultures, religions and peoples were shaped by these evangelical and nationalistic perspectives ... (They) ... viewed other societies critically, condemning their religious world view and attempting to replace it with their own' (Davidson 1997: 8). Missionaries were consciously and conscientiously agents of change. Their task was not so much to sympathetically understand, but to evangelize and convert.

They had a message to share, but they tended to identify the message with the cultural package that, for them, went with it. From the perspective of Maori, Christian missionaries were the agents of the 'fickle' for they introduced disruption and change in their attempts to introduce a new form of the 'fixed'. Two English Protestant missionary societies were the first to set up in New Zealand in the early nineteenth century: the Anglican Church Missionary Society (CMS) and the Methodist Wesleyan Missionary Society (WMS).

The Anglican Mission

The CMS was founded in 1799. At first it had trouble getting English workers, particularly ordained clergy, so it relied on German recruits, some of whom came to New Zealand and had a considerable impact (cf. Oettli 2008). However, the society was able to send, initially, the English clergyman Samuel Marsden, who had been a chaplain in Australia. He was also a prosperous farmer, landowner, and magistrate. He had had some contact with Maori who had gone to Australia and had been impressed with one he met, *Te Pahi*, of the major northern *Nga Puhi* tribe (*iwi*), who had gone to his church in Sydney. Marsden arranged support for a CMS mission to New Zealand on the principle of inculcating 'civilization' as the precursor for introducing Christianity. This attitude reflects both the perspective of cultural superiority from which the missionary society operated, together with the difficulty in recruiting clergy: supposedly if the posting were to a 'civilized' place they would be the more easily enticed. Marsden set sail from England in 1809 accompanied by two artisans: John King, shoemaker and ropemaker, and William Hall, a carpenter. En route, Marsden befriended a sick Maori chieftain who had had an unsuccessful voyage to England to meet the King. He was *Ruatara*, also of Nga Puhi. As a result, Marsden was offered the hospitality and protection of the Nga Puhi people, which was eventually taken up.

After a delay of a few years in Australia, Marsden eventually made a trial journey to the Bay of Islands in 1814 accompanied by Ruatara and also *Hongi Hika*, a great Nga Puhi chief. Marsden had acquired his own ship and he hoped to combine evangelization with business – to return with a good cargo of kauri (a New Zealand native tree prized for its hard wood), spars (for sailing ships), and flax (for weave-able fibre). The first recorded service of Christian worship took place on Christmas Day 1814 at Oihi Bay in the Bay of Islands. Marsden was optimistic and the Mission settled where they could take advantage of Ruatara's Nga Puhi protection. But Marsden left for Sydney in March 1815 and did not return to NZ until 1819 – by which time the CMS mission was in serious trouble. Ruatara had died and the mission became more closely associated with

Hongi Hika, whose military ambitions clashed with missionary intentions. Further, the land of the mission site was unsuitable for farming. Therefore, missionaries became more dependent upon Maori for material support. Some missionaries got involved in trade and commerce, especially muskets, and a mixture of interpersonal difficulties amongst the mission staff also emerged. Things had become very fickle indeed. The upshot was that Marsden's desire to first bring civilization had failed. However, in 1823 Marsden returned with the Revd Henry Williams and the mission was re-established where the land was good for farming. The mission built its own schooner, thus ensuring a link to the outside world. Greater emphasis was placed on the tasks of evangelization, education and literacy. Henry's brother, William, made an important contribution to the study of Maori language and worked on the first translation of the Bible. The first baptisms, constituting something of a 'breakthrough' so far as the missionary endeavour was concerned, occurred in 1825. The cause of the Anglican mission was now underway. From the missionaries' perspective one might say a very fickle era was ending as a new form of identity and purpose – a reconfiguring of the fixed – emerged. But Anglicans were not the only Christian missionaries at that stage. How had the Methodists fared?

The Methodist Mission

The Revd Samuel Leigh, the first Wesleyan (Methodist) minister to Australia, began a mission to Aotearoa, also in the north of the North Island, in 1822. A station was established but, as with the Anglicans, this also proved a difficult beginning with considerable tension between the local Maori community and the Mission station. Interpersonal difficulties among the missionaries arose here as well. The mission itself was sacked by some Maori in 1827, and so the Wesleyans withdrew for a while. Then, in 1828, the mission was re-commenced at another site in the North, and Wesleyan missionary activity expanded from there down the west coast of the North Island. The Anglicans likewise expanded southwards – but by a gentleman's agreement, they stuck to the east coast. The legacy of this division of territory is marked still; Maori from east coast tribes are typically Anglican; West Coast Maori more likely Methodist. However, in these early years of the Methodist cause, personal problems continued to flare up with rivalry leading to sudden departures: dismissal on the grounds of engaging in trade and even dismissal on the grounds of adultery.

By 1830, little missionary success had been achieved. In reality, the missionaries were ill-prepared; there was little or no understanding of the real task. Physical, spiritual, and psychological isolation took their toll.

There was difficulty in language acquisition, and the missionaries had little of perceived value to offer Maori. Thus, the Methodists encountered their own very fickle situation. But all was not a total failure; Maori language was eventually learned, nonetheless, and some significant points of contact made that bore fruit in terms of missionary outreach. Gradually, the Wesleyan Mission established itself and paved the way for the eventual emergence, in the wake of European settlement, of the Methodist Church. But if these two Protestant missionary movements had a head-start, they did not enjoy a relative missionary monopoly for long.

The Catholic Mission

A French Roman Catholic bishop, Jean Baptiste Pompallier (1807–71), arrived in New Zealand in January 1838 together with two members of the Society of Mary (Marists), a then newly formed French missionary order. The first Mass in New Zealand was celebrated on 13 January in a private home on the Hokianga harbour – just across the water from the Methodist Mission Station. Appointed to oversee a vast region, and given few resources, the enthusiastic bishop was charged with combining mission work and ministry to settler immigrants. Pompallier himself was able to preach in Maori only three months after his arrival. He also had to learn English. But a twofold suspicion and animosity immediately attached itself to the Catholic missionary endeavour. There was Protestant–Catholic rivalry on the one hand and French–British rivalry on the other, and both rivalries would have their extreme protagonists. Pompallier himself had urged his missionaries to be sensitive to Maori customs, but also to attack 'Protestant errors'. On the whole, however, the approach of the Catholics was much more accommodating towards Maori life and customs. 'Catholic missionaries opted for a life of poverty which had difficulty competing with the attractions of the Protestant missions' (Davidson 1997: 16), but it meant they had less to offer the Maori, by way of material benefits, than did the Protestants with their emphasis on education, health, and agricultural technology and so on.

However, it has been acknowledged that the 'Catholic missionaries, without the demands of families and mission stations, were often able to get closer to Maori than their Protestant counterparts' (ibid.). More French Marists joined Pompallier, who established his headquarters at Kororareka in the Bay of Islands (which soon became the town of Russell and was, for a short time in the nineteenth century, the capital of New Zealand). He set up a printing press to rival the Protestants. By the 1840s, Catholic missionary work extended down to the central North Island (thus largely steering clear of Anglican advances to the east, and Methodists to the west), and ministry to incoming settler communities of Catholics had begun in Auckland and Wellington. In 1850, the Catholic enterprise in New Zealand divided into two dioceses: the upper North Island run from Auckland; the lower North Island and the whole of the South Island from Wellington. The demands of servicing the fixed needs of the incoming settler community, made up substantially, but not only, of Irish Catholics, dictated a change of direction and strategy. Nevertheless, the legacy of Pompallier and the Marist Mission has had a lasting impact – there are many Marist schools, sports clubs, and so on that are now well-integrated into wider society.

Maori Reactions and Interactions in the Nineteenth Century

Although other Christian denominations, as well as members of other traditions such as Jews and Mormons (Church of Jesus Christ of Latter-Day Saints, or LDS), also arrived in the latter half of the nineteenth century, it was the three missionary societies outlined above that introduced competing versions of Christianity and, in the process, established new forms and options of religious identity for Maori. It was these missions that brought about the initial encounter of Maori and Christianity. But, as with the history of missionary endeavour virtually anywhere, the actual outcome of the work of evangelization is less a matter of re-creating the 'fixed' of the incoming religion with respect to a new people and context as it is an unforeseen production of novel responses, reactions, and appropriations that register a considerable dimension of the fickle. The 1830s is the decade regarded as the period of first indigenous movements formed as a result of the interaction of Maori with missionary Christianity – Maori New Religious Movements (Elsmore 1985).

But religious *reaction* began earlier. The early period of contact occurred during the second two decades of the nineteenth century. Up to 1830 there was a period of mutual cultural adjustment in which a two-way exchange and learning took place. However, major differences in worldviews and religious outlook began to emerge. There is evidence of an early missionary view, based on the missionaries' own understanding of what constitutes a 'developed system of religious belief and life', of regarding Maori as having no religion: they 'observed the customs of the Maori and seeing no rites they regarded as set apart as sacred observances, concluded the New Zealanders had no religion' (Elsmore 1989: 16). Elsmore goes on to argue:

> If it were true that the Maori had no religion of their own, then no period of adjustment would have been necessary as regards sacred matters; they would have been completely free to adopt or reject the new teachings without any theological conflict ... Changes in social customs, as demanded by the new religion, would have been merely a matter of altering habits ... the fact that conflicts did occur shows that the Maori did have a well-developed system of religion; and as this was the case, the rise of a series of adjustment movements was inevitable. (ibid.)

Whereas, initially, in the 1830s there was an upsurge in converts and baptisms – Maori were 'signing on' to the new religion – correlated with this apparent 'going over' to a new 'fixed' of religious identity there was a range of significant changes to social customs and practices. For example polygamy, the suicide of wives of deceased chiefs, cannibalism, and so on, previously part of the 'fixed' Maori worldview were challenged, depreciated and rejected. Religion was not necessarily the primary cause of such change, but it certainly provided a *mana*-saving reason for social changes brought about inevitably by, for instance, new technologies of warfare. In other words, non-religious motivations played a part, even where conversion was sincere.

A Maori New Testament was officially completed in 1837 and was well circulated by 1840. Maori had already obtained much knowledge of biblical content through missionary teaching, although this was necessarily selective and limited and so gave rise to much misunderstanding. Missionaries would effectively (and quite naturally) use scripture to advance their own worldview and agendas in respect to Maori. Some of this was to do with the sheer fact that nineteenth century missionaries tended to preach 'Christian civilization' in their image, and some stemmed from issues of translation. However, once the Bible could be read in Maori, reactions to the missionaries and their teachings set in. The 1840s saw publication of the full Old Testament. Literacy, perceived as a skill to acquire, coincided with an increase in the publication of biblical material in Maori and so an upsurge during the 1840s of Maori interest, both popular and intellectual, in the religion of the Pakeha. This meant that, alongside the purely 'Christian' teaching as propounded by the missionaries, Maori began to learn of the history and story of the Israelites – the tribal people of Israel.

The next period, 1830–50, saw a number of adjustment movements reacting to the missions and settlements in distinctly positive or negative ways. Attempts were made to reconcile traditional beliefs with those of the missionaries, and responses varied. Positive examples included responding to themes of religious ecstasy and messianic expectation on the one hand, and the phenomenon of the formation of Christian villages, on the other. Millennial teachings, including ideas of a second-coming and prophecies of an impending new age, excited the imagination and contributed to Maori interpretation of, and their own resultant development of, Christian religious thought. Negative responses included setting up a rival deity to be worshipped, rejecting the incoming Christian doctrines outright and taking on a new identity as *Hurai* – Jews, or Hebrews. So New Zealand became yet another location of the 'lost tribe of Israel' phenomenon. Elsmore describes the situation well:

> The traditional religious concepts of the Maori were not static and the addition of new rituals and beliefs to the Maori views was quite natural (e.g., rites of passage – missionaries introduced the wedding ritual) ... So it was not so much a matter of the Maori being 'converted' to Christianity, as their choosing to add to their own beliefs those aspects of the other religion which suited them. (Elsmore 1989: 32)

The 1850s was the decade of the healers. Social and religious factors provoked the formation of a series of healing movements. Most particularly, the introduction of new diseases provoked a religious interpretation: in response to health disasters the emphasis on religion lay with physical healing through the Spirit, or the spirits. The overall religious response focused on matters of physical health: accessing the realm of the transcendent in order to obtain material benefit became the chief concern. In this respect, biblical figures and imagery were often involved, and there was a notable group of women healers. At the same time, there was also a variety of negative social consequences of the coming of Europeans that led to a growing feeling, for Maori, of a betrayal by the Christian mission: 'interest in the religion declined as it seemed it was not living up to the principles it preached' (ibid.: 96). Further, the growing variety of Christian denominations with their competitive praxis did not help: the European missionaries became identified as the bearers not so much of a new and appealing 'fixed', but a threatening 'fickle'.

With disruption to the fixed structures of identity, the context of change and adjustment ushered in a period of comparative fickle-ness: new identities had begun to emerge. In the nineteenth century these were substantially of a religious nature but there were also some significant allied political developments, such as the evolution in the latter nineteenth century of the

Kingitanga (Maori King Movement) in the Waikato region where there had been substantial land confiscations, and in the early twentieth century the emergence of the Ratana political party. Both of these had their roots in religious reactions that involved recourse to the biblical model of a prophet figure, and both also attempted to unite Maori across tribal divides in an effort to counter the apparent monolith of a substantially Christian colonial presence. So it was that there emerged, in the latter half of the nineteenth century, a new type of movement which featured a prophetic figure who differed in status and purpose from the leadership of movements and reactions of the preceding eras. Many social, political and demographic factors also played a part – in particular, the growing sense of cultural inferiority relative to the technologically advanced Europeans and continually increasing mortality rates coupled with declining fertility rates. By 1858, Maori were outnumbered by Europeans. Thus was signalled the seemingly endless road of disadvantage, soon brought into focus over land wars which raged through the central North Island during the early 1860s. In response, there was an increasing sense of isolation and withdrawal on the part of Maori in a self-imposed reaction and direct consequence of negative interaction with the growing dominant Pakeha culture.

The discovery of parallel experiences and identity with the Israelites of the Old Testament fed a more pronounced shift towards a Hebraic, as opposed to a more overtly Europeanized-Christian, focus of new religious activity. The phenomenon of Maori prophets and prophetic movements, very much in the model of Old Testament prophets, was fuelled largely by a sense of dissatisfaction and injustice combined with religious backing and fervour. The prophets were themselves agents of religious and ethical revelation. Religiously, this indicated a move from *atua* as agents of spiritual revelation/power, to a focus on 'messengers' (prophets – the mouthpiece of God) of one sort or another conveying a divine 'word'. Significantly the millennialism of this period changed from the earlier, more orthodox Christian pattern which looked to the return of Christ, to a more Hebraic-oriented vision of a 'new Jerusalem in which the chosen could reside free from domination by their enemies' (Elsmore 1989: 174). Such a vision was 'a message of hope, dealing with social salvation rather than the individual promise of Christianity' (ibid.). In effect, in response to an external change agent (colonial Christianity) Maori responded with their own innovative-cum-reactive change agencies. The 'fickle' could become 'fixed' to the extent it could be controlled or at least owned.

The Settler Impact: Religion Transplanted

When Christianity first came to Aotearoa the focus was on missionary outreach to the native population. By the 1850s the tide of incoming settlers had overtaken the Maori population. The priorities and attentions of the missionary churches shifted accordingly. Although missionary work continued with Maori, the combined effect of the Land Wars of the mid-nineteenth century and the consequent rise of prophetic New Religious Movements meant that the settler churches retained and fostered their European heritage and thus by default became identified as Pakeha-only churches so far as the Maori were concerned. At this juncture it needs to be noted that land is a significant component of Maori identity and the threat to, and loss of, land as a result of colonial incursion has had a lasting impact. For some major tribal groups in the North Island who fought the British and colonial troops during the Land Wars, the confiscation of large tracts of their land as an outcome of this conflict amounted to much more than simply losing a means of livelihood, for land was never a possession of Maori to be used, traded, or otherwise disposed of – although commercial transactions with incoming European settlers involving land were by no means unknown. Rather, the relationship of belonging to their ancestral land – 'the place where the bones of one's ancestors were buried' (Mol 1982: 8) – meant it was Maori who *belonged to* the land; their land was an inalienable part of their identity. It still is. One of the appellations of Maori identity is *tangata whenua* – people of the land. And individuals know their place of belonging as their *turangawaewae* – the 'place of standing' where the self truly belongs.

The vision and goals of many nineteenth century immigrants to New Zealand was to create the ideal society: 'People left Britain to seek a new world and new opportunities' (Davidson 1997: 28). This can be seen in the aspirations and intentions of the secular settlement process which concentrated on Auckland and Wellington in the North Island on the one hand, with more overtly Christian immigration – the Canterbury settlement of the central South Island that was predominantly Anglican; the Otago-Southland settlement which was a Scottish Presbyterian-led venture – on the other. Four factors need to be grasped in order to gain a fuller picture of nineteenth century Christianity in New Zealand. First, Anglicans dominated the early statistics (40 per cent of the population in the 1886 census). This meant that the Church of England as, in effect, a 'transplant' into New Zealand could operate as an unofficial establishment church. Second, however, is the fact that census denominational allegiance was not reflected in active attendance at, or membership in, the churches; people claimed an affiliation which they did not necessarily demonstrate in action. This has been well-documented (cf. Webster and Perry 1989; Davidson 1997; Stenhouse and Thomson 2004; Phillips and Hearn 2008) and remains the case today. Third, British Christianity was already deeply affected by attitudes and perspectives of the modern era. Scepticism, secularism, indifference, and even hostility toward religion were gaining momentum and this was given free rein in New Zealand. Finally, there was also, from the late nineteenth century onward, a very distinct thread of sectarian rivalry and bigotry, especially Protestant–Catholic that originated out of Britain and Europe. This persisted within New Zealand well into the twentieth century (cf. King 1997).

Denominational institutions, including the churches, might be transplants, but a colonial indigenous identity soon emerged. There was strong resistance in the fledgling colony to the idea that there should be an 'established Church' as such. By the 1870s, New Zealand was a self-declared secular nation. Christianity might be the predominant religion, but no one denomination was to dominate. This, together with the reality of sectarian tension and religious bigotry, resulted in a strong secular flavour emerging in the political development of the country from colonial outpost to self-governed dominion of the British Empire. Denominational religious plurality was a fact of life that everyone had to embrace. Regional religious variation also reflected different patterns of migration and settlement: together with Scot's Presbyterianism in the lower South Island, there were pockets of German and Scandinavian Lutherans in the North Island.

Immigrant Diversity

Whilst the first immigrants in the early nineteenth century were European, and predominantly from Great Britain, other ethnic groups also arrived, especially later that century and in the wake of the South Island gold rush.[1] These included, most notably, Indians and Chinese. Chinese first arrived in 1842 in the upper South Island and from the 1860s there was an influx into the Otago goldfields. The census of 1874 records some 15 Chinese Muslims working these gold claims (NZ Government 1875). Such non-European migrants encountered racial prejudice as in other colonial countries of the time. The new colony enacted restrictions, imposing first an 'entry tax'

---

[1] I am grateful for statistical information supplied by doctoral student Todd Nachowitz from a presentation entitled 'How Diverse Are We Really: Quantifying Religious Diversity in New Zealand' presented to the Religion in New Zealand class of the Religious Studies Programme as the University of Waikato, September 2012.

(poll tax) on Chinese immigrants of £10 in 1881, raising it to £100 in 1896. In the 1890s, and beyond, there were many attempts to regulate the activities of Asian migrants and to limit their immigration. However, prior to 1899 Indians were treated as British subjects and were allowed free entry; all other Asian migrants faced restrictions as 'race aliens'. Then the Immigration Restriction Act of 1899 made it necessary for anyone 'not of British birth or parentage' to fill out their immigration application in a European Language. Interestingly, records show a relative spike in Chinese residents in New Zealand of some 5,000 in 1881, dropping by more than half to around 2,100 by the time of World War I.

By contrast, Indians were an almost invisible group: around 50 in the country in the late nineteenth century (1896) and only about 150 some 20 years later. And whereas the European population early in the nineteenth century was far outnumbered by Maori, that had reversed by the early twentieth century. In 1906 the total population was 93.7 per cent European to 5 per cent Maori, with all others comprising just 1.3 per cent. (A century later, in 2006, these ratios had become 67.6 per cent European to 14.6 per cent Maori, with all others now amounting to 17.8 per cent.) In 1916, Maori numbered less than 50,000 whereas the European populace had risen to almost 1.1 million. Such statistics reflect a shifting demographic that, in turn, belies a very complex story of change, loss, adaptation and development – involving the interplay, in the arena of religion, of the dynamics of fixed and fickle as the swirling forces of inevitable change require an adjustment one way or another by everyone caught up in them.

Religious Diversity

Although Christianity was by far the dominant religion of incoming migrants during the nineteenth century, along with Mormonism and Judaism as noted above, other religions such as Islam, and to a lesser degree Hinduism and Buddhism, were at least notionally present in as much as adherents were known to have immigrated. In some cases, fledgling communities were in formation (cf. Beaglehole and Levine 1995; Donovan 1996). Few Muslim migrants are recorded as having entered New Zealand during this time and of those who did, most were Indians from Gujarat with some from Fiji (Drury 2006; Kolig 2010). It was in the middle of the twentieth century, in the aftermath of World War II, that immigration into New Zealand picked up and so brought about an increase in the diversity of ethnicities, cultures and religions. Certainly, in the last quarter of the century the rise of immigrant communities bringing their various cultures and religions, adding to the changing demographic profile, has brought about an increase in visible manifestations of the diversity of religions. If at the outset of the twentieth century the basic dynamics of religious diversity encompassed Christian denominationalism on the one hand, and various Maori movements on the other, by the end of that century the profile of religious diversity in New Zealand had changed utterly.

Consequently, issues of inter-communal and interreligious relations, together with the wider issue of the relationship of diverse religions to a secular society, have surfaced and have been addressed both within New Zealand and regionally (cf. Pratt 2010b). A National Statement on Religious Diversity (Human Rights Commission 2007) has been promulgated with the aim of articulating aspirational ideals for the guidance of the wider community. The introduction of this statement attracted some resistance from evangelical conservative Christians who did not wish to admit diversity, rather they wanted to promote the notion that New Zealand is a Christian country; and it was resisted by secular humanists who did not wish to see any apparent privileging of religion as such.

Islam: A Case Study

Whereas at the beginning of the twentieth century the issue of religious diversity was focused on Christian and Maori contexts, in the opening decade of the twenty-first century New Zealand is undeniably multi-ethnic and religiously diverse. The way in which this development has occurred can be illustrated with reference to Muslim immigration (cf. Pratt 2010a). The 1945 New Zealand census recorded only 67 Muslims in the country (NZ Government 1952), but six years later that figure had almost tripled. In the late 1940s, a boatload of post-war European refugees brought some 50 Muslim men from Albania, Bulgaria, and Yugoslavia. In the 1960s, a number of Muslim Asian students also began arriving, and the early 1960s saw a relatively rapid rise of Muslims, from 260 recorded in the 1961 census to 551 in 1966. Although for some years the total number of Muslims in the country fluctuated, one thing remained virtually constant: the gender balance as at the census remained overwhelmingly male dominated. The Muslim population again trebled between 1961 and 1971 with, during the 1970s, an influx of Indo-Fijians, a large minority of whom were Muslims (most were Hindu) who settled mainly in Auckland, New Zealand's largest city. The 1981 census recorded a total of 2006 Muslims residing in New Zealand, with 825 living in Auckland (NZ Government 1983). Then, in the 1990s, as a result of significant change to immigration policy, Muslims from many countries, especially from the Middle East and notably also from Somalia – mainly refugees – began arriving in increased numbers (Shepard 2002).

The 1991 census was the first to provide a detailed ethnic breakdown of the Islamic population nationwide. Ethnic Indians constituted 49 per cent of the total Muslim population. Other Asians (Malaysian, Indonesian, etc.) made up a further 20 per cent while the census category 'Other' (i.e., Arab, African) comprised some 22 per cent. Europeans made up only 6.6 per cent of the Muslim community (NZ Government 1994). Since the 1970s immigration has been supplemented with a steady trickle of local converts to Islam, including some indigenous Maori. The 2001 census recorded over 23,000 Muslims (NZ Government 2002) and the 2006 census recorded 36,000. Most Muslims in New Zealand live either in the large commercial city of Auckland, or in the national capital, Wellington, both located on the North Island. There is a scattering of smaller communities found in many of New Zealand's major towns and elsewhere. Most have integrated well; some who have come as immigrants or refugees have found the New Zealand context too isolating and so have moved on – often to join larger communities in Australia.

Islam in New Zealand is certainly a diverse, not a homogeneous, phenomenon; the Muslim community is variegated and growing. Today, Muslims in New Zealand are estimated to number around 45,000 (Kolig 2010). They constitute a relatively small proportion, around 1.1 per cent, of the total population of some 4.2 million. According to recent census data, only some 23 per cent of all Muslims in New Zealand were born in this country. However, there are now several Muslim Justices of the Peace, police and military officers, and one Muslim Member of Parliament – a Pakistani-born academic who has been an MP since 2002. The Muslim population has a younger profile than the overall population, and males still outnumber females, although much less so than was the case earlier. Muslims in New Zealand typically support and understand multicultural diversity within the bi-cultural context that sets New Zealand apart from other western nations, including its nearest neighbour, Australia (Clarke 2006; Kolig 2006; Kolig and Kabir 2008). They seek to participate within a context of an 'incorporated multiculturalism' rather than, as elsewhere, find themselves set apart within what sociologists often refer to as 'silo multiculturalism', the form of multiculturalism that has arguably predominated in the UK and Europe. In keeping with a general stance of positive integration into New Zealand society, whilst yet maintaining a Muslim identity, there are also many in New Zealand's Muslim community who are very active in interfaith affairs and multi-faith organizations.

Identity and Religion

Mol asserts the identity model of religion 'places religion in a dialectical context of identity (order) and change (disorder)' (Mol 1982: 2). It is the function of religion to reinforce order and harness disorder, thus mitigating the deleterious effect of change by in some sense controlling or subsuming it. Mol applied the model in his study of religion in New Zealand by way of exploring the four chief elements whereby religion sacralizes – and so embeds and secures – identity at the personal, group, and social levels. These four – objectification, commitment, ritual and myth – are the components of the sacralizing process and so allow for research into 'the order-provision, the emotion-anchorage, the rite-reinforcement, the belief-consolidation of religion' of whatever sort (Mol 1982: 3). Mol notes the particular interest for the social scientist of studying religion in New Zealand 'because of the abundant examples of the Maori, change-absorbing, charismatic movements of the nineteenth and twentieth centuries' which 'revitalized Maori identity by stripping the old tribal patterns and by welding new ones, better adjusted to changed conditions', with much borrowed and adapted from the incoming Christian religion in the process (ibid.). In the process of his sketching and discussing religion in New Zealand, Mol highlights the distinction and shift from considering religion in respect to cultural function and religion in respect to social organization. In classical Maori society, religion was functionally integrated into daily cultural praxis whereas the Christian religion, whilst perhaps proclaiming an ideal of such cultural integration, was by the nineteenth century subject to great organizational complexity and structural differentiation. Hence there was never a single incursion of Christianity into this land; rather the initial two relatively compatible variants were soon joined by a third, radically differentiated, form and before long many others beside.

If in the early years of the nineteenth century religion in New Zealand comprised Maori and Protestant Christian of an evangelical ilk, by the early twentieth century there were a plethora of Christian denominations, sectarian alternatives, and first signs of other major religions to boot. The change that Christianity brought into the Maori domain – the fickle that disturbed the Maori fixed – during the nineteenth century spawned a myriad of Maori adjustments and even new religious movements which, in the early twentieth century settled into new patterns of fixity. The middle decades of the nineteenth century were relatively tumultuous, religiously as well as socio-politically. But the challenge of change was, relatively speaking, resolved as a new equilibrium of Maori religious identity – especially Ringatu and Ratana – consolidated and settled. By the 1920s, these were two Maori Christian

Churches, and later in the twentieth century they were foundation members of the National Council of Maori Christian Churches, alongside the Maori components of the Anglicans, Methodists, Presbyterians, Catholics and others. As this ebb and flow of fixed and fickle occurred for Maori, so the incoming Europeans experienced their own forms of challenging change, disruption, and patterns of consolidating identity re-formulation. For example, the Methodist experience of arriving initially in one form (Wesleyan Missionary Society), to be joined later by settlers belonging to the Wesleyan Church, then others in the form of Primitive Methodists and later in the nineteenth century the Bible Christians – all of which stemmed from Methodism which arose from the eighteenth century English evangelical revival – to eventual unite to form the Methodist Church of New Zealand (in 1913) as a self-governing (i.e., free from Australian oversight) religious institution of the now British Dominion (no longer merely a colony) of New Zealand, was not an isolated phenomenon. Other denominations appeared initially in the guise of sectarian variants, only to form some form of unified whole as colonial variability settled into dominion-status stability. The nation was growing up and so were its (Christian) religious institutions.

Mol's investigation of religion in New Zealand ends just before some very interesting developments emerged. The predominant pattern of settled Christian denominations, each with its Maori component in a relatively subsidiary position, was challenged to change during the last quarter of the twentieth century by the eruption, onto the societal stage, of the Maori renaissance and accompanying upsurge of interest in addressing Maori grievances stemming from a century or more of flagrant disregard of, if not outright disrespect for, the 1840 Treaty of Waitangi – the moment in which the modern nation state of New Zealand was arguably forged. For the churches this meant a radical reassessment and even the forging of a new constitution (as with the Anglicans) in pursuit of what was widely regarded as a 'gospel imperative' of the bi-cultural journey. The subject of race relations and religion, which Mol addressed, took a whole new turn toward equal partnership and complementary autonomy in the closing decades of the twentieth century and this process is still underway. However, the negative corollary of a societal and religious (that is, Christian) focus on the bi-cultural bedrock of New Zealand society tended to down-play, or simply ignore, what by the latter decades of the twentieth century had emerged as an unstoppable change-factor for New Zealand society and religion: increasing immigration bringing with it increasing range and numbers of ethnic, cultural and religiously diverse communities. The bi-cultural focus took place in an increasingly multicultural context.

The call for greater prominence to Maori language, at times contentiously so, took place when our largest city, Auckland, was displaying increasing numbers of shops and their signage in Asian and Polynesian languages.

The Challenge of Religious Diversity

The future of New Zealand is one of increasing diversity across the board – racially, ethnically, linguistically, and religiously. Yet by and large the self-image portrayed is one of secular homogeneity; diversity is at best a little flavouring on the side, but not the main menu. To that extent, Mol's analysis of religion fixed and fickle needs to be revisited in the New Zealand context. Religious diversity is here to stay. And this diversity brings with it challenges to the pattern of things fixed; the security of the known is disrupted by the incursion and presence of the foreign. More and more, our city skylines are marked by mosque-domes and the temples of the religions of the East. Being of more recent and modern construction, despite the ancient architectural tropes displayed, such buildings also are more likely to survive the shaking of these earthquake-prone isles than the Christian stone- and brick-built edifices of the late nineteenth and early twentieth century, as was demonstrated by the recent Christchurch earthquake. Whereas many churches, and both the Anglican and Roman Catholic Cathedrals, have tumbled down, the more recently built Masjid-al-Nur, at one time Islam's southern-most house of prayer, survived. Contrary to any presumption of divine favour, the outcome reflects a century or more of different building codes and structural design. Most churches in Christchurch had been of stone or brick-veneer construction; recent religious buildings, including the mosque, are more likely to be of steel-reinforced steel and the like. It was these latter that could survive an earthquakes shaking, even with some moderate damage.

Religious plurality, in New Zealand and elsewhere, is the contemporary challenge par excellence. The fact of religious plurality can be responded to, broadly speaking, by way of one or other of three lead paradigms, viz., exclusivism, inclusivism and pluralism (Pratt 2005, 2007a). Exclusivism and inclusivism are premised on the notion that there is but one universal truth or religion whereby the relationship between the universal and specific religions is problematic. Either way, it is taken as a *sine qua non* for whatever is 'universal' that there can be only one valid expression of it in terms of particular form. The religious exclusivist makes an assumption that his or her religion is, in fact, the only universally true one. All others are necessarily false. The inclusivist holds views that allow for a measure of universal religious truth being found in more than one particular religion, but that, nonetheless, it is his or her religion that fully contains, or is the full expression of, the universal truth. The paradigm of pluralism promotes the idea that the diverse religions, if not exactly or necessarily equal in all things, at least all have an equal right to exist, and that all religions – as well as the secular society in which they are set – need to allow for and acknowledge the rights of others. This is spelt out in the New Zealand context by the statement on religious diversity mentioned above. It is the absence of the spirit of pluralism that arguably lies at the heart of so much interreligious and inter-communal difficulty within the world at large (cf. Pratt 2007b). In New Zealand and, as we will see in the next chapter, Australia it is the dialectical tension between the tradition of being a secularized Christian nation in which religion has a muted sense of place on the one hand, and the emerging reality of highly diverse and potentially mutually competitive or complementary – the former leads to heightened forms of exclusive reaction, the latter to increasing efforts of interfaith détente – religions on the other, that constitutes the arena of future development and, for the scholar of religion, a fascinating field of study.

References

Beaglehole, A. and Levine, H. (1995) *Far from the Promised Land: Being Jewish in New Zealand*. Wellington: Pacific Press/GP Publications.

Clarke, I. (2006) 'Essentialising Islam: Multiculturalism and Islamic Politics in New Zealand', *New Zealand Journal of Asian Studies*, 8(2): 69–96.

Davidson, A. (1997) *Christianity in Aotearoa: A History of Church and Society in New Zealand*. Wellington: New Zealand Education for Ministry Board.

Davidson, A.K. and Lineham, P. (1989) *Transplanted Christianity*. Palmerston North: Dunmore Press.

Donovan, P. (ed.) (1996) *Religions of New Zealanders*. 2nd edition. Palmerston North: Dunmore Press.

Drury, A. (2006) *Islam in New Zealand: the First Mosque*. Christchurch: Xpress Printing.

Elsmore, B. (1985) *Like Them That Dream*. Tauranga: Moana Press.

Elsmore, B. (1989) *Mana from Heaven: A Century of Maori Prophets in New Zealand*. Tauranga: Moana Press.

Human Rights Commission (2007) *Religious Diversity in New Zealand: Statement on Religious Diversity*. Wellington: New Zealand Human Rights Commission.

Irwin, J. (1978) 'Mana-Tapu-Noa in Maori Religion', in J. Hinchcliff, J. Lewis and K. Tiwari (eds), *Religious Studies in the Pacific*. Auckland: Colloquium Publishers, 17–28.

Irwin, J. (1984) *An Introduction to Maori Religion*. Adelaide, Bedford Park: Australian Association for the Study of *Religions / AASR*.

King, M. (1997) *God's Farthest Outpost: A History of Catholics in New Zealand*. Auckland: Penguin Books.

Kolig, E. (2006) 'Interfacing with the West: Muslims, Multiculturalism and Radicalism in New Zealand', *New Zealand Sociology*, 21(2): 215–46.

Kolig, E. (2010) *New Zealand's Muslims and Multiculturalism*. Leiden: Brill.

Kolig, E. and Kabir, N. (2008) 'Not Friend, Not Foe: The Rocky Road to Enfranchisement into Multicultural Nationhood in Australia and New Zealand', *Immigrants and Minorities*, 26(3): 266–300.

Mol, H. (1982) *The Fixed and the Fickle: Religion and Identity in New Zealand*. Dunedin: Pilgrims South Press.

NZ Government (1875) 'Results of a Census of the Colony of New Zealand taken for the Night of the 1st of March, 1874', *Religions of the People*. Wellington: NZ Government.

NZ Government (1952) 'New Zealand Population Census 1945: Volume 6', *Religious Professions*. Wellington: Government Printer.

NZ Government (1983) 'New Zealand Population Census 1981: Volume 3', *Religious Professions*. Wellington: Government Printer.

NZ Government (1994) '1991 New Zealand Census of Population and Dwellings', *Population Overview*. Wellington: Government Printer.

NZ Government (2002) 'New Zealand Census of Population and Dwellings 2001', *Regional Summary*. Wellington: Government Printer.

Oettli, P.H. (2008) *God's Messenger: J.F. Riemenschneider and Racial Conflict in 19th century New Zealand*. Wellington: Huia Publishers.

Phillips, J. and Hearn, T. (2008) *Settlers: New Zealand Immigrants from England, Ireland and Scotland 1800–1945*. Auckland: Auckland University Press.

Pratt, D. (1993) *Religion: A First Encounter*. Auckland: Longman.

Pratt, D. (2005) 'Religious Plurality, Referential Realism and Paradigms of Pluralism', in A. Plaw (ed.), *Frontiers of Diversity: Explorations in Contemporary Pluralism*. Amsterdam and New York: Rodopi, 191–209.

Pratt, D. (2007a) 'Pluralism, Postmodernism and Interreligious Dialogue', *Sophia*, 46(3): 243–59.

Pratt, D. (2007b) 'Exclusivism and Exclusivity: A Contemporary Theological Challenge', *Pacifica* 20(3): 291–306.

Pratt, D. (2010a) 'Antipodean Angst: Encountering Islam in New Zealand', *Islam and Christian-Muslim Relations*, 21(4): 397–407.

Pratt, D. (2010b) 'Secular Government and Interfaith Dialogue: A Regional Asia-Pacific Initiative', *Studies in Interreligious Dialogue*, 20(1): 42–57.

Shepard, W. (2002) 'Muslims in New Zealand', in Y. Haddad and J. Smith (eds), *Muslim Minorities in the West: Visible and Invisible*. Walnut Creek: Altamira Press, 233–54.

Stenhouse, J. and Thomson, J. (eds) (2004) *Building God's Own Country: Historical Essays on Religions in New Zealand*. Dunedin: University of Otago Press.

Webster, A.C. and Perry, P.E. (1989) *The Religious Factor in New Zealand Society*. Palmerston North: Alpha Publications.

Chapter 7
From Secularist to Pluralist: Post-World War II Australia

Desmond Cahill

Introduction

It is said that religion may be part of culture, constitute culture, include and transcend culture, be influenced by culture, shape culture or interact with culture (Saroglou and Cohen 2011). But what happens in culturally and religiously pluralist nation states where the bidirectional links, firstly, between religion and culture and, secondly, between religion and state are manifestly complex and evolving? What impact does this bi-directionality have on broader governance processes and the narrower, state-focused government processes? Much as we saw in Chapter 6 concerning New Zealand, contemporary Australia provides an interesting case study of these links where the model of the separation of religion and state follows a more moderate path than other developed countries such as France and the USA.

In Australia, in the early stages of British colonialism after settlement began in 1788, the Church of England attempted to assert itself across the eventual six colonial states as the potential established Church (Hilliard 2009). This was fiercely resisted by the Nonconformist churches driven by their English narrative of tensions and hostility in separating themselves or at least differentiating themselves from Anglican majoritarianism though they were happy to be included under the Protestant umbrella (Breward 1993; Carey 1996). More strongly opposed was the Irish Catholic community whose emotionally driven narrative about the plight of Ireland made them determined to prevent embryonic Australia from becoming a class-ridden society (O'Farrell 1987: 162–3).

Up until federation in 1901, religious groups did have a special status, though it should not be over-stated. But it continued in evolving ways under the fledgling Australian state. Through the process of accommodation, legal and financial privileges and exemptions were granted in the nineteenth century to church bodies until an aggressive wave of secularism overwhelmed the status quo in the early 1870s, especially in the schooling sector where the government funding of private religious schools ceased for almost a century – after a bitter sectarian battle, it would be restored gradually in the 1960s and 1970s.

The changes in Australia's religious profile in the three decades after World War II were documented by Hans Mol (1971, 1985) in his two major Australian works which helped lay the foundations of Australian religious sociology. Another three decades brought even more changes regarding Australia's cultural and religious profile, and the complex Australian scenario has become full of continuities and contradictory discontinuities such as the increased number of secularists combined with a partial and changing quarantining of the secularist ideology.

This chapter will document the emergence of a paradoxically secularist and multi-faith Australia which rests on the tripod of the many Christian traditions (led by the Catholics and the Anglicans), an assertive secularism that has always been at the core of European Australian society and, thirdly, the rise over the past four decades of the non-Christian religious communities, most notably, the Buddhist, Islamic, Hindu and Sikh in the context of religious freedom and religion-state relationships.

Australia's Religious Profile in Historical Context

In the past two decades Australia, along with many other societies, has become aware that its religious composition is changing profoundly as the global movement of people, ideas, new technologies and media images (Apparadurai 1996) reshape the religious profile. Australian census data allow us to focus on small geographic units, enabling us to conclude that nowhere in Australia is there anything closely resembling a religious ghetto even if there are zones of religious and ethnic concentration, particularly around faith-based schools and shops and restaurants catering to particular food and other cultural needs and in areas of initial immigrant and refugee settlement (Bouma 1997; Cahill, Bouma, Dellal and Leahy 2004).

Religious affiliation tells us only a little about a person's religious beliefs or practices though differences in religious identification alone have been shown to correlate with many other variables Religious identification does provide an indication of the religio-moral culture of a person and the basis for assessing the religious composition of a nation or other geographic unit. The regularly conducted Australian census makes possible a moving series of snapshots of the changes in Australia's religious composition and culture over more than 100 years. What becomes clear is that the primary factor that has shaped and continues to shape Australia's religious profile is immigration.

By the latter decades of the nineteenth century after the population explosion from the gold rushes beginning in the 1850s, the religious profile of the Australian colonies remained settled until after World War II. While the gold rushes had brought a diversity of religious and ethnic groups – Revivalist Methodism, Buddhism and Islam as well as Chinese, Afghanis, and others – the ethnic diversities had been either absorbed or pushed out by the end of the nineteenth century. As the major religious group with its intellectual and psychological base still firmly in the UK, the Church of England, albeit never a majority, helped generate the sentiment of Australian nationalism that would underpin the formation of a federated commonwealth in 1901 and ensure that Australia would be a nation within the family of the British Empire, committed to Great Britain and its welfare. 'Anglicanism still purported to be the spiritual cement of the British Empire that needed to be protected against the allegedly disruptive creeds and claims of other denominations' (Frame 2002: 5). For too long Anglicanism was tied to its English parent; it was not until 1962 that a constitution for the Australian Anglican Church came into operation, and it was not until 1981 that it began calling itself the Anglican Church of Australia (Hilliard 2009). The net effect was a profoundly English Protestant establishment.

From 1860 till 1947, Australia's religious profile had remained relatively stable and dominated by Anglicans, Presbyterians and Methodists who together comprised just over 60 per cent of the population. The period from the 1910s to the late 1940s (see Table 7.1) was the time of least migration in Australia's post-1788 history. These were also the formative years of those Australian leaders who served in the two decades following World War II when assimilationist policies were at their height, and this explains why they were so tardy in changing the White Australia policy and constructing a multicultural society. However, the 'yellow peril' fear remains deep in certain compartments of the Australian psyche.[1]

---

[1] 'Yellow peril' refers to the racist, derogatory label used to describe all Asians, but especially Chinese, after the 1850s gold rush and the fear that they would flood the Australian continent. The huge influx of Chinese gold-seekers was the main instigator of Australia's infamous White Australia policy which, although it had been slowly breaking down from the end of World War II to the mid 1960s, ultimately lasted until the early 1970s.

In 1947, Roman Catholics comprised 20.9 per cent of the population at 1.57 million compared with 2.96 million Anglicans and 1.68 million identifying themselves with Methodist, Presbyterian, Congregational or Reformed Churches. Buddhists, Muslims and Hindus did not rate on the demographic map, though in that year 32,019 Australians identified themselves as religiously Jewish (Tables 7.1 and 7.2).

Table 7.1   Major religious and secularist groups in Australia: 1911–2011 (in raw numbers)

Religious group		1911	1947	1961	1981	2001	2011
Anglicans	N	1,710,433	2,957,032	3,669,940	3,576,641	3,881,162	3,679,907
Baptists	N	97,074	113,527	149,628	190,259	309,205	352,499
Buddhists	N	3,269	411	n.a.	35,073	357,813	528,977
Catholics	N	996,804	1,586,738	2,619,984	3,786,505	5,001,624	5,439,268
Eastern Orth	N	2,896	17,012	154,924	421,281	529,444	563,074
Hindus	N	414	244	n.a.	n.a.	95,473	275,534
Jehov. Witnesses	N	n.a.	n.a.	n.a.	51,815	81,069	85,638
Jewish faith	N	17,287	32,019	59,329	62,126	83,993	97,335
Lutherans	N	72,395	66,891	160,182	199,760	250,365	251,930
Muslims	N	3,908	2,704	n.a.	76,792	281,578	476,291
Pentecostals	N	n.a.	n.a.	16,572	72,148	194,592	237,986
Presbyterians and Ref	N	558,336	743,540	976,721	637,818*	650,148	599,520
Sikhs	N	n.a.	n.a.	n.a.	n.a.	17,401	72,297
Uniting Church	N	–	–	–	712,609	1,248,674	1,065,794
No Religion	N	177,209	189,801	263,051	1,576,718	2,905,993	4,796,786
Not Stated	N	119,616	827,533	110,481	1,595,195	1,835,598	1,839,598

Note: From 1977 many Presbyterians identified themselves with the Uniting Church of Australia which was formed in 1977 from the Methodist Church and large portions of the Presbyterian and Congregationalist Churches; n.a. = not available from the census figures.

Source: Based on Hughes, Fraser and Reid (2013) and Australian Census figures.

Changes on Religious Profile since 1947

It should be noted that, apart from the religious scene outlined above, 1947 also saw Australia embark upon its immigration programme to the sound of the 'populate or perish' drum. It was done for security reasons after the Japanese incursions into the islands north of Australia and the bomb attacks upon Darwin. The associated fear, born on the goldfields of the nineteenth century, was that Australia needed to populate its 'empty spaces' to offset envious Asian eyes and to repel Soviet invasion. A third reason was that the Australian birth-rate had fallen during the depression years of the 1930s, and by the late 1940s those leaving the labour force were more numerous than those entering it. Finally, the Australian aim to populate rural areas and develop secondary manufacturing increased the demand for labour. The Labour government of the day had sufficient confidence in its own administrative abilities to maintain full employment and a migration programme (Price and Martin 1975).

Table 7.2   Major religious and secularist groups in Australia: 1911–2011 (in percentages of total Australian population)

Religious group		1911	1947	1961	1981	2001	2011
Anglicans	%	38.4	39.0	34.9	24.5	20.7	17.1
Baptists	%	2.2	1.5	1.4	1.3	1.6	1.6
Buddhists	%	0.07	0.01	n.a.	0.24	1.9	2.5
Catholics	%	22.5	20.9	24.9	26.0	26.6	25.3
Eastern Orthodox	%	0.07	0.22	1.5	2.9	2.81	2.82
Hindus	%	0.01	0.00	n.a.	n.a.	0.51	1.28
Jehov. Witnesses	%	n.a.	n.a.	n.a.	0.4	0.53	0.40
Jewish faith	%	0.39	0.42	0.60	0.43	0.45	0.45
Lutherans	%	1.6	0.88	1.5	1.4	1.3	1.2
Muslims	%	0.09	0.04	n.a.	0.53	1.5	2.2
Pentecostals	%	n.a.	n.a.	0.16	0.49	1.0	1.1
Presbyterians and Ref	%	12.5	9.8	9.3	4.4*	3.4	2.8
Sikhs	%	n.a.	n.a.	n.a.	n.a.	0.09	0.34
Uniting Church	%	26.5	22.2	20.2	4.9	6.7	5.0
No Religion	%	0.4	0.4	0.4	10.8	15.5	22.3
No Stated Religion	%	2.7	10.9	10.5	10.8	9.8	8.6

Note: From 1977 many Presbyterians identified themselves with the Uniting Church of Australia which was formed in 1977 from the Methodist Church and large portions of the Presbyterian and Congregationalist Churches; n.a = not available from the census figures.

Source: Based on Hughes, Fraser and Reid (2013) and Australian Census figures.

The original intention was for the immigration to be 90 per cent British and to be rurally oriented (Price and Martin 1975) – on both counts it was a spectacular failure, beginning with the arrival of the 160,000 displaced persons from central and eastern Europe, the so-called 'DPs', or 'Refos', with a substantial Jewish component. As the years went by, the immigration programme increasingly diversified as the British component declined (though a small reversal between 2006 and 2011 occurred) and the demand for labour continued to rise. The late 1960s, a high point of intakes, saw diversification shift beyond the eastern, northern and southern European groups to the Balkans and the choice of Turkey in preference to Mexico as the next source of immigrants (Keceli 1998). The 'White Australia' policy legislated by the first Australian parliament in 1901 had begun breaking down by the mid-1960s and after its dissolution in 1973, the diversification in immigrant intake was further broadened with the Fraser Government's welcome of Vietnamese 'boat people' and increased migration from Asia.

Tables 7.1 and 7.2 paint a picture of this increased diversity corresponding with rises in those declaring 'no religion' and a cultural decline in the hegemonic power of English Protestant groups. For the first time, in 2001, it took three religious groups to make up 50 per cent of the population. Other indicators of increased diversity and the decline of an English Protestant hegemony are revealed in the facts that, as of 2011 there are more Muslims (2.2 per cent) than Lutherans (1.2 per cent), more Buddhists (2.5 per cent) than Baptists (1.6 per cent), and more Hindus (1.3 per cent) than Salvationists (0.3 per cent). There are about the same number of Baha'is (13,706) as Reformed (14,700). Atheism also grew, rising from 24,464 in 2001 to 31,305 in 2006 to 58,899 on 2011, following its previous decline in the 1996–2001 period. Of course, the diversification of mainstream Australian Christianity is illustrated by the Uniting Church of Australia. Given its Methodist, Presbyterian and Congregational origins, it is perhaps surprising to learn that in 2002 this church had 117 ethno- and language-specific (other than British) congregations, including (in order of size) Korean, followed by Tongan, Fijian, Indonesian, Samoan, Tamil, Hindi, Cook Islander, Chinese, Sudanese, Dutch, Vietnamese, Niuean, Rotuman, Filipino, Armenian, Cambodian, Farsi, Taiwanese, Macedonian, Nauruan and Tokelauan (Cahill, Bouma, Dellal and Leahy 2004).

Moving Away from British Protestant Australia

These trends away from hegemonic British Protestantism in Australia since 1947 are attributable primarily to five socio-cultural factors. The first is the decline of British Protestant denominations in proportional terms by essentially 50 per cent to their present situation where they constitute just over a quarter of the population. While the proportional decline of these groups has been occurring for nearly a century, the fact that these denominations are seriously aged – with well over 40 per cent aged over 55 years – augurs for more decline in the near future. The proportion who was Christian varied between 98 and 96 per cent until 1933. At that time, it fell 10 percentage points to 86 per cent and stayed at that level until it began to decline consistently after 1976 from 88.2 per cent to 61.1 per cent in 2011.

The mainstream Protestant decline is greater than it first appears; since in 2011 Anglicans were much more sacramentally oriented and less 'protestant' than they were in 1947. Those who have retained a 'Protestant' orientation do not express it in the ways commonly found in 1947, but in ways that are often laced with charismatic influences. Moreover, many Australians who once would have listed themselves as 'C of E', or some other Protestant group on their census form now say 'no religion'.

The religious climate thus changed in the three decades following World War II after the stable maintenance period for the first half of the twentieth century. The end of the twentieth and commencement of the twenty-first century has witnessed a religious response to these declines in religious moral order in the form of calls for a renewed focus on values, rises in faith-based education, and the return of religious voices to the policy arenas as conservative Christians are joined by Muslim and other groups seeking to influence the political order (Bouma 2006).

The Catholic Church and Australian Cultural and Religious Fermentation

The second factor changing Australia's religious profile has been the global movement of Catholic majority and minority groups to Australia. No mainstream Christian group has benefited more from post-World War II migration than the Roman Catholic Church which is now, by a considerable margin, the largest religious group. In 1981, it became the largest religious group when it surpassed Anglicanism in the number of adherents (see Table 7.1).

Hence, the Catholic Church in Australia is probably the most multicultural in the Catholic world. The overall profile of the Catholic Church in Australia has been one of increasing diversification, including in its priests and religious adherents. For instance, overseas priests are being imported to fill the many parish gaps in both metropolitan and rural Australia. The Catholic Church of the future, then, will be a very different and much more culturally diverse entity than its Irish background history would have presaged. The future of the Australian Church is as an immigrant Church with an Anglo-Irish and continental European remnant.

Yet, there is the temptation to identify Irishness and Catholicism when, in fact, Australian Catholicism had other tributaries – in colonial times one-quarter of Irish immigrants were not Catholic and one-quarter of Catholics were not from Ireland (O'Brien 2009). The first wave of Irish immigrants was, of course, the almost 50,000 Irish convicts, about a quarter of the overall total. Once in Australia, the Catholic Irish were not prepared to reject their identity or their religion. 'Losing the faith' was seen as a betrayal. For them, as underdogs and outcasts, Ireland was both an inspiration and a warning that Australia must not become 'the little Britain of the South'. They would not accept subordination, however nicely delivered, nor exclusion. In O'Farrell's view, the Irish were the galvanizing force at the centre of Australian history until quite recent times, and the battle was as much political as religious. There would be much cultural and religious conflict, but essentially it would be a situation of cultural fermentation in which core Australian values would be forged (O'Farrell 1987).

Since World War II, the Catholic population has continued to increase, led principally by the Italians and other European groups, including the Maltese, the Croatians, the Poles and the Dutch. The Latin Americans began arriving in the late 1960s, but it was the arrival firstly of the East Timorese and then the huge influx of Vietnamese refugees, quickly followed by the Filipinos in the 1970s, that signalled the move away from a European church. The Vietnamese have become particularly significant. An important fact here in the context of the severe priest shortage is that there are now about 150 Vietnamese priests and other religious working in the Australian Catholic Church. Symbolic of this was the appointment in 2011 of a Vietnamese Australian bishop.

Since the turn of the millennium, the Catholic population has continued to grow at a greater rate than expected with 5.439 million in 2011 (Table 7.1) though its proportion has begun to slip (Table 7.2). This rise in raw numbers has occurred for six reasons:

1. The greater longevity of Catholic Australians together with other senior Australians.
2. The unexpected rise in Catholic immigrants from English-speaking countries as a result of the economic difficulties flowing from the global financial crisis, including from the UK, Ireland and the USA.
3. The strong flow of South Africans, including the Catholic component, exiting because of the lukewarm performance of the local economy over the past two decades and the perceived problematic situation of white South Africans.
4. The continuing immigration of Filipinos, especially female Filipinos marrying Australian men, in an emigration movement that began in the 1970s under the Marcos regime (Cahill 1990).
5. The increased immigration of Catholic Asian minorities from countries such as India, Indonesia, Malaysia, Pakistan, Sri Lanka, Singapore and Vietnam.
6. The entry of Eastern rite Catholics over the past 15 years, particularly Chaldean refugees from Iraq and Syro-Malabar immigrants from southern India, especially Kerala.

Accordingly, Australian Catholicism whilst much more diversified has also been haemorrhaging large numbers of those raised as Catholics. While estimates are difficult to reach, the figure is at least over 1 million, extrapolating from data from the 2009 International Social Sciences Project. Sunday Mass attendance is now just over 12 per cent, mainly because of the exit of Anglo-Australians as a result of the secularization process and disenchantment with Church policies on birth control, homosexuality, priestly celibacy, second marriages and women's ordination.

The Movement to Multi-Faith Australia

The third factor altering Australia's religious landscape is the rise of what we call multi-faith Australia. While British Protestantism has declined, other groups have increased in strength and grown substantially, not least the Christian Orthodox. The Greeks, Macedonians, and Serbs were followed by, beginning in the late 1960s, Turks, Lebanese and Egyptians who began the significant expansion of Islam in Australia – though the Turkish Cypriots helped lay Muslim foundations in the 1950s. Additionally, from the mid-to-late 1970s, the Vietnamese arrived and began building their Buddhist temples.

In fact, these religious groups were themselves ethnically diverse comprising a wider range of immigrants. Australian Buddhists represent many birthplaces in addition to Vietnam (19.7 per cent of Australian Buddhists were born in Vietnam) – China (9.7 per cent), Thailand (6.3 per cent), Sri Lanka (6.2 per cent), Malaysia (5.5 per cent), Cambodia (4.3 per cent) and Taiwan (1.9 per cent) (see Table 7.3).

Between 1996 and 2001 there was a 79 per cent increase in the number of Buddhists who, with 528,977 persons as of 2011, are the second largest religious group after Christianity representing 2.5 per cent of the population. The 'Australian born' component includes converts as well as children born to Australian Buddhists, comprising 30.2 per cent of the total. While children are likely to predominate in the data, it is impossible to disentangle converts from those born Buddhist. Buddhism in Australia has exhibited a haphazard historical development after the earlier pre-World War II migration of Buddhists to Australia made little permanent impression (Abeyagunawardena 2009). As well, many of the Anglo-Australian converts, the Lao and Cambodian immigrants followed the Theravada form of Buddhism which is quite distinct from the Mahayana Vietnamese form. Other groups follow the Vajrajana and Tantrayana forms of Buddhism. While these internal differences reflect the diversity of global Buddhism they have made the development of local and national representative bodies just about as difficult as it has been for Christian and other groups.

Islam is the third largest religious group in Australia. Saeed (2003) documented the diversity of Australia's Muslims who come from over 70 countries. What is more, in the years since Saeed's data was gathered the Muslim population has become even more diversified, now including members from both Pakistan and Bangladesh. In 2011 the major birthplace group is Australia (37.5 per cent), reflecting the youthful profile and comparatively high birth-rate within this community with 50 per cent under the age of 24. Other countries of origin include Lebanon (7.0 per cent), Pakistan (5.6 per cent), Afghanistan (5.5 per cent), Turkey (5.3 per cent), Bangladesh (5.0 per cent), Iraq (3.2 per cent) and Iran (2.7 per cent). Just over half of Australian Muslims are male, and the majority of them are working class. Most live in either Sydney or Melbourne, but recent years have seen the emergence of significant Muslim communities in most capital and some regional cities. A policy of locating new migrants in rural communities has revitalized some small country towns, like Shepparton and Cobram in Victoria (Cahill 2007), Young in New South Wales and Broome and Katanning in Western Australia, resulting in a diversification of rural areas.

Table 7.3 Major religious and secularist groups in 2011 Australia: seven largest source countries

Religious group	First country	Second country	Third country	Fourth country	Fifth country	Sixth country	Seventh country
Anglicans	England	NZ	Sth Africa	Scotland	Wales	India	Malaysia
Baptists	England	Sth Africa	NZ	China	Myanmar	Hong Kong	Philippines
Buddhists	Vietnam	China	Thailand	Sri Lanka	Malaysia	Cambodia	Taiwan
Catholics	Italy	Philippines	England	NZ	Ireland	India	Vietnam
Eastern Orthodox	Greece	FYROM	Serbia	Cyprus	Russia	Lebanon	Croatia
Hindus	India	Fiji	Nepal	Sri Lanka	Malaysia	Sth Africa	Singapore
Jehov. Witnesses	England	NZ	Italy	Philippines	Germany	Sth Africa	Greece
Jewish faith	Sth Africa	Israel	England	Ukraine	USA	Russia	Poland
Lutherans	Germany	Finland	Denmark	Latvia	USA	Sweden	England
Muslims	Lebanon	Pakistan	Afghan	Turkey	Banglad	Iraq	Iran
Pentecostals	NZ	England	Sth Africa	Malaysia	Philipp	India	Fiji
Presbyterians and Ref	Scotland	NZ	Sth Korea	Sth Africa	England	Netherlds	Nth Ireland
Sikhs	India	Malaysia	England	Singapore	NZ	Kenya	Fiji
Uniting Church	England	NZ	Sth Africa	Sth Korea	Scotland	Malaysia	China
No Religion	England	China	NZ	Scotland	Hong Kong	Vietnam	Germany
No Stated Religion	England	NZ	China	Scotland	German	Vietnam	India

Source: Based on Hughes, Fraser and Reid (2013) and Australian Census figures.

That being said, in the period between 2006 and 2011, the Hindu community exploded in size due to a large Indian influx with those born in India representing over 50 per cent of the total Australian Hindu population. In 2011, the major national sources of Hindu migration were India (50.7 per cent), Fiji (9.6 per cent), Nepal (7.1 per cent), Sri Lanka (5.6 per cent), Malaysia (1.6 per cent), South Africa (1.4 per cent), Singapore (0.9 per cent), the UK (0.8 per cent), and New Zealand (0.8 per cent).

As another significant religious group, Jews have had a long and distinguished history in Australia, being 'represented' among the earliest migrants and influential in establishing Australia's commercial life (Goldlust

2009; Rutland 2009). Indeed, just over half of the Jewish constituency report being born in Australia. However, in recent years it is South Africa which has become the major source country – 13.4 per cent of the religious Jewish group were born in South Africa, followed by Israel and the UK Being long established in Australia, the community is well served by a range of synagogues, schools, welfare and service organizations.

The Rise of the Pentecostal, Charismatic and Nature Religion Movements

The fourth factor changing Australia's religious and spiritual life has been the emergence of new religious groups and spiritualities largely through conversion, or the adoption of teachings and practices brought to Australia not by migration of persons but through the globalization of religious and spiritual practices.

One of the most influential of these conversion-based changes has been the growth of Pentecostal and charismatic movements in Christianity. Not only have Pentecostals risen to just over 1 per cent of the population, Pentecostal and charismatic forms of Christian renewal play a substantial role in the rapidly growing category of 'other Christian' which grew by 28 per cent from 1996 to 2001 and another 27 per cent from 2001 to 2006 to attract the identification of 2.07 per cent of Australians. Moreover, no Christian denomination has been untouched by this experiential, enthusiastic and musically energetic force which has been adopted wholeheartedly by some, resisted by others and is an influence in nearly all Christian groups. However, whilst Pentecostal and charismatic groups grew significantly from the 1960s, they seemed to have reached a plateau in the new millennium.

In addition to the rise of Pentecostal Christianity, the adoption by Australians of other largely imported religious teachings and practices has led to the rise of such groups as New Age and Earth based religions like Gaia, Goddess religions, and Witchcraft which had spectacular growth during the 1990s followed by steady growth in the first decade of the new millennium, a trend especially true for Paganism. Paganism grew vigorously from 2001 to 2011, increasing by 58.4 per cent. The numbers identifying with Wicca/Witchcraft have levelled off following a spectacular growth from 1,849 to 8,755 (a growth rate of 374 per cent) between 1996 and 2001. If the 'nature religion' cluster of religious groups is added together, a total of about 32,086 or 0.15 per cent of Australians is reached (Hughes, Fraser and Reid 2013). These religions also tend to be less formal and not quite so hierarchical and patriarchal, making them more appealing to women. They are very disproportionately female. Spiritualities of choice as opposed to religions of birth are growing substantially in Australia. This resonates with the understanding that a secular postmodern society is not anti-religious or even irreligious but one where the religious and spiritual is less under the control of religious organizations. This reflects the postmodern viewpoint, 'I believe but do not belong', a sentiment that – as we saw in previous chapters – arguably challenges the understanding of religious identity promulgated by Hans Mol.

The Rise of Australian Secularism

The fifth factor affecting the religious scene, however, is the notable growth of Australian secularism (Bouma 2006). The secularist voice has always been strong in Australian society, and it continues to express concern about the growth of political religion in Australia, the religious lobby groups and their influence on political parties and the perceived attempt to re-Christianize the nation. The secularists want freedom from religion. Other concerns are tax exemptions and subsidies as well as the outsourcing of welfare, health and educational services to religious organizations, especially when they involve discriminatory practices or missionizing in their service delivery. Of course, some are extremely anti-religious in the spirit of Richard Dawkins and the late Christopher Hitchens. Others feel that religion should remain privatized. In their view, the secular voice is the only appropriate public voice. Also questioned are issues such as whether or not religious leaders have any particular expertise in questions of morality since secular views are more rational and logical. However, some such as the Humanist Society of Queensland in a recent government submission felt that 'Religion and Humanism should be understood as different systems of Belief' (see Bouma, Cahill, Dellal and Zwartz 2011).

Historically, the period from the early 1870s to the early 1970s was one where there was a quite rigid separation of religion and state. It can be rightly called the secularist era of Australian history with the Catholics agitating strongly for the funding of their schools. The philosophical basis of the Catholic position would be the mantra that parents have the right to send their children to whatever school they like. The secularist legacy would last beyond World War II. Government policy towards religious communities was largely that of negative neutrality though relations between political and religious leaders were generally positive.

The legacy of the strict separation was not sustainable in the context of globalization, the decline of the welfare state and religious extremism.

Education, of course, has always been the touchstone of interreligious relationships and the religion–state relationship. As a result the poorer private, mainly Catholic, schools were able to move from survival mode to an era of professionalization once they began receiving almost total funding from 1973 onwards according to a formula weighted in favour of schools in economically poorer and higher migrant density areas.

In our discussion of secularism, and in analysing the census data, it is important to resist the temptation to combine those who declare that they have no religion with those who, exercising their freedom to privacy on this issue, do not respond (8.6 per cent). Doing so gives a false reading of almost one-third with no religion. Other studies indicate that many of those who will not answer the question have higher than average participation in religious and spiritual activities. They are simply not saying what they are.

Regional Variation in Religious Diversity

Of course such individuals could belong to any of a wide variety of religious groups. Even so, that religious diversity is not evenly spread across Australia. Table 7.4 presents the religious composition of each state and territory of Australia. Buddhists are present at levels above the national in New South Wales, Victoria and the Australian Capital Territory (ACT) Muslims are concentrated in New South Wales and Victoria, while Hindus are in New South Wales, Victoria and the ACT. This is to be expected of migrant groups as Melbourne and Sydney have been the primary recipients of migrants for decades. In comparison, those declaring 'no religion' are disproportionally high in South Australia, Western Australia, the Northern Territory and the ACT. Each Christian denomination has a different spread across Australia. Anglicans are weakest in Victoria, South Australia and the Northern Territory. Catholics are notably underrepresented in Tasmania, whilst the Anglicans are overrepresented.

The fact of these regional differences means that Australians experience religious diversity differently depending on where they live and work. Most capital cities are richly diverse, but not in the same ways. Brisbane Muslims and Hindus are more likely to come from Fiji than South Asia or the Middle East, for example. Many country towns, once bastions of '1947' style Australia, are now in some cases religiously diverse due to the settlement of migrants in rural centres or they are in serious decline because of the lack of immigrant and refugee settlement (Cahill 2007). While not all stories of migrant settlement are positive, the vast majority are. Australians have done much to make welcome a rich diversity of peoples with many religious, cultural and linguistic backgrounds which in turn has enabled the productive diversity that characterizes Australia.

Table 7.4   Major religious and secularist groups in Australia X state/territory (in percentages of total state/territory population)

Religious group		NSW	Victoria	Qld	SA	WA	Tas.	NT	ACT	AUST
Anglicans	%	19.9	12.2	18.9	12.6	18.8	25.8	12.2	14.6	17.1
Baptists	%	1.4	1.4	2.0	1.7	1.9	1.7	2.6	1.2	1.6
Buddhists	%	2.9	3.2	1.5	1.8	2.1	0.7	1.7	2.6	2.5
Catholics	%	27.5	26.7	23.8	20.0	23.6	18.0	21.3	26.1	25.3
Eastern Orthodox	%	3.1	4.4	0.8	2.9	1.2	0.4	1.7	1.9	2.6
Hindus	%	1.7	1.6	0.7	0.9	0.9	0.3	0.7	1.7	1.3
Jehov. Witnesses	%	0.4	0.3	0.6	0.4	0.5	0.4	0.3	0.2	0.4
Jewish Faith	%	0.6	0.8	0.1	0.1	0.3	0.1	0.1	0.2	0.5
Lutherans	%	0.5	0.8	1.8	4.5	0.6	0.5	3.6	1.0	1.2
Muslims	%	3.2	2.9	0.8	1.2	1.7	0.4	0.7	2.1	2.2
Pentecostals	%	1.0	0.9	1.5	1.2	1.1	1.0	1.1	1.0	1.1
Presbyterians and Ref	%	3.1	2.6	3.5	1.1	2.2	2.4	1.7	2.4	2.8
Sikhs	%	0.3	0.6	0.2	0.3	0.2	0.0	0.1	0.3	0.3
Uniting Church	%	3.9	4.6	6.4	8.8	3.4	4.8	7.1	3.3	5.0
No Religion	%	18.0	24.0	22.0	28.1	25.5	28.8	23.6	28.8	22.3
No Stated Religion	%	7.7	8.3	9.2	8.9	9.8	8.9	14.7	7.7	8.6

Source: Based on Hughes, Fraser and Reid (2013) and Australian Census figures.

Social Cohesion in Australia and Religious Freedom

By most indices, Australia's migration and settlement policy and practice has been successful, though this is not to deny some failure. Policy and its implementation have been underpinned by the twin principles of gradualism and accommodation as well as by policies on family migration and on equality of pay.

The principle of gradualism refers to the refined social engineering process that moved away from the introduction of European immigrant groups to later more culturally and racially different groups from Asia and Africa. If migration policy has been gradualist in approach, it has been monumentally self-centred, if not selfish. Australia did not take refugees from Idi Amin's Uganda because it was felt that refugees from Africa at the time might affect the fragile social consensus that supported the programme. In tandem with gradualism has been the accommodation mechanism, which implies the change in policy, programme or law to accommodate a particular custom. Cemetery regulations have been changed to accommodate Islamic burial practice; criminal justice laws have been adjusted to accommodate the Sikh wearing of turbans rather than helmets on motor cycles and the carrying of the ritual *kirpan* or dagger in contravention of the laws on offensive weapons.

In the aftermath of 9/11, it was inevitable that focus switched to social cohesion. Since the London bombings of 7 and 21 July 2005, the social cohesion and religious extremism debate has focused very much on home grown terrorism. The Scanlon Foundation in association with the Australian Multicultural Foundation and Monash University, for example, published a collection of papers on social cohesion in Australia (Jupp, Nieuwenhuysen and Dawson 2007) and funded a major research project on the issue (Markus 2008). There is no agreed definition of social cohesion but generally descriptions revolve around a shared vision held by a well-functioning core group or community that acts in a continuous and interminable process of achieving social harmony. For his work on the topic, Markus (2008) based his notion of social cohesion on the five domains:

1. **Belonging** which incorporated shared values, trust and identification with Australia.
2. **Social justice and equity.**
3. **Participation** with regard to voluntary work and political and cooperative involvement.
4. **Acceptance** regarding newcomers and minorities and the lack of racism and discrimination.
5. **Worth** which incorporated people's general happiness and life satisfaction and their future expectations.

With that in mind, it is important to realize that Australia has made citizenship relatively easy to obtain with a requirement of four years' residency before becoming eligible to have naturalization. In the Scanlon study (Markus 2008), the overwhelming majority of respondents (96 per cent) expressed a strong sense of belonging to Australia as did a similar number (94 per cent) in having pride in the Australian way of life, a figure consistent with surveys over the past two decades. In other results, 89 per cent of the respondents indicated they were happy with their lives, and 80 per cent agreed with the statement that 'Australia is a land of economic opportunity where in the long run hard work brings a better life'.

Despite the fact that some 10 per cent of overseas-born respondents reported a discrimination experience at least once a month, Markus concluded that the level of disaffection and the threat to social cohesion is at historically low levels in contemporary Australia. But other results warned against complacency. In a series of targeted surveys in high migrant density urban areas, a minority of mainstream Australians, like Anton Breivik, harboured negative attitudes towards migration and multicultural policy.

Conclusion: Religious Freedom and the Religion–State Relationship

In the Australian context, the constitutional fathers took a minimalist approach to religion, not even defining it. In retrospect, this was probably very wise. Section 116 of the Commonwealth of Australian Constitution Act states that 'The Commonwealth shall not make any law for establishing any religion, or for imposing any religious observance, or for prohibiting the free exercise of any religion, and no religious test shall be required as a qualification for any office or public trust under the Commonwealth.'

After an earlier 1998 survey of religious freedom in Australia, the Australian Human Rights Commission published *Freedom of Religion and Belief in Twenty-First Century Australia* in March 2011. The overall conclusion was that 'the accommodation of genuine religious differences has not become easier. Religious leaders have a key role to play, through both example and teaching. The context is made more complex by the internal diversity of religious groups and voices as well as by media coverage. The roles of government and legislation are not clear for the various groups seeking protection of their rights and redress for injuries. The Australian Human Rights Commission needs to continue to monitor issues of freedom of religion and belief, including non-belief' (Bouma, Cahill, Dellal and Zwartz 2011: 83).

Other issues which arose during the project included:

1. Whether religious adoption agencies are able to refuse child adoption to gay or lesbian couple.
2. Whether religiously committed owners of hotels, apartments and other accommodation outlets are able to refuse their rooms to be used by gay or lesbian couples.

3. Whether Muslim women wearing the full *burqa* are able to give court evidence whilst still wearing their face cover.
4. Whether Sikh men can wear their *kirpans*, especially in venues where there are security restrictions, e.g. cricket grounds.
5. Local popular opposition to the building of non-Christian, especially Muslim, schools and places of worship.
6. Anti-Jewish billboards placed alongside major urban roads.
7. The issue of cyber-racism, including hate websites and virtual museums with their extremely skewed versions of religious history.
8. The campaign from selected medical circles opposed to male circumcision on health grounds because of the pain caused to the young male baby.
9. The use of the Christian cross and other Christian symbols on official insignia as inappropriate in a multi-faith society.
10. The use of the Christian Our Father to begin each Parliamentary day instead of a rotational prayer system that gives a regular opportunity to each faith.
11. The use of immigration laws to disallow the entry of religious monks, nuns and other religious workers into the country, even on a temporary basis.

It seems that mechanisms for managing global, regional and local ethnic and religious diversity depend on broadening understanding about the functional equality of all persons and all faiths and building common foundational norms. It also depends on the creation of a unified and cohesive multi-faith culture. Separation of religion and state does not imply a secularist or a majoritarian stance on the one hand, or a theocratic approach on the other. The role and function of civil authorities is to adopt what Laycock (1990) has called 'a substantive neutrality'. Certainly it is a form of neutrality that is positive towards religion though this has to be further nuanced to accept that there are bad religions or there are religions with negatively destructive elements, practices or doctrines.

The Australian stance might be better described as 'a facilitating, brokering and monitoring neutrality' to create a culture of tolerance, acceptance and reconciliation through its legislative, judicial and policing agencies and to prevent the development of any heady brew of religious extremism or a religiously supported ethno-nationalism or to counter pathology such as clerical sexual abuse.

The responsibilities of this stance in the governance of religious diversity are to keep an open religious market to prevent the emergence and growth of ultra-fundamentalist religious movements, and to facilitate religious practice in meeting the needs of many of its citizens. The second role of the state is to encourage harmony, contact and cooperation between the different faith communities – in this sense, it has to play more of a brokering role. It also has a monitoring role to detect, at the earliest possible moment, causes of difference and tensions between the religious groups, then to act purposefully in preventing such tensions from escalating into violence and to unmask the real motives behind the conflicts. It has to monitor and take action against harmful religious practices that threaten the state or its citizens.

In the creation of a 'civic ethos' or 'a culture of reconciliation and co-operation', the regulation of religious diversity is, firstly, a process and in Australia has had the following features:

1. The state through its constitutional, legislative, judicial and policing processes treats all faith and non-faith traditions on the basis of equality and neutrality.
2. The state establishes the appropriate legislation to regulate the place of religion in civil society with the legislation being administered fairly and in time.
3. The leaders of faith communities show how they contribute to the nation's social capital through their teachings and activities.
4. The faith communities have the political, economic and educational space to safeguard, develop and transmit their traditions, and are able to worship and meditate, own property, form associations and establish educational facilities freely but within an intercultural and interfaith climate.
5. The state put into place mechanisms to accommodate essential religious practices in conflict with either state legislation or core national values and practice through a process of cultural/religious impact assessment and accommodation.
6. Religious law has no place in or direct impact upon civil and criminal law.

As Mol recognized decades ago – when he initiated the sociological analysis of Australian religiosity – the Australian case is interesting because of its very high multicultural profile, its various religious and ethnic diasporas, the stability of its democratic system and the recent repositioning of its religion-state separation. It suggests that a moderate position in the separation of religion and state is the appropriate course of action because the encouragement of religious moderation is the key strategy. Aggressive secularism and aggressive majoritarianism are inimical to such a strategy in perhaps encouraging violent responses. The Australian example contrasts with the French model of *laïcité* and its 'strongly positive commitment to exclude religion from state institutions and, in its place, to inculcate principles of nonreligious rationality and morality' (Beckford 2004: 32). The importance of a strong state is also evidenced by the Australian case study.

The managing and regulating of ethnic and religious diversity has taken on a new urgency; it has to be a committed process by both the state and faith communities themselves who need to recognize the new exigencies based on dialogue and education. In the messy aftermath of 9/11 and two unnecessary wars, the best strategy lies in supporting religious pluralism and in a strategy of religious moderation rather than a retreat into an aggressive secularism (Beckford 2004). The increasingly transnational nature of faith communities and the rise of religiously inspired terrorism suggest that the evolution of praxis needs to keep pace with the concrete realities. The management and regulation of diversity is an issue for all nation states, as we will see with even greater strength in the next chapter where the dilemmas of pluralism and globalization are explored in relation to theological beliefs.

References

Abeyagunawardena, D. (2009) 'Buddhists in Australia', in J. Jupp (ed.), *Encyclopaedia of Religion in Australia*. Melbourne: Cambridge University Press, 182–213.

Appadurai, A. (1996) *Modernity at Large: Cultural Dimensions of Globalisation*. Minneapolis: University of Minnesota Press.

Beckford, J. (2004) '"Laïcité", "dystopia" and the reaction to new religious movements in France', in J. Richardson (ed.), *Regulating Religion: Case Studies from Around the World*. New York: Kluwer Academic/Plenum Publishers, 27–42.

Bouma, G. (1997) *Many Religions, All Australian: Religious Settlement, Identity and Cultural Diversity*. Melbourne: Christian Research Association.

Bouma, G. (2006) *Australian Soul: Religion and Spirituality in the 21st Century*. Melbourne: Cambridge University Press.

Bouma, G., Cahill, D., Dellal, H. and Zwartz, A. (2011) *Freedom of Religion and Belief in 21st Century Australia*. Sydney: Australian Human Rights Commission.

Breward, E. (1993) *A History of the Australian Churches*. Sydney: Allen & Unwin.

Cahill, D. (1990) *Intermarriage in International Context: A Study of Filipinas Married to Australian, Japanese and Swiss Men*. Manila: SMC Press.
Cahill, D. (2007) 'Regional and Rural Migration in the 21st Century: Historical and Contemporary Perspectives', Keynote address at ECCV conference, 'Regional Settlement for Migrants and Refugees', Bendigo, May 2007.
Cahill, D., Bouma, G., Dellal, H. and Leahy, M. (2004) *Religion, Cultural Diversity and Safeguarding Australia*. Canberra: Department of Immigration and Multicultural and Indigenous Affairs and the Australian Multicultural Foundation.
Carey, H. (1996) *Believing in Australia: A Cultural History of Religions*. Sydney: Allen & Unwin.
Frame, T. (2002) 'Introduction', in B. Kaye (ed.), *Anglicanism in Australia: A History*. Melbourne: Melbourne University Press.
Goldlust, J. (2009) 'Jewish Religious, Educational and Secular Organizations', in J. Jupp (ed.), *Encyclopaedia of Religion in Australia*. Melbourne: Cambridge University Press, 361–9.
Hilliard, D. (2009) 'Church of England in Australia', in J. Jupp (ed.), *Encyclopaedia of Religion in Australia*. Melbourne: Cambridge University Press, 128–40.
Hughes, P., Fraser, M. and Reid, S. (2013) *Australia's Religious Communities: Facts and Figures*. Melbourne: Christian Research Association.
Jupp, J., Nieuwenhuysen, J. and Dawson, E. (eds) (2007) *Social Cohesion in Australia*. Sydney: Allen & Unwin.
Keceli, B. (1998) 'Boundaries Within; Boundaries Without: Turkish Immigrant Settlement in Melbourne', PhD thesis. Melbourne: RMIT University.
Laycock, D. (1990) *Populism and Democracy in the Canadian Prairies 1910–1945*. Toronto: University of Toronto Press.
Markus, A. (2008) *Mapping Social Cohesion: The Scanlon Foundation Summary Report*. Melbourne: Monash Institute for the Study of Global Movements.
Mol, H. (1971) *Religion in Australia: A Sociological Investigation*. Melbourne: Nelson.
Mol, H. (1985) *The Faith of Australians*. Sydney: Allen & Unwin.
O'Brien, A. (2009) 'The Irish Origins of Australia Catholicism', in J. Jupp (ed.), *Encyclopaedia of Religion in Australia*. Melbourne: Cambridge University Press, 235–45.
O'Farrell, P. (1987) *The Irish in Australia*. Sydney: NSW University Press.
Price, C. and Martin, J. (1975) 'The Demography of Post-War Immigration', in C. Price and J. Martin (eds), *Australian Immigration: A Bibliography and Digest*, 3(1). Canberra: Department of Demography, Australian National University, 1–51.

Rutland, S. (2009) 'The Modern Australian Jewish Community', in J. Jupp (ed.), *Encyclopaedia of Religion in Australia*. Melbourne: Cambridge University Press, 349–53.

Saeed, A. (2003) *Islam in Australia*. Sydney: Allen & Unwin.

Saroglou, V. and Cohen, A. (2011) 'Religion and Culture: An Introduction, *Journal of Cross-Cultural Psychology*, 42: 1309–19.

Chapter 8

Contextual Theology and Religious Discourse in Indonesia

James Haire

Introduction

Serving as both an acknowledgement of Hans Mol's ministerial and theological work in the Reformed tradition as well as an earnest analysis of yet another setting in which religion acts as the nexus of complex social encounters, this chapter seeks to examine the concept of 'contextual theology' or, more precisely, 'contextual theologies' in relation to the traditions of western Trinitarian belief. This is accomplished in three ways. First, we look at the theological issues and questions surrounding the concept of contextual theologies. Second, a detailed description and analysis of a series of original and interrelated contextual theologies from one area of Indonesia is provided. Third, we evaluate the ways in which these contextual theologies relate primarily to the western tradition of Trinitarian theology.

This is an important issue in relation to the work of Hans Mol. On the one hand, Mol came from the Reformed tradition within Christianity, and throughout his long and distinguished career always maintained his strong identity with that tradition. In English-speaking countries that Calvinist tradition is normally referred to as Presbyterian (relating primarily to church polity). In countries influenced by the Calvinism of the European continent it is referred to as Reformed (relating primarily to doctrine). Mol viewed the world very much from the ethos and values of Reformed Christianity. On the other hand, Mol carried out his life-long work on the social-scientific theories of religion and, in particular, on the sacralization of identity. It seems appropriate, then, to explore some of the interactions between these two backgrounds: the Reformed tradition within Christianity and the social-scientific analysis of religion. The geographical area examined is Indonesia, the former Netherlands East Indies (or, more precisely, The Netherlands' India), the major country overseas related to The Netherlands, the land of Mol's birth and formative years. The Netherlands' India, later Indonesia, is, in international terms, by far the most significant place of interaction between Reformed Christianity and other religions. It is thus the most significant place of contextual theology in the Reformed tradition.

Theological Issues Surrounding Contextual Theologies

The starting point in this chapter is Christianity, and the notion of Christian 'contextual theologies' needs to be examined before we can proceed with our exploration of the particular case of Indonesia. In the first instance, it is necessary to look at the plural term, 'theologies'. By using the plural, many would seek to be entirely descriptive; however, it is necessary to be aware of the discourse here. One end of the scale is classically stated by Stephen Bevans: 'There is no such thing as "theology"; there is only contextual theology, feminist theology, black theology, liberation theology, Filipino theology, Asian American theology, African theology, and so forth' (2003: 3). There are a number of issues here. For example, what makes Filipino theology Filipino? What makes black theology black? Or, for this chapter, what makes Indonesian theology Indonesian? In a descriptive sense, these words are quite bland. Nevertheless, Bevans is patently seeking to go further. He is attempting to challenge certain concepts of a Christian theological meta-narrative. However, in addition, he in fact, consciously or unconsciously, uncovers other concerns: how do we theologically evaluate context? If there is no such thing as theology, what then is to be the relationship between, say, Filipino theology and Indonesian theology? In other words, is one simply describing things, or is one claiming something more? Even if, as we have noted, some do seek to be purely descriptive, it has to be admitted that others who use the term 'contextual' do so with additional intentions.

This leads us on to a second issue, that of the use of the adjective 'contextual'. Its intention can be varied. It can be used to correct a perceived lack of historical consciousness. As a corrective, contextual theology has drawn attention to the culturally and socially conditioned presuppositions with which theological writers and the Christian community work. Again, contextual theology has sought to challenge the close relationship between Christian theology and the academic world. As such it has sought to encourage an engagement and an exploration in theology in the areas of race, nation, class, gender and gender-orientation. Again, contextual theology has pointed to the perceived power relations that have been seen in so-called classical western Trinitarian theological discourse. These are indeed issues to be addressed. However, this issue has itself been problematic.

For the assumption has been that such motivations are in the minds of the theological writers producing contextual material. Such may, in fact, be very far from the truth. It may rather be a projection of those who believe that they themselves can accurately interpret the motivations of those who produce these theologies. Another, more trenchant, caution regarding the concept of 'contextual' is that of Kathryn Tanner. She argues that the encounter between Christianity and context (or culture, the term which she tends to use) is highly complex with no direct epistemological access to what context, or culture, is. For her, the Christian engagement with culture is an engagement between two internally disputable realities (Tanner 1997: 135). Thus, it is clear that this area is highly contested. Work needs to be cautious and detailed, and part of a larger discourse.

The Issue of Non-Western Theological Discourse

However, the issue cannot simply be left there. Andrew Walls states that, while at the beginning of the twentieth century more than 80 per cent of Christians lived in Europe and North America, at the beginning of the twenty-first century 'well over half of the world's Christians live[d] in Africa, Asia, Latin America, and the Pacific' (2002: 171). He contends, moreover, that at the beginning of the next century two-thirds of the world's Christians may be living in the southern continents. Walls argues that the Christianity of the west cannot avoid primarily being the Christianity of the European Enlightenment (ibid.). The majority Christian world may, then, be a community in which the effects of the Enlightenment are not apparent. The existence of the Enlightenment world is simply part of being a Christian for a great many people. Equally the non-existence of the Enlightenment world now is simply not part of being Christian for many more. It must, of course, be said that the lines of demarcation between these two worlds cannot be sharply drawn. Of course, they affect each other. Nevertheless, the differences between these spheres of influence need to be recognized.

So, this leads to what for many is a significant discourse. Many Christian theologians, especially those outside Europe and North America, are highly conscious of the epistemological difficulties with contextual theologies, as has been noted. Many of them are clearly aware of the dangers highlighted by Tanner and others. They are also cognizant of the significance of the European Enlightenment for Christianity, particularly in the west. Nevertheless, they face a dilemma. On the one hand, their cultures provide not just images and paradigms but wider 'intellectual furniture' through which there can, in their estimation, be a real meeting between the Christian faith and the cultural dynamics of their societies, however fluid those dynamics may be (Akkeren 1970: 3–48, 147–86). That intellectual furniture is, in their view, both sophisticated and resonant of their cultural dynamics. Moreover, it is a means by which discourse can be opened up with the theologies of other religious faiths. On the other hand, they are conscious that Christian theology must always be, in some sense, catholic, ecumenical, international, interracial, inter-gender and inter-confessional. In that context, then, let us look very carefully and very precisely at one specific set of contextual theologies.

Analysis of Interrelated Contextual Theologies in Indonesia

Indonesia provides a helpful example of such discourse. It is home to over 230 million people, in a society of many interrelated cultures. In religious terms, its regional ethnic faiths have had waves of Hinduism, Buddhism, Christianity and Islam (in that order) enter their lives and communities. Indeed, in recent years, there has been great debate as to whether Christianity or Islam arrived first in the archipelago. There is strong evidence now of Christian presence from the ninth century CE. Islam appeared slightly later, although with much greater continuing impact. Within Christianity the largest traditions are Reformed, then Catholic, and then Lutheran. The Reformed tradition represents about 14.5 million, or about 75 per cent of Protestants, and thus about 18 per cent of the over 80 million Reformed Christians worldwide (the membership of the World Communion of Reformed Churches) (Siwu 2010: 41–2).

This specific examination is concerned with the northern group of the Molucca Islands in eastern Indonesia. From an anthropological viewpoint it is a very useful area to examine, primarily for four reasons. First, a comparison of historical accounts by travellers over the past four centuries indicates that only the very slightest changes to indigenous cultural forms have occurred over that period (Baretta 1917: 116; Campen 1882: 438–51, 1883: 284–97). This is very different from the situations, for example, in some South Pacific islands (Garrett 1982) or among the varied Australian Aboriginal groupings (Turner 1974: 189, 192–3) where Asian or European influences have so changed pre-literary forms that today it is often difficult to know what they were just two centuries ago. As a result, it is very difficult to comprehend how a whole system worked or even which are the genuine vestiges of any original system (Turner 1986: 18). Second, population change through immigration has been very limited.[1]

---

[1] The only significant movement of population was that of the Sangihe and Talaud Islanders into the area.

Third, the heartlands of the cultural systems have been very isolated. An almost 'laboratory-type' situation has occurred. Fourth, over half the population is Christian, almost all belonging to a church in the Reformed tradition.

There is a French proverb, which may have come from French experience throughout the world, which runs: 'Il n'y a que les details qui comptent' ('Only the details are really important'). Mircea Eliade found it very illuminating in relation to cultures (1969: 37). We thus need to work carefully through the elements of belief and practice in this geographical area. Our 'way-in' is not to be via a study on the history of religions, nor via a dialogue with non-Christian living faiths, nor via a phenomenological analysis of religious appearances, although naturally all of these will impinge upon the work. We shall not, therefore, be primarily concerned in this study to discuss the various beliefs in terms of structural-functionalism or any other socio-anthropological models.[2] In other words, we are vicariously involved in 'being there' in all senses, as far, of course, as that is possible. To the North Moluccan, of course, could be applied the words of Williamson concerning the Akan of Ghana, that 'the integration of his [sic] religious views and practices lies not in the fashioning of theological and philosophical structures, but in his socially inculcated personal attitude to the living universe of which he [sic] is a part' (1965: 86).

It is impossible, from a Moluccan point of view, to dissociate in any way so-called religious beliefs from a total understanding of life and the world (Thomas 1968: 19). For theological reasons, however, I have chosen that particular part or aspect of the totality of life which is the particular focus of the meeting of the Christian message with other beliefs as our departure point in this investigation. In doing so, however, we must attempt to be true to the Moluccan viewpoint in not extrapolating one particular part of the whole but rather in using one particular 'way-in' to view the whole.

In the north part of the Molucccas, the term *gikiri* was and is used as a generic word for one of the many local or personal divinities. However, it is clear that the word originally had a much wider meaning. Hueting, in 1908, understood the basis of its meaning as 'levend wezen, mensch, iemand' (Dutch; 'living being, spirit, human being, someone/anyone') (1908: 100). In other words, he sees in it the elements of *mana* (Hadiwijono 1977: 11, 17), permeating nature in general and human beings in particular. Elsewhere, Hueting notes that '[D]e mensch bestaat

---

[2] I.e., we are not dealing with the issue primarily from such a stand-point. On this, see J. Rex (1970) *Key Problems of Sociological Theory*. London: Routledge, 175–90.

uit roehe,[3] gìkiri of njawa[4] en gurumini' ('[H]umanity consists of body, gìkiri or njawa and gurumini') (1903). What is significant here is that it would seem there are two kinds of *mana* operative in North Moluccan religious understanding. For Kruijt has observed that, while *gikiri* is found in human beings, animals and plants, *gurumini* is found additionally in animals and especially in human-kind (1903). What seems clear is that among the Moluccans the *gìkiri* was originally a *mana*-type concept more connected with a supreme being,[5] while *gurumini* was originally a *mana*-type concept more related to the physical needs, particularly in relation to mobility, in creatures.[6] In humanity, however, the two were very closely connected (Kruijt 1903: 23).[7] Even so, it is the *gikiri* which 'is het onstoffelijke van den mensch, datgene wat ook na den dood voortleeft' ('is the immaterial element of humanity, that which also lives on after death') in all cases (Hueting 1928).[8] Moreover, the *gikiri* has a connection with plants and agricultural and forest areas which the *gurumini* has not (Hueting 1903; Fox 1971: 219–52). It is for this reason that 'spirit' or 'god' seems a more appropriate translation than 'soul', although no translation exactly covers the meaning-spectrum.[9] This *mana*-type concept is still seen today in that the power of the *gikiri* is particularly seen in 'objects, for example stones or tree-roots which have extraordinary forms' (Indonesian: 'benda-benda, umpama batu, akarkaju jang bentuknja gandjil-gandjil') (Rudjubik 1978: 3). It is also seen too, however, in humanity.

It is doubtless from the breadth of the applications of the *gikiri*-concept that the term *Gikiri Moi* was related to the concept of a High God. We can see that, from *gìkiri*, which we translate 'spirit' or 'god', and *moi*, the general North Moluccan word for 'one', *Gikiri Moi* implies 'the One God' or 'the One Spirit'. Thomas sums up the present understanding of *Gikiri Moi* as 'the One God' (or 'Lord'), who is head of all powers which are animistic, dynamistic or mana' (Indonesian: 'Tuhan Jang Satu, jang mengepalai segla kekuatan-kekuatan jang

---

[3] I.e., Tobelorese for 'body'.

[4] 'Njawa' is a Malay word which as used in the North Moluccas has a meaning very close to that of 'gìkiri'.

[5] Nothing specific is here implied about such a being.

[6] Despite his uncertainty as to how to translate this term, Hueting uses the word 'levenskracht' ('vital strength') for 'gurumini'.

[7] Kruijt uses the term *zielestof* for both; he uses *zielestof* rather than *ziel* because the *gikiri* and the *gurumini* are not in particular places (or in a particular place) in the body or plant but rather are diffused like a fluid or ether throughout it. ('ziel' means 'soul'; 'zielestof' means 'soul-material').

[8] In limited cases; the *gurumini* also has a life after death.

[9] E.g., Hueting moves between *geest* (spirit) and *ziel* (soul) in translating *gikiri*, but seems partially dissatisfied with both.

animistis, dinamistis maupun mana') (1968: 20).[10] Hueting defines the term in a similar way as 'het opperste wezen, de eerste der geesten (God?)' ('the supreme being, the first of the spirits (God?)') (1908: 100). However, it would seem to be inaccurate to think of Gìkiri Moi in terms of a *deus otiosus* (Tobing 1956: 21–3). His connection with the life of the world is rather as 'misschien *de* gìkiri of de *voornaamste* gìkiri' ('perhaps *the* gìkiri or the *principal* gìkiri') (Hueting 1903). For this reason Gìkiri Moi is regarded as the Great God or Spirit in whom all the various *gìkiri* have their unity and meaning. Although each *gìkiri* might appear to be more powerful than Gìkiri Moi, this power is the power of immanence or presence. Gìkiri Moi holds the unity in that the Moluccans do not tend to distinguish between higher and lower powers, but rather to experience each microcosm as the pertinent presence of the macrocosm at a particular time (Tobing 1956: 21).

It would seem that Gìkiri Moi was the most original term associated with this Unifying God. However, other terms too are found, the most common being *Djou Ma Datu* and *Djou Latàla*. The word *Djou* is found in Tobelorese, Galelarese and Ternatenese,[11] and means 'Lord'. As such it was the primary title applied to the Sultan of Ternate, who was formerly regarded as having the status of a demi-god.[12] It seems that the meaning of the term was then widened and applied to Gìkiri Moi. However, in general it was used together with an epithet. *Ma Datu* (or *Madutu*) originally may have meant either 'the true' or 'the possessing' ('eigenlijke' or 'eigenaar') (Hueting 1903). There is similarity, of course, between the two, in that 'the Lord who is the Possessing One' or 'the Possessor' is for that reason 'the true' or 'real Lord'. At the present time, *Djou Ma Datu* is similar to Hueting's 'de Opperheer, het Opperwezen, de eigenlijke Heer' or '*de* Heer' ('the Sovereign, the Supreme Being, the true Lord' or '*the* Lord') (1908: 66; 1903). *Latàla* is associated with another Moluccan phrase, *Unanga Daku*, which implies 'The One from above' or 'The One above' (Hij daarboven'). However, it would seem that *Latàla* or *Lahatàla* is a localized form of the Malay/Indonesian expression for the Arabic-Muslim divine name, *Allah ta'ala*. Therefore, *Latàla* (or *Lahafàla*) is, at source, a loan-word from Malay/Indonesian and has replaced the Moluccan *Unanga Daku*. It has been given the thrust of the meaning of *Unanga Daku* ('above') because the Muslim God has been implied to be superior to the Highest Being (*Gìkiri Moi*) in the pre-literary

---

[10] *Tuhan* is the usual Indonesian for (the Christian) 'Lord'; it is also frequently used for (the Christian) 'God', in order to avoid using the standard Indonesian for 'God' (including 'the Chrsitian God', 'Allah'.

[11] It is also a loan-word in other North Moluccan languages.

[12] *Djou* is also sometimes written (and so pronounced) *Djoü* or *Djoöe*.

belief. From this it would seem that originally perhaps *Gìkiri Moi* was given the additional names of *Djou, Djou Ma Datu, Unanga Daku* and *Djou Latàla*.

It would seem that a tendency to pose a *deus otiosus* above *Gìkiri Moi*, although, of course, related to him, gradually arose. Such a God was associated with the names *Djou Ma Datu* and *Djou Latàla*, and he was the God who was the true and real Lord as well as the Possessor of all and the One Above All. Nevertheless, there was always a tension with this dualism between *Gìkiri Moi* and *Djou Ma Datu/Djou Latàla*. On the one hand, *Gìkiri Moi* was the very same as *Djou Ma Datu/Djou Latàla*; on the other hand, he was no *deus otiosus*.

Below *Gìkiri Moi* are the company of the *gòmànga*, the spirits of the dead or, more accurately for the Moluccans, the living-dead ('geest van afgestorvenen, zielen die men vereert' ('souls of the dead, spirits whom people revere')) (Hueting 1908: 109). All *gòmànga* are *gìkiri*.[13] These living-dead engage a very considerable amount of the thinking of the Moluccans. The basis of this concern with the *gòmànga* is the uncertainty as to the future relationship between a Moluccan and a near-relation of anyone of great influence in the village or tribe (Indonesian: *suku*) who died and so now lives in this new way (Noss 1956: 21–4). The *gòmànga* or living-dead can become a true friend, guardian, guide and counsellor or a very dangerous personal enemy. For this reason the customs carried out at death must be done so with the utmost care.

Campen reported in 1883 that on the death of the head of a household it was customary to destroy most of that person's property, especially that of any value, so as to prevent the person's *gòmànga* from later having any regrets or jealousy over possessions which that person could now no longer use (293). Funerary rites, then, involved the building of a small, separate *dooden huisje* (house of the dead) beside a family's house, where the corpse was guarded for up to 40 days (Hueting n.d.: 12). Thereafter, sometimes the bones were buried, sometimes they remained in this small house, and sometimes they (or some of them) were placed in the roof-space of the family's home. In any case, the *gòmànga*, after the due observation of these rites, was regarded as living with the family and the total village community. Daily food would be offered to the person by being placed in the roof-space. These living-dead existed in so far as they had had influence in their previous life and had been given due funerary rites, and those with the greatest influence in the past had the greatest 'presence' or 'existence' after death (Rudjubik 1978: 3). The *gòmànga*, as such,

---

[13] However, of course, not all *gìkiri* are *gòmànga*. North Moluccans say that the *gòmànga* are 'more refined than "gìkiri"' (Indonesian: 'lebih halus dari "gìkiri"'); by this it would seem that the *gòmànga* are deemed higher than the other types of *gìkiri* associated with birds, etc.

were neutral in their attitude towards their families and community. However, a *gòmànga* of great influence who was properly cared for both in the original funerary rites, as well as daily and annually thereafter, could become the main guide, guardian and hope of a person and that person's family. If, on the other hand, the rites were poorly observed both at death and thereafter, a living-dead person could become a fearful enemy. However, forms of the *gòmànga* from the outset were mainly implacable enemies. For example, the *gòmànga madorou* was one of the living-dead who was insulted at death by being given improper funerary rites (Pederson 1970: 25). He thus brought disaster at every opportunity, especially upon his immediate family (Rudjubik 1978: 4).

Religious and Theological Discourse in Indonesia

From what we have seen, it can be observed that in the cultural understanding of the Moluccans the security-creating harmony most closely related to the Christian concept of salvation concerns protection from the village spirits, the correct relationship with other creatures and nature, the right ties with the *gòmànga* and the hoped-for respect to guarantee one's future *gòmànga*-status. It seems that for the Moluccans in general it is accurate to follow Cooley's observations in the central Moluccas, that is, that 'the indigenous religion and *adat* [customary law] should be seen as two halves of a whole' (1962: 482). Although *Gìkiri Moi* or *Djou Ma Datu/Djou Latàla* has not been given a specific law-code, the *gòmànga* and the village spirits are they who provide the sanctions for the *adat* system, and it is *Gìkiri Moi* who sums up and holds together the various *gòmànga* and other *gìkiri*.

For this reason the *adat* (customary law) system has a close connection with the security-creating harmony which is dependent upon the relationship of a person with the *gòmànga* and all the other *gìkiri* (including all of the village spirits). This we can see in relation to that part of the *adat* which most concerned the population – that is, the issues of marriage and sexual relations. The correct actions in these matters were determined by what was correct within the tribal grouping. That is, in general, moral action only concerned those within the tribe. In the coastal regions of the Moluccas, a man was quite free to have sexual relations with an 'outside' unmarried girl.[14] However, an adulterous wife and her lover could be killed by the husband and his brothers. The effect of this outlook was to cause great stability in family life among the coastal peoples. This self-preserving intolerance to *howono*, 'the breaking of the *adat*', was presumably related to the fact that the coastal

---

[14] I.e., with a girl from outside the village, and even more with a girl from outside the tribe (*suku*). Even with a girl from within the village, penalties were not very severe.

people were traditionally a sea-faring people who had set up communities at great distances from their homeland. Therefore, they needed a strict marriage *adat* in order to protect their stability. On the other hand, in some interior agricultural plains, there was an annual fertility feast known as *waleng*, the term referring to both the feast and the *gìkiri* of fertility. The feast was held for 7 to 10 days at the end of harvest and before the new planting. During this time there was worship to the *gìkiri waleng*, *Gìkiri Moi* and the *gòmànga* in addition to communal eating and merry-making for a number of villages. Also, from dusk until dawn, there were communal sexual relations. During the period of the *waleng* one did not concern oneself about who was one's wife or one's husband. The purpose of this was to give honour to *gìkiri waleng* and to ask for fertility of the soil and of the produce in the coming planting-season. Unlike the situation of the coastal, sea-faring peoples, the significant difference of this interior *adat* was that it had in general very little sanction against adultery. Adultery in recent times, especially by the wife, has been considered of little consequence.

The Formation of Contextual Theologies

It is important to look closely at the above structures, so as to appreciate the interrelationships of such a system. Therefore, we now move on to look at the outworking of the interrelated Christian contextual theologies in this system. As noted above, our approach in terms of examining these contextual theologies is based on the traditional agenda of western Christianity. We have chosen such a method due to its utility for understanding and comparing these contextual theologies. It should be noted that the internal agendas of these contexts may be quite different.

With that in mind, we first look at the contextual Christian doctrine of God of the Moluccans. Here, there was an attempt to work out an integrated system between the Christian Triune God and the *gìkiri* and village spirits. A tendency towards Sabellianism could be expected, in that *Gìkiri Moi* had been integrated into the greater Christian God and this God was the unifying basis of all the *gìkiri*.[15] This in fact seems to have happened.[16] In this tendency to Sabellianism

---

[15] Sabellianism, an influential movement within Christianity named after the third-century CE theologian Sabellius (who seems to have taught in Rome), which expounded that the three persons of the Trinity were simply different modes of being of the One God. The teaching was opposed by the theologians Hippolytus and Tertullian.

[16] This tendency towards Sabellianism has, of course, often been inherent in Reformed thinking; cf. K. Barth (1936) *Church Dogmatics I: The Doctrine of the Word of God, Prolegomena to Church Dogmatics, Part I*. Edinburgh: T&T Clark, 403.

'a la Moluccas' Christians regarded the various *gikiris*[17] as the microsmic presence in each place of one of the three facets of the triune God, although the doctrine of the Holy Spirit tended to be minimised. Unlike the situation in Ceram in the Central Moluccas, in the North Moluccas the Christian God tended to be regarded more in terms of power-through-presence (Cooley 1962: 490; Haire 1981: 256).

A second example relates to the North Moluccan outlook on Christology. As the *gìkiri*, as we have just seen, were related in general to the facets of the Triune God, so the *gòmànga* were specifically related to the sonship.[18] As we have seen, there were concepts of the Senior Living-Dead and the Unseen Leader. These pre-literary outlooks were to have considerable influence on the Moluccan Christian understanding of the relation between the divine and human in Christ. Thus the North Moluccan Christians began to base their Christological understanding on the Senior-Living-Dead who was the Unseen Leader. They were the people (*bala*) who had been called out to follow the Lord Jesus as their leader. He could be related to them (that is, they could understand his humanity) because he had been alive but was now living after death in their villages in their midst, and as such was their Unseen Leader. That is to say, in the first instance he was quantitatively but not qualitatively different form their greatest ancestral *gòmànga*. Because of this, the following New Testament theme is of great frequency in their preaching. The Church and particularly the village-congregation as the body of Christ are often used to stress the relationship of each humble villager's future *gòmànga* with the *gòmànga* (*the gòmànga*) of Christ.[19] Christ as the forerunner and pioneer in Hebrews 12 is also used to relate the believer's *gòmànga* to that of Christ.[20] It has been noted that the pre-literary influence of the *gòmànga*-concepts tended to set no ontological difference between Christ and believers, although there was a great quantitative difference.

Set against this, however, and stressing the divine in Christ, was the 'Moluccan Sabellianism' which we have just seen, and which regarded Christ as the microcosmic presence in each congregation of the whole macrocosmic Christian God. However, it must be said that this tended not to result in a systemized

---

[17] Here used in the generic sense, including the *gòmànga* and village-spirits (the latter at least in part). Where the *gìkiri* was potentially favourable or unfavourable, then it was related to the Christian God. When it was entirely unfavourable, then it was related to Satan.

[18] The Fatherhood of God was related to Gìkiri Moi as the unifying and meaning-giving basis of all the *gìkiri*, including the *gòmànga*.

[19] Based mainly on Romans 12:3–8; I Corinthians 12:12–30; Ephesians 1:22–23 or Colossians 1:18–20, the last reference, especially Colossians 1:18 where Christ is also-called 'πρωτότοκος' being most supportive.

[20] Based particularly on Hebrews 12:1–17.

understanding of Christ such as the *vere deus, vere homo* of Chalcedon. For the *gòmànga* influence in Moluccan thinking rendered a clear distinction between the divine and the human both impossible and incomprehensible in Moluccan terms. They thought of Christ as the Great *Gòmànga*. The *gòmànga*-concept explained and integrated for the Moluccans what was the Christological problem in Latin terms. On the one hand, as all the *gòmànga* in pre-literary terms found their meaning in *Gìkiri Moi*, so Christ was the aspect of God most related to the lives of believers both before and after death. On the other hand, as the Unseen Leader of all Christian *gòmànga*,[21] he was the Head of the village congregational Body of the faithful. Yet these two were not mutually opposed, but could conceptually be easily integrated. Thus, we see the significance of the Moluccan de facto interaction with the definition of Chalcedon,[22] and indeed a more integrated Christology. Chalcedon insists on three factors. First, it insists that Christ is truly divine. Second, it insists that Christ is truly human. Third, it insists that Christ is one. Undoubtedly, this Moluccan Christology sees Christ as one just as it sees Christ as truly human. It may arguably even see him as truly divine. However, Moluccan Christology also seeks to explain Christ to a degree that Chalcedon's definition does not. Thus, the Moluccan understanding seeks to do for this specific context, and the Moluccan Christians would say achieves, much more than Chalcedon is able to do for western Christianity.

A third issue is the Moluccan contextual theology of salvation. We have seen how the pre-literary concern for security-creating harmony, the concept most closely related to the Christian understanding of salvation, was based upon guarding the correct relationships in and around the village community, including the relationships with the *gikiri*, the *gòmànga*, the village spirits, other creatures and nature in general. Implied in this also was a forward-looking concern for each person's *gòmànga*-status after death. What seems to have happened with the advent of Christianity is that these concerns were baptized into Moluccan Christian practice, while in addition an eschatologically oriented concept of salvation related to the grace and sovereignty of the Christian God

---

[21] I.e., both the *gòmànga* of the already living-dead and the anticipated *gòmànga* of believers still alive. The Christian eschatological emphasis stimulated the application of *gòmànga*, in the eschatological 'already-but-not-yet' sense found in the New Testament, to still-living believers.

[22] The Definition of Chalcedon is the Christological formula drawn up at the Council of Chalcedon in 451 CE, and accepted by the majority of churches at that time, apart from the Monophysite and Armenian Churches. Today most churches regard this Definition as a high point in the search for a Christological statement. In it, among other things, are affirmed that Christ is one; that both natures of Christ, divine and human, are each unimpaired; and that the two distinct natures of Christ are each fully God and fully human.

was pursued. Moreover, there seems to have remained an unresolved tension between these two outlooks. On the one hand, the pre-literary salvation outlook had been primarily oriented to the present (the guarantee of the security-creating harmony), with the *gòmànga* status concern as an addendum to that. Regarding the *adat* and illness and death the thinking seemed to be that, as the *gikiri* sanctioned the *adat* and also had to be in correct harmony with the community for there to be security, and as through *Gikiri Moi* they had all been incorporated into the Christian God, so the correct observance of a Christian *adat* and the righting of wrongs through the Church would guarantee security and harmony for all of the village. Running parallel with this outlook, on the other hand, was the eschatologically oriented understanding of salvation. Salvation in these latter terms seems to have been related to the fact that the Christian God was now ultimately responsible for the majority of the previous pre-literary religionists, and so would be responsible in his grace. However, there tended in this eschatologically oriented outlook to be less emphasis on salvation from sin. As sin was so closely connected with the breaking of the *adat*, salvation from the consequences of sin was almost always related to the former, 'baptized' pre-literary security-and-harmony concept of salvation. Thus, a security-and-harmony-related understanding of salvation, primarily oriented to the present and largely baptized into Christianity, remained in unresolved tension with a more eschatologically oriented concept.

There was a very significant example of this regarding ecology and the integrity of creation. In the 1980s, during the logging boom in the eastern Indonesian islands, a licence was granted to an overseas company to log in an area of high density timber of the highest international value and uniqueness in the North Moluccas. The concession set out terms for the logging. Only one tree in ten was to be felled, and that tree was to be replaced through planting. The villagers, almost entirely Christian, saw that the terms of the licence were not being carried out. Moreover, they saw great danger in any logging of this proposed scale taking place in any case. In fact, their overwhelming outlook was controlled by their concept of salvation, both present-orientated and eschatologically orientated. They regarded the overseas logging company as merely irresponsible, endangering the integrity of creation and being unfaithful to their concept of salvation. In their eyes, the villagers were humanly powerless but divinely empowered. Thus, in darkness, day-by-day and week-by-week, they removed small parts of the logging machinery and hid them in the forest. The logging company brought in more and more equipment, with great trouble and at great expense. The villagers continued to remove and hide the small parts. The logging company was greatly frustrated, but could not work out how the parts of their equipment were disappearing. Finally, the logging company gave up, returned the licence to the government, and left the area. No more logging took place. After this, the deeply pious villagers gave thanks to God for God's guidance and empowerment. They had absolutely no concept of carrying out sabotage, or of acting illegally. For them, it was clear simply that irresponsible outsiders, like irresponsible children, were engaging in activity that was, and would be, detrimental to both present-orientated salvation and eschatologically orientated salvation. They carried out, in their perspective, a theological *praxis* of salvation.

Fourth, there was a clear contextual sacramentology of the Lord's Supper. If the Bible was the day-to-day contact point with God, so the Lord's Supper was the pre-eminent contact point where God, through the Great Living-Dead Jesus Christ, was supremely present. It was thus a truly 'aweful' occasion, potentially fraught with great danger but also capable of giving great blessing. In this understanding there were clearly influences from the high-feasts of *Gìkiri Moi* and the *gòmànga*. Fear was expressed in that any person attending the Lord's Supper with a hidden unresolved sin was liable to face serious illness or death in the near future. It was also seen that the slightest flaw in the carrying-out of the service could result in grave trouble for the community, as Lord Himself was in the process of holding his feast. Blessing, however, could be obtained both for each individual attending the Supper or especially for the whole community through the correct carrying-out of the ordinance.[23]

Fifth, and closely related to this, is the contextualized understanding and celebration of Christ's Passion. Thus in the Moluccas there was often a very close following of the details of Christ's suffering and death week-by-week and sometimes day-by-day up until the celebration of the Lord's Supper. For Christ was the Great and Senior *Gòmànga* who was also the Hero (as Unseen Leader) who had undergone a violent death. Therefore the careful following and examination of the details of the passion, death and resurrection of Christ could help guarantee his leadership and support of the congregation as his dependent *bala* (people) in the year ahead, and help protect them from the dangers always attendant upon their contact with such a great *gòmànga*.[24]

The sixth example involves the presence of visions and the general intensity of worship within Christianity. Within congregations, although visions had largely been adapted to Biblical forms, a contextualized theology can be seen. Visions

---

[23] In North Moluccan thinking material and spiritual (i.e., that related to the whole *gikiri*-complex) blessing could not be sharply differentiated.

[24] On this following of Christ's suffering, cf. *Heidelberg Catechism*, Question 79.

of Christ's appearance, particularly at the time of Reception to the Lord's Table (Confirmation), often also carried concepts of the heroism of a great *gòmànga*.

Likewise, then, the seventh issue concerns Confirmation. A very severe and humiliating procedure for the candidates was undergone at the hands of the Session at the end of catechizing, and if a potential communicant could show his or her resilience in this then confirmation would ensue. Underlying this would seem to be the concept that through the catechetical trial culminating in confirmation the initiate's connection with the Great *Gòmànga* (Christ) as Head of the Body, and through him with God, was guaranteed.

The eighth example, however, is essentially a moral or ethical one. The attitude towards adultery and marriage-sanctity in Christian communities was very strongly influenced by the differing outlooks on the subject in coastal and inland areas. In coastal areas the wife's adultery was a very serious breaking of the *adat*, while in inland, agricultural areas it was considered to be of little consequence. This was, of course, related to the much greater significance of inland fertility-cults.

Finally, in Church Order, much of the thinking and aspirations formerly applied to traditional religious leaders, some in the *shaman* tradition, were applied to the minister. The religious leader's leading of the worship each year to seek protection and blessing for the village, despite the dangers of dealing with the 'aweful', seemed similar to the minister's task in the twice-yearly celebration of the Lord's Supper. This melding of times and traditions, beliefs and behaviours, effectively highlights the creative interface between the emerging contextual theology and long-established western doctrine.

Relationship of Contextual Theologies to the Western Tradition of Trinitarian Theology

Having explored the interrelated contextual theologies and their practical outcomes above, against their backgrounds, we can now delineate three types of interaction. First, there is the tendency for pre-literary views to be 'baptized', partially or 'in toto', into Christianity. Second, there is the struggle or, more precisely, the 'double-wrestle' between pre-literary and Christian outlooks. Third, there is the producing of new insights into Christian faith and life, communal and individual.

So now we need to evaluate how such contextual theologies, or, as we have seen to be more likely, such a grouping of contextual theologies and practices, come to be a kind of *theologia in locō*. In doing so, we can begin to answer an important question: how do these contextual theologies relate to the western tradition of theology? For Christianity, it is perhaps because the Christ Event can never be exclusively identified either with one culture or one type of culture that Paul employs the ambiguous 'ἡ ἀκοή' ('*hē akoē*'; 'the hearing') to describe the action by which the Christ Event enters a person's or a community's life, that is, the crucial step that leads to faith (Taylor 1958: 254).[25] For, in a sense, in all the interactions described before and since H. Richard Niebuhr,[26] the Christ Event must become *pagan* in the original meaning of that term (that is, *earthed*) and yet must also be under the opposing Divine criticism. This, in fact, is seen in the varied theologies in the New Testament (Käsemann 1951/52: 13–21; 1952/53: 455–66).

Transition, translation, transposing, transplanting, transferring, transforming, transfiguring are varying expressions of the intercultural activity to which Christians are called and in which theological writers bear a special responsibility. However, these very theological writers are very often conscious that they may be accused of not speaking of God, but of simply speaking of themselves 'with a loud voice', in Barth's words. For some contextual theologians, *contextuality* itself may simply remain the central driver. Yet for many contextual theologians, these contextual theologies do not in any way seek to replace the Trinitarian theological models of the western church, Catholic and Protestant, as they witness to the glory of God in the face of Jesus Christ. On the contrary, they seek to add to the models of the classic expressions, especially of western Christianity.[27] They do so now increasingly because of the new world in which humanity finds itself – that is, the world of pervasive inter-religious interaction which has been extensively surveyed in this and the preceding chapters. For this reason, this discourse becomes more significant. It would be easier if it could simply be written off as a corrective, or even as an exercise in polemical discourse. However, it has now moved far beyond that, to a much more serious discourse, now involving both interaction with the theologies of other faiths and a theological existence which is outside

---

[25] See, e.g., Romans 10:16–17; Galatians 3:2.

[26] H. Richard Niebuhr (1894–1962), the United States theologian, served for many years as Sterling Professor of Theology and Ethics at Yale Divinity School. His work involved the interweaving of sociological, theological ethical analyses, including ground-breaking analyses of the interrelationships of Christianity and culture, entitled *Christ and Culture* (1951). He is to be distinguished from his elder brother, also a theologian, Reinhold Niebuhr (1893–1971).

[27] I am not here speaking of eastern (Orthodox) Christianity, in that the written interaction between eastern Christian theology and contextual theologies is only now developing to any great degree.

the scope of the inheritance of the European Enlightenment. For that reason it is also not directly related to the debates on modernism and post-modernism. For many contextual theologians, inter-religious and cross-cultural discourse seeks to add to the western Trinitarian tradition its own Trinitarian traditions. It is the language of a new and rapidly growing Christian world, a new style of dialogue. To engagement with such new discourse, and to the intersection of sincere theological reflection and responsible sociological investigation, Hans Mol has given much of his extraordinary academic life, and thus it is an honour to share in this *Festschrift* to him.

References

Akkeren, P. van (1970) *Sri and Christ: A Study of the Indigenous Church in East Java*. London: Lutterworth Press.

Arndt, W.F. and Gingrich, F.W. (eds) (1957) *A Greek–English Lexicon of the New Testament and Other Early Christian Literature*. Cambridge: Cambridge University Press.

Baretta, J.M. (1917) 'Halmahera en Morotai', *Mededeelingen van het Bureau voor de Bestuurszaken der Buitenbezittingen, bewerkt door het Encyclopaedisch Bureau*, 13. Weltevredan, 116 ff.

Barth, K. (1936) *Church Dogmatics: I, The Doctrine of the Word of God, Prolegomena to Church Dogmatics, Part I*. Edinburgh: T&T Clark.

Bevans, S.B. (2003) *Models of Contextual Theology*. Maryknoll: Orbis.

Campen, C.F.H. (1882) 'De Godsdienstbegrippen der Halmaherasche Alfoeren', *Tijdschrift voor Indische Taal-, Land-en Volkenkunde (uitgegeven door het (Koninklijk) Bataviaasch Genootschap van Kunsten en Wetenschappen)*. Batavia, 438–51.

Campen, C.F.H. (1883) 'De Alfoeren van Halmahera', *Tijdschrift voor Nederlandsch Indië*, 4e Serie, 12/1: 284–97.

Cooley, F.L. (1962) 'Altar and Throne in Central Moluccan Societies: A Study of the Relationship between the Institutions of Religion and the Institutions of Local Government in a Traditional Society Undergoing Rapid Social Change'. Unpublished PhD thesis, Yale University.

Eliade, M. (1969) *The Quest: History and Meaning in Religion*. Chicago: The University of Chicago Press.

Fox, J.J. (1971) 'Sister's Child as Plant: Metaphors in an Idiom of Consanguinity', in R. Needham (ed.), *Rethinking Kinship and Marriage*. London: Tavistock Publications, 219–52.

Garrett, J.R. (1982) *To Live among the Stars: Christian Origins in Oceania*. Suva/Geneva: University of the South Pacific/World Council of Churches.

Hadiwijono, H. (1977) *Religi Suku Murbu di Indonesia*. Jakarta: BPK Gunung Mulia.

Haire, J. (1981) *The Character and Theological Struggle of the Church in Halmahera, Indonesia, 1941–1979*. Frankfurt-am-Main and Bern: Peter Lang.

Heidelberg Catechism (1563) Question 79.

Hueting, A. (1903) 'De Tobèloreezen in hun Denken en Doen', *Verslagen en Mededeelingen der Koninklijke Academie van Wetenschappen* (Amsterdam), Afdeeling Letterkunde, Vierde Reeks, 4: 361–411.

Hueting, A. (1908) *Tobèloreesch-Hollandsch Woordenboek, met Hollandsch-Tobèloreesche inhoudsopgave*. Gravenhage: Het Koninklijk Instituut voor de Taal-, Land- en Volken-kunde van Nederlandsch-Indië/Martinus Nijhoff.

Heuting, A. (1928) 'Geschiedenis der Zending op het eiland Halmahera (Utrechtsche Zendings-Vereeniging)', *Medeelingen: Tidschrift voor Zendingswetenschap*. 72: 1–24, 97–128, 193–234.

Hueting, A. (n.d.) *Van Zeeroover tot Christen*. Oegstgeest: Zendingsbureau.

Käsemann, E. (1951/52) 'Begründet der neutestamentliche Kanon die Einheit der Kirche?' *Evangelische Theologie*, 1: 13–21.

Käsemann, E. (1952/53) 'Zum Thema der Nichtobjektivierbarkeit', *Evangelische Theologie*, 12: 455–66.

Kruijt, A.C. (1903) 'De Rijstmoeder in den Indischen archipel', *Verslagen en Mededeelingen der Koninklijke Academie van Wetenschappen*. Afdeeling Letterkunde, Vierde Reeks, 361–411.

Niebuhr, H.R. (1951) *Christ and Culture*. New York: Harper and Row.

Noss, J.B. (1956) *Man's Religions*, 2nd edition. New York: Macmillan.

Pederson, P.B. (1970) *Batak Blood and Protestant Soul: The Development of National Batak Churches in Northern Sumatra*. Grand Rapids: Eerdmans.

Rex, J. (1970) *Key Problems of Sociological Theory*. London: Routledge.

Rudjubik, M. (1978) 'Kepercayaan Agama Kafir' (unpublished paper). Kao, Indonesia.

Siwu, R.A.D. (2010) 'Carry the Burden Together, Whether Heavy or Light: An Indonesian Perspective on Communion and Justice', *Reformed World*, 60(1): 41–56.

Tanner, K. (1997) *Theories of Culture: A New Agenda for Theology*. Minneapolis: Fortress.

Taylor, J.V. (1958) *The Growth of the Church of Buganda: An Attempt at Understanding*. London: SCM Press.

Thomas, P.H. (1968) 'Penjebaran Agama Ksisten dan Pengaruhnja bagi Pendidikan Penduduk Halmahera' (The spread of Christianity and its influence on the education of the population of Halmahera) (unpublished thesis). Ambon: Pattimura University.

Tobing, P.L. (1956) *The Structure of the Toba-Batak Belief in the High God*. Amsterdam: Jacob van Kampen.

Turner, D.H. (1974) 'Tradition and Transformation: A Study of the Groote Eylandt area Aborigines of Northern Australia'. Australian Aboriginal Studies, No. 53. PhD thesis. Canberra: Australian Institute of Aboriginal Studies, University of Western Australia.

Turner, D.H. (1986) 'Terra Incognita: Australian Aborigines and Aboriginal studies in the 80s' (typed manuscript).

Walls, A. (2002) 'Christian Scholarship and the Demographic Transformation of the Church', in R.L. Peterson, and N.M. Rourke (eds), *Theological Literacy for the Twenty-First Century*. Grand Rapids: Eerdmans, 166–83.

Williamson, S.G. (1965) *Akan Religion and the Christian Faith: A Comparative Study of the Impact of Two Religions*. Accra: Ghana Universities Press.

Postscript
Reflections of a Sociologist-Priest

Gary D. Bouma

It seems that many scholars have been clerics or have had clerical forbears. Hans Mol lived an integrated life combining being an active pastor and a productive sociologist. Some have seen these roles as incommensurable, and others have found them mutually reinforcing. There remains space within the sociology of professions for a study of the ways these professional orientations are managed. Below, I provide my own brief look at this phenomenon, beginning with insights from Hans Mol garnered from a recent interview with him and moving on to some reflections from my own experience in order to provide a window on the problems and possibilities of combining pastoral/priestly and academic sociology roles.

While I had read Mol before coming to Australia, I only got to know him as a person after we met in 1983 at a meeting of The Australian Association for the Study of Religions in Brisbane. There has been a rapport between us, arising from the similarities in our backgrounds and the way we have conducted our professional lives. Hans Mol was raised in Holland as a Dutch Calvinist. I was raised in Grand Rapids, Michigan as a Dutch Calvinist. Hans learned his sociology in the early 1950s finishing a PhD at Columbia. I began learning sociology when my father took his Master's in 1944 at the University of Michigan under Guy Swanson and then his PhD at Michigan State University in 1952 under John Useem. Hans and I have both spent significant time in Canada and have both 'retired' in Australia. While Hans found a spiritual home in the Presbyterian Church in Canada and Australia following service in the Presbyterian Church USA, I found mine as a priest in the Anglican Church of Australia, following service in the Presbyterian churches listed along with the United Church of Canada and the Religious Society of Friends. All this is to say that, having quite similar life experiences and academic careers, I understand Hans, and this kind of interwoven biography provides a special richness. What is more, this is the same richness that being a person of faith affords to the student of religions.

Mol's Own Views

In order to gain more direct information regarding Hans as Pastor and Sociologist I visited him and his wife Ruth in their apartment in the suburb of Deakin in Canberra. Ruth assisted Hans with some elements of memory, but he was very clear about how he viewed his two professional roles. For Hans, the intersection of religion and sociology began in the late 1940s and early 1950s. This happened almost accidentally. Hans emigrated to Australia on the first ship to bring Dutch immigrants. While onboard he was informally recruited and appointed by the Protestant Dutch to be their chaplain and to represent Protestant interests both on the ship and later in the migrant camp at Bonegilla. Hans adds that 'they did this although I was young'. He was called by the people to the ministry in order to fill a gap. The Roman Catholics had been much better organized with priests appointed to sail with migrants, providing religious services and leadership. The Protestants, however, were alone with no chaplains and no leadership in place.

Following his informal election to the roles of chaplain and spokesperson, Hans served as a chaplain among Dutch migrants to Australia in the migrant camps at Bonegilla and Bathurst from 1950 to 1954. He dealt with immigrants' religious issues because, unlike British immigrants who could be welcomed by the existing Anglican, Methodist and Presbyterian churches, there was no Dutch Reformed Church to welcome them to Australia. He did pastoral work and helped the immigrants find employment. He said, 'I tried to imitate the work of the Catholic chaplains. I cooperated with Catholic chaplains in the migrant camps and regarded them as friends.'

While acting as a chaplain at the Bathurst migrant camp he began attending St Andrews College in Sydney in preparation for the Presbyterian ministry. The Presbyterian Church had offered Hans direct entry to theology on the basis of his gymnasium (high school) studies in Holland. He was ordained by the Presbyterian Church in 1952 in Bathurst. Then in 1954 he went back to Holland to recruit Dutch Reformed pastors to minister to the rapidly growing Dutch communities in Australia.

Hans was awarded a scholarship to study at Princeton Theological Seminary but convinced the donors that instead he should go to Union in New York City to work with Reinhold Niebuhr. Hans was critical of sociologists at Union and Columbia because 'it had become a religion in itself' and in some forms 'reduced religion and faith to an illusion, rather than a potent force in society'. He said, 'I preferred Niebuhr to old fashioned liberalism, and I was critical of sociology through my theology. I argued with how they approached religion, they looked down on orthodoxy, while I took orthodoxy seriously. I was the only one who took orthodoxy seriously.' The optimism of the social gospel movement did not sit well with his Dutch Calvinist pessimism about human nature, and Hans could sense the rising tide of secularism which in decades to come would deny the role of religion in society.

While studying at Columbia, Hans had to work to pay the bills and support a wife and growing family. He was appointed to the Bethel Presbyterian Church in White Hall, Maryland. It was a large congregation, 'one of the largest on the Eastern seaboard of the United States' according to Hans. 'Many members of the congregation were yeoman farmers and some workers in industry. Having been raised on a farm I could talk about farming with farmers.' His PhD thesis was on Dutch emigration to New Jersey in the seventeenth century and the role of Calvinist piety and theology in their adaptation to the new setting (Mol 1968). In pursuing this topic, Hans began to combine his experience of migration with his sociology while also ministering to a congregation. He argued for the positive impact of theology on economic activity.

After finishing his PhD, Hans said he 'wanted to meld sociology and religion in a sociology department'. He accepted a position at Canterbury University in Christchurch New Zealand where he studied the impact of migration on the religious lives of Dutch migrants to New Zealand (Mol 1961). He also prepared a report for the National Council of Churches in New Zealand on racial integration (Mol 1966). He was then invited to a position in the demography section at the Australian National University where he stayed for six years. He was one of three sociologists at the ANU, and one of very few in Australia at that time. Following a sabbatical, Hans was offered a chair in the sociology of religion at McMaster University in Hamilton, Ontario, Canada from which he retired after 18 years.

When asked to reflect on how sociology and being a pastor related Hans said, 'Sociology was my big thing. I started as minister, on the evangelical side because they took religion seriously and did not apologize about its importance or role in life. Yes, my sociology influenced my preaching and my pastoral work influenced my sociology'. Hans' life was an ongoing interweaving of pastoral work involving the experience of working with people of faith and interpreted through the two lenses of theological reflection and sociology. Books such as *Christianity in Chains* (Mol 1969) were sociological analyses directed at the churches and clergy, unabashedly applying current theory and research to critiques of and suggestions for ecclesiastical policy and program. In retirement, he became a regular preacher at St Andrews Presbyterian Church in Canberra and conducted services at the Dutch war memorial in Canberra.

He last preached about four years ago. When I asked Hans how he understood his two vocations he was very clear and said, 'Sociology was my talent, as a Presbyterian minister I could not neglect or negate my gift.' Both were God-given and there was no conflict in his mind or person.

Seeing Religion Sociologically (with Eyes of Faith)

Many have asked me (and I am sure that Hans shares this experience), 'How can you be a sociologist and a pastor/priest at the same time?' The notion that there might be an inherent conflict between being a person of faith and a scholar or scientist, and later particularly a social scientist, arose as the Enlightenment progressed and reactionary church leaders defended untenable positions; some scientists claimed they knew all that was able to be known. Against all of this, there was a continuing stream within Christian thought that agreed with John Calvin who argued in the Second Book of his *Institutes of the Christian Religion* that to learn of the world was to learn about God, there could be no enduring conflict only temporary confusion. The discipline required to pursue rigorously and without clerical or political interference any academic enterprise was seen by many scholars as a religious calling and duty. The conflict between these perspectives on the relation of religious commitment and science persists today. Some, but far from all, scholars and universities presume that there is a necessary contradiction between being a person of faith and a social scientist. I have had the good fortune to be educated in and employed by universities that were open to the study of religions. This was, for the most part, also the case for Hans. Some sociological traditions have been strongly anti-religious it is true, but not all.

Many European and British universities, for instance, have highly respected departments of theology. Given the strong role played by religion in the foundation and continuing life of its society, openness to the study of religion also characterizes many American universities. For example, many Ivy League universities have their own or are affiliated with theological schools – Harvard, Yale, Princeton, and Columbia. The American Academy of Religion attracts over 10,000 scholars to its annual meetings and there are a host of other professional associations devoted to the study of religions – The Society for the Scientific Study of Religion, The Association for the Sociology of Religion, The Religious Research Association (Hans would have been a member of each of these), along with Psychology of Religion groups and then international associations such as the International Society for the Sociology of Religions. Hans served as Secretary-Treasurer of the Sociological Association of Australia and New Zealand and

President of the Sociology of Religion Research Committee of the International Sociological Association. There has been a vibrant and exacting professional discourse focused on the study of religions in the United States and in many other countries. Hans made a major contribution to this discourse promoting the rigorous sociological study of religion as a serious factor in social life.

A related, and recurring, issue is the assumption that a person of faith must necessarily be biased when examining religion, especially if studying their own religion. It is true that the outsider is capable of seeing things to which the insider is blind. Weber claimed to be religiously 'unmusical', but he had lasting insight into relations between religious cultures and social organization. It is equally true that insiders can be blind to negative aspects of a religious group, or prone to defend rather than critique. At the same time, the insider may have a better idea of how a particular social phenomenon works and feels as well as knowledge of the subtle but important nuances that the outsider is unable to detect. Indeed, an insider's critique can be much more trenchant, perceptive, and powerful. Likewise, outsiders can be so distant from the phenomenon that they are unable to see significant aspects of their object of study. For example, I tire of reading research proposals from researchers who clearly have little understanding of the religions that they seek to study or who begin with undeclared, but very evident, negative assumptions about religion.

A Protestant View of Protestant Societies

Hans was not only a religious insider but a Presbyterian with a deep Dutch Calvinist foundation and orientation. As a Presbyterian pastor, Hans was enabled to understand Protestant societies in a way that a non-Protestant would not have. On the other hand, being an 'outsider' to Scottish Presbyterianism when in Canada, New Zealand, and Australia and having experienced a very different form of Presbyterianism in the United States, Hans would have had a capacity to see the cultural entrapments of the denomination and people he served. I know this having also served as a Presbyterian in these contexts. Sharing with Hans a similar religious background and history, I am aware that I too am less able to interpret Catholic societies and that, however much I discipline myself to do otherwise, my instinct is to view religions through a Protestant lens.

American Sociology was a very Protestant discipline well into the 1970s. In fact, American, New Zealand (English), Canadian and Australian societies were very Protestant until quite recently. It is in this light that I note that Mol's last treatment of religion in Australia was published in 1985 and was based in part on 1981 census data (Mol 1985b). I find it interesting that 1981 was the last year that Anglicans were more numerous than Catholics and the last year that the combined presence of Presbyterians, Methodists and Congregationalists exceeded 10 per cent of the population. After this point, those declaring 'no religion' exceeded the numbers of Presbyterians and Uniting combined. At the same time detectable populations of Muslims, then Buddhists, and now others began to make their presence felt, ushering in the post-Protestant and multi-faith features that now characterize Australia (Bouma 2006). In the 2011 Australian Census, Presbyterians had declined to 2.8 per cent of the population and those declaring 'no religion', at 22.3 per cent, were closing in on Catholics at 25.3 per cent (ABS 2012). Once a potential advantage, being Protestant and Presbyterian no longer serves as a helpful sensitizing orientation to the religious life of Australia (Bouma 2006, 2011). Similarly, while being a Dutch migrant helped one to understand other migrants in the 1950s and 1960s, migration to both Canada and Australia is no longer primarily from Britain or Europe.

Hans has been active in ministry throughout his adult life, and relating regularly to congregations of believers keeps one in touch with the data for the sociology of religion, at least some of the data. Some issues are persistent, like death, disease, and accidental injury, child rearing and marital relations; but the approach taken to these issues changes, in both their theological and societal framing. In the mid twentieth century, Australian Presbyterians were among those who led the way in accepting the ordination of women, but in the late twentieth they reversed their position. Of course, the social location of congregations and denominations will shape their views of social change. Today, in Australia, many Presbyterians actively oppose the acceptance of Muslims by seeking to prevent the building of mosques and Islamic schools. Once proud, prosperous and influential as British Protestants, Presbyterians must now share the civic platform with Muslims, Buddhists, Hindus and a host of others. I doubt that Mol shares this view, but his church which actively welcomed British and Dutch immigrants in the 1950s and 1960s now takes a different and defensive view of more recent immigrants to Australia.

Sociologist and Theologian

While being a religious insider both opens the eyes to some aspects of religion and directs them away from others, there are some strong similarities between being a theologian and a sociologist. First of all, they both study similar objects. God and society are unseen, unseeable and known only in their effects. In that sense, both theologians and sociologists require faith. Yet, there are both theologians and sociologists who do not believe that their object of study actually 'exists'. There are of course other objects of study that are known only in their effects. No one has ever seen a quark. The Higgs Bosun was detected in its effects. No one saw it, or for that matter, touched it. Mol believed in both God and society; both were real and valuable objects of study. Experiences of each could be encountered and analysed rationally, and both exhibited detectable patterns which could be expressed in language even if not exhausted by such expressions.

Given the intangibility and invisibility of their subject matter, sociologists like theologians are prone to use analogical language in their reports about the object of study. Society is like a network, like a system, or to revert to the nineteenth century, like an engine, or a body, or some other thing. Some reduce the societal to social interaction using economic metaphors or communication analogies. Mol's focus on identity risks reducing the societal to a form of psychological process, but this is a problem faced by all sociologies not just that produced by Mol. Scientists studying more tangible objects and processes do not as a rule resort to analogical thinking.

Sociology through Theology

Yes, being an insider holding to a particular theology can and will obstruct, or at least channel, the view taken of religious phenomena. Presbyterians will be prone to look for creeds, to intellectual formulations of faith, and to the rational in the religious. Less, if any attention is likely to be paid to the emotional, experiential or charismatic elements of the religious life. This rational focus sat comfortably with 1950s consensualist sociology with its assumptions about the causal influence of beliefs and attitudes, its seeking cultural uniformity and behavioural conformity. Following from this focus on the rational was a confidence in the power of education (proper socialization) to solve the social ills of the day – poverty, racism, class distinctions, and even the propensity to war. Leading social reformers often had religious roots or were religious – the Niebuhrs, Buber, Tillich, Martin Luther King, etc. But then so did those opposed to change. They all looked to education to fix the problems.

However, with the late twentieth-century cultural shift from reliance on rational modes of authority to more experiential forms (Bouma 2006, 1991), the Presbyterian and 1950s consensualist sociological approaches no longer provide the best lenses through which to understand the societies Mol once studied. The forms of being religious (and now we must add of being spiritual) have changed, and if the lenses that worked in the 1960s are used much will be missed.

After all, Presbyterians now make up less than 3 per cent of the Australian population and have a seriously elderly age profile such that they look to be less numerous than Buddhists and Muslims in less than a decade.

Theology through Sociology

We should note that the social has been observed to affect the theological as well. Guy Swanson (1960) made a strong case for the influence of social structure on the structure of theology found in a society. Some sociologists have highlighted the manner by which sermons preached differed by the social class of the congregation (Pope 1942). Others have noted the ways in which images of God have changed with changes in society (Bouma 1999; Blombery 1989). I do not consider it to be coincidental that the declarations of the 'death of god' made from the mid 1960s happened at the same time that some sociologists began to doubt the existence of society. The very social conditions for belief in a transcendent god, according to Swanson, were eroding. At the same time, the independence of national societies and their capacity to maintain internal, coherent organizational structures was passing. Moreover, Swansons' prediction about the social conditions for the rise of witchcraft – a decrease in trust in or satisfaction with the justice processes of a society – fits neatly with recent trends.

Hans Mol was a product of his times and creatively wove together being a Presbyterian pastor, a theologian, and a sociologist in ways that enabled him to make a major contribution to the sociology of his time and to the churches he served. Without a doubt, Mol believed that the theological had social consequences. Following Max Weber, he argued for the positive role of Calvinist piety and theology in the settlement of migrants to colonial America (1968). He often refuted those who saw only negative or counter-productive effects of strongly held religious beliefs. He also considered theology often to have more sophisticated understandings of humans and of social life (1985a). Theological ideas about the nature of humanity, what is wrong and how it is to be fixed, were understood to have consequences for social policy. Mol recognized that Protestant and Presbyterian theologies of individual responsibility as well as the corresponding structures of representative governance not only informed the framers of the American constitution but continue to inform current social ethics and basic ideas about the constitution of societies, making it difficult for westerners to understand or appreciate more communal populations. This – as well as the insights of the preceding chapters – highlights just one way in which Mol's work is still relevant and urges others to acknowledge that he is an excellent example of the productive integration of the religious pastor and the sociologist.

References

Australian Bureau of Statistics (2012) *2011 Census of Population and Housing (Time Series Profile – Cat. 2003.0)*. www.abs.gov.au/census (accessed 8 January 2013).

Blombery, T. (1989) *God through Human Eyes*. Melbourne: Acorn Press.

Bouma, G. (1991) 'By What Authority? An Analysis of the Locus of Ultimate Authority in Ecclesiastical Organisations', in A. Black (ed.), *Religion in Australia*. Sydney: Allen and Unwin, 121–31.

Bouma, G. (1999) 'Sociology and Theology in the Re-imagination of God', in P.H. Ballis and G.D. Bouma (eds), *Religion in an Age of Change*. Kew: Christian Research Association, 12–22.

Bouma, G. (2006) *Australian Soul: Religion and Spirituality in the Twenty-First Century*. Melbourne: Cambridge University Press.

Bouma, G. (2011) *Being Faithful in Diversity: Religions and Social Policy in Multifaith Societies*. Adelaide: Australasian Theological Forum.

Mol, H. (1961) *Churches and Immigrants*. The Hague: Albani.

Mol, H. (1966) *Race and Religion in New Zealand: A Critical Review of the Policies of the Churches in New Zealand Relevant to Racial Integration*. Christchurch: National Council of Churches of New Zealand.

Mol, H. (1968) *The Breaking of Traditions: Theological Convictions in Colonial America*. Berkeley: Glendessary Press.

Mol, H. (1969) *Christianity in Chains: A Sociologist's Interpretation of the Churches' Dilemma in a Secular World*. Melbourne: Nelson.

Mol, H. (1971) *Religion in Australia: A Sociological Investigation*. Melbourne: Thomas Nelson.

Mol, H. (1985a) 'Religion and Identity: A Dialectical Interpretation of Religious Phenomena'. Keynote address opening the 5th Congress of the International Association for the History of Religions, University of Sydney, Australia. http://rsh.anu.edu.au/Hans Mol/rel-identity.php (accessed 8 January 2013).

Mol, H. (1985b) *The Faith of Australians*. Sydney: Allen and Unwin.

Mol, H. (1987) *How God Hoodwinked Hitler*. Sutherland: Albatross Books.

Mol, H. (2003) *Tinpot Preacher*. Queanbeyan: Talpa.

Pope, L. (1942) *Millhands and Preachers*. New Haven: Yale University Press.

Swanson, G. (1960) *The Birth of the Gods*. Ann Arbor: University of Michigan Press.

Select Bibliography of Hans Mol

Books

Mol, Hans (1966) *Race and Religion in New Zealand*. Christchurch: National Council of Churches in New Zealand.
—— (1968) *The Breaking of Traditions*. Berkeley: Glendessary Press.
—— (1969) *Christianity in Chains*. Melbourne: Thomas Nelson.
—— (1971) *Religion in Australia*. Melbourne: Nelson.
—— (ed.) (1972) *Western Religion*. The Hague: Mouton.
—— (1976) *Identity and the Sacred*. Oxford: Basil Blackwell.
—— (ed.) (1978) *Identity and Religion*. Beverly Hills: Sage Publications.
—— (1982) *The Fixed and the Fickle*. Waterloo: Wilfrid Laurier University Press.
—— (1982) *The Firm and the Formless*. Waterloo: Wilfrid Laurier University Press.
—— (1983) *Meaning and Place: An Introduction to the Social Scientific Study of Religion*. New York: The Pilgrim Press.
—— (1985) *Faith and Fragility*. Burlington: Trinity Press.
—— (1985) *The Faith of Australians*. Sydney: Allen & Unwin.
—— (1987) *How God Hoodwinked Hitler*. Tring: Lion Publishing.
—— (1990) *The Regulation of Physical and Mental Systems: Systems Theory of the Philosophy of Science*. New York: Edwin Mellen Press.
—— (2008) *Calvin for the Third Millennium*. Canberra: Australian National University Press.

Articles

Mol, Hans (1963) 'The Function of Marginality', *International Migration*, 1(3): 175–7.
—— (1970) 'Secularization and Cohesion', *Review of Religious Research*, 2(3): 183–91.

—— (1972) 'Religion and Competition', *Sociological Analysis*, 33: 67–73.

—— (1974) 'Marginality and Commitment as Hidden Variables in the Jellinek/Weber/Merton Theses on the Calvinist Ethic', *Current Sociology*, 22: 279–97.

—— (1974) 'The Sacralization of Identity', *Current Sociology*, 22: 267.

—— (1979) 'Belief: Its Contribution to Whole-making', *Religious Traditions*, 2(2): 6–23.

—— (1979) 'The Origin and Function of Religion: A Critique of, and Alternative to, Durkheim's Interpretation of the Religion of Australian Aborigines', *Journal for the Scientific Study of Religion*, 18(4): 379–89.

—— (1979) 'Theory and Data on the Religious Behaviour of Migrants', *Social Compass*, 26: 31–9.

—— (1981) 'Time and Transcendence in a Dialectical Sociology of Religion', *Sociological Analysis*, 42: 317–24.

—— (2008) 'Religion and Political Allegiance', *Australian Journal of Politics & History*, 16: 320–33.

Index

Numbers followed by 'n' refer to footnotes.

abortion 72, 74
academic life 20
adaptation 37, 95n
Afghanistan 132
Africa 92, 137–8, 147
afterlife 150, 156
age 172
Albania 115
Amsterdam 14, 16
ancestors 112
Anglicanism 92, 105–7, 112, 118, 123, 165, 170
animism 92, 150
anomie 20
Aristotle (lian), 57, 59
Austin, A.L. 43
Australia 17, 18, 19, 28, 43, 51, 79, 92, 101, 123–42, 165, 170
Australian National University 22, 167
Austria 70

Barth, K. 18, 19, 29, 50n
Batnitzky, L. 49
BBC 14
believe-belong 135
Bellah, T. 34
Berger, P. 4, 25, 39, 101
betrayal 110, 130
Bevans, S. 146
Bible 106, 109
bioethics 94
birth control 73, 131
blessing 158
Bloch, E. 90

blood transfusion 91
Böckenförde, E.W. 88, 94–6
brain studies 48
Britain 170
Brooks, P. 53–5
Brown, R. Mc. 20
Buddhism 50n, 97, 114, 124, 132, 148, 170
Bulgaria 115
bullying 132
Bultmann, R. 47

California 25
calling 168
Calvinism 38, 165–70
Canada 28, 40, 91, 165, 170
cannibalism 109
Casey, M. 5
Cassirer, E. 44, 45
Castells, M. 34, 41
Catholic Church 40, 69–70, 107, 108, 118, 123, 166, 169
causality 48–9
cemeteries 138
census 126–33, 169
Chalcedon 156
China (ese) 40, 92, 113
Christianity 101, 103, 117, 140, 148
    charismatic 129, 134, 171
    competing 108, 110, 113
    missionaries 104–5
    Orthodoxy 131
    Reformed 145
Christianity in Chains 23
Churches and Immigrants 22

circumcision 140
cities 38
civil religion 94–5
civilizing mission 105
class 123, 132, 172
clocks 69
colonialism 111, 123
Columbia University 20, 165
commitment 36
communicative action 88
concentration camp 45, 53
Confucianism 40
conversion 104, 132
convicts 130
Cox, H. 40, 87
creationisn 91
creeds 5, 156
culture 123

danger 158
Darwinian thought 34
dead 152
    living-dead 152, 155, 158
death 16, 170
deconstruction 46–7
democracy 97
Denmark 59
denomination 33, 113, 115, 117
    entrapment 169
despair 15
detective novels 55
differentiation-integration 34, 36
dignity 15, 98
Dinterloord 16
discrimination 139
divorce 72
Durkheim, E. 34, 36–7
Dutch Reformed Tradition 17

Eckhart, Meister 45, 49
ecology 157
economics 131, 167
education 135–6, 171
egoism 19
Eliade, M. 149

elites 12, 17, 92
emigration 17, 22, 167
emotion 4, 16, 117, 171
Enlightenment 147, 161, 168
equality 94
Erikson, E.E. 27, 30
Essentialism 44
ethics 20, 44, 52, 57, 72, 81, 88
    committee 75
    prophets 111
    secular 96
European colonization 101
    Values Survey 67, 72
euthanasia 72, 73–7
evangelicals 21, 104, 115, 118
experience absolutized 52

factory 16
faith 15, 50, 58, 160, 165, 170
    scholarship 168
farming 12, 13, 167
fascism 38
feminism 35, 37
Fenn, R. 27, 38
fertility 154, 159
Feuerbach, L. 50n
Filipinos 131
financial crisis 131
France 18
Freedom 46, 52
Freud(ianism) 44
Function(alism) 27, 29, 44
    differentiation 67
fundamentalism 40, 52, 89, 93–7, 140

Gaia 134
gender 115, 132, 134, 170
Germany 18, 38, 95
Gestapo 14, 15
gift 168
Gikiri 149
globalization 34, 41, 135
Glock, C. 20, 24
God 19, 45, 53, 58, 59, 62, 72, 104, 151–2, 160, 172

Dead 34, 87, 172
Society 170
grace 62, 156
gradualism 137
Greece 95
Greenspan, L. 33–42

Habermas, J. 88–90, 94
harmony 17
healing 110
Hegel (ian) 34, 36, 37, 59
Heidegger, M. 45–9
hero-heroism 159
Hindu 97, 114, 124, 133, 148
history 37
Holocaust 29
Holland 165
Holy Spirit 155
Homosexuality 72, 74, 131, 139
hope 15, 111
hospitals 71
human rights 16, 139
Humanae Vitae 72
Humanists 115, 135
Hume, D. 51n
hypocrite 60

iconoclasm 52
identity (theory) 19, 27–2, 35, 54, 71
    context 102
    crisis 38, 39
    essential 44
    fortress 38
    narrative 53–64
    sacralized 5
Identity and the Sacred 24, 33, 35–8, 44, 90
immigration 17, 20, 113–14, 148, 136–66, 170, 172
imperialism 104
Indeterminism 48
India 28, 40
Indians 113–14
indifference 113
individuality (ism) 12, 24, 38
Indonesia 97, 145–61

industrialization 38, 55, 57, 61
initiation 159
insider/outsider 169, 170–71
integration-adaptation 28
intellectualism 13
Iran 40
Ireland 130–31
Irwin, J. 102
Islam-Muslims 92, 97, 98, 113, 115–16, 131, 140, 148, 170
Israel (ites) 40, 109, 111
Italy (ians) 18, 78, 130

Japan 92
jealousy 152
Jehovah's Witnesses 91
Jesus Christ 5, 49n, 104, 111, 155–6
    Passion 158
Jevons, F.B. 6
Jews 5, 14, 49n, 91, 108, 110, 114, 133, 140
Jihad 41
Judaism 5, 34, 40, 49–50
    becomes 'religion' 49
justice 55, 71, 97, 138

Kant, I. 45
kerygma 47
ketuhanan 97
Kierkegaard, S. 52, 57–61
Kleinwanzleben 14
Kraemer, H. 18
Kuhn, T.S. 49

laïcité 95, 142
land 112
language 43
Latin America 147
law 74, 153
Liberalism 166
Life 79, 81, 96
Lifton, R.J. 44
loneliness 15
longevity 131
Lord's Supper 158
Luhmann, N. 67

Luther, M. 47
Lutherans 113

MacIntyre, A. 57
Majoritarianism 141
Mana 149
Maori 24, 101–16
Marburg 47
marginalization 24
marriage 159
Marx, K. 39, 44
masonic lodges 74
McIntyre, R. 18
McMaster University 26, 28, 33, 43, 49n, 167
Meaning and Place 19
meaning in life 78
media 69
medicine 71
Mendelssohn, M. 49, 52
Merton, R. 21, 69
Methodism 106–7, 118
Mexico 91
migrants, *see* immigration
millennialism 110–11
Mol, Jacoba 11
Mol, Johannis (Hans) Jacob 101, 117–18, 124, 145, 161, 165–72
 Autobiography 11
 bereavement 27
 bibliography 30–31
 birth 12
 Canberra 23
 Canterbury Christchurch 21
 doctorate 21
 faith 27, 44
 identity 15–16
 marriage 17, 18
 ordination 18, 21, 166
 prison 14, 15
 retirement 29, 165
 science 47
 teaching 22, 165–7
 USA citizen 21
money 13

mono-polytheism 51n
Moral Majority 40
Mormons 5, 6, 91, 108, 114
mortality rates 111
Moscovici, S. 5
multiculturalism 116, 130, 139
multi-faith 131
music 13, 14
myth 19, 33, 36, 47, 88, 102

narrative 53, 62, 146
nationalism 97
Nazis 13, 15, 62
Netherlands 12, 13
neuroscience 48
New Age 134
new religious movements 112
New Zealand 2, 21, 28, 101–20, 167
Niebuhr, H. Richard 160, 171
Niebuhr, R. 18, 19, 20, 166, 171
Nietzsche 34, 49
nothing human alien to me 34
Nussbaum, M. 91

objectification 36
O'Dea, T. 25
Otto, R. 19

Paganism 134
pain 75
palliative care 75
Pancasila 97
Paris 91
Parsons, T. 34
paternalism 104
Pentecostalism 134
performative utterance 44
phenomenology 93
philanthropy 104
Pietism 21
pillarization 70
Plato 13
Pluralism 34, 95, 101, 142
politics 74, 91, 92, 111, 135
polygamy 91, 109

pomposity 19
Popper, K 33
post-modern(ism) 46, 161
post-secular 39, 40, 90
poverty 171
Powell, A. 6, 11–31
prayer 12
Presbyterians 17, 29, 113, 118, 145, 169, 171
pride 19
priest-sociologist 165
Princeton Seminary 166, 168
prison 15–16
progress 37
projection 147
prophets 111
Protestant(ism) 38, 49, 52, 91, 104, 117, 123, 129, 166, 169–70
    Post 170
providence 59
psychology 15, 27
Purchas, S. 49
Puritanism 21

Quakers-Friends 165

race-relations 118, 140, 167
RAMP 72
rationality 13, 15, 16, 19, 24, 89, 93
Ratzinger, J. 94
reciprocity 98
reductionism 44, 166
religion (ious) 19, 28
    associations 168
    birth 135
    civil 94
    definition 139
    diffused 87
    diversity 102, 115, 119
    experience 48
    identity 28
    order 24
    paradigms 119
    plurality 119
    process 28

    scholars of 50n, 165
    state 140–41
    study of 19, 168
    usage 49
repentance 34
revelation 111
revolution 91
right to die 79
rites of passage 110
ritual 4, 33, 36, 88
    purity 103
Robinson, J. 23
Rokkan, S. 70
Rusconi, G.E. 96

Sabellianism 154
sacralization of identity 19, 34, 36, 145
    desacralized suffering 79
    four factors 117
sacraments 70, 88, 158
sacrifice 88
salvation 4, 5, 34, 88, 104, 111, 153, 156
    pre-literary 5, 157
    religions 4
sanctity of life 79, 81
Sanders, E.P. 49
Scanlon Study 138
schools 124
Schleiermacher, F. 11
Schneider, L. 25
Scholem, G. 50
science 19, 47, 51
Secularism 39, 89, 93, 101, 113, 124, 135–6, 141, 167
    Post-secularism 39
Secularization 33, 34, 39, 52, 67–85, 89, 97, 131
security of life 15
self-deception 58, 60–61
sexuality 15, 39, 82, 153
shaman 159
Sherlock Holmes 55–6
Shinto 51
Sikhs 5, 124, 138
sin 19, 34, 58, 104, 157

Singer, P. 73, 79, 80, 82
slavery 104
Smart, Ninian 28
Smith, Wilfred Cantwell 49n
Society (ial) 43, 171
    change 67n, 104
    cohesion 138
    Gospel 167
    harmony 17
    solidarity 88
sociology 13, 14, 20, 166
    American 169
    associations 26, 28, 168
    professions 165
    religion 168–9
South Africa 133–4
Soviet Union 40
spirits 152
spirituality 171
    of choice 135, 136
Stanner, W.E.H. 4
State, the 140–41
substantive neutrality 140
suffering 15, 77
sugar industry 14
suicide 15, 109
suspicion 61
Sydney 18, 28, 105, 136, 166
symbols 38, 44, 46
sympathetic scholarship 19
systems-theory 4
Swanson, G. 165, 172
Switzerland 70

Tanner, K. 147
Tasmania 136
Tawney, R.H. 38
Terence 34
terrorism 138, 142
theocracy 40, 140
theology (ical) 4, 18, 19, 146, 168, 170, 172
    anthropology 20

contextual 145–61
dialectical 19
Tillich, P. 19, 20, 171
time 69
transcendence 19
Trinity 145–61
truth 98, 119
turkey 132
typhus 15

Union Seminary 18, 19, 166
USA 21, 25, 91, 101
Utopia 90

values 129
Vatican 37, 78
vegetative state 79
Vietnam (ese) 130–31
violence 142
virtue 57
visions 158–9

Walls, A. 147
war
    memorial 167
    post- 114
    Second World 13, 15, 19, 45
    Vietnamese 44
Weber, M. 5, 21, 24, 35, 39, 169, 172
welfare 71, 135
    state 135
wellbeing 71, 97
Wilson, B.R. 5
witchcraft 134, 172
Wittgenstein, L. 43
working class 12, 18
World Council of Churches 18, 22
world-views 82, 95, 109, 149
worship 105

Yale 168
Yugoslavia 115